JIM CROW'S DEFENSE

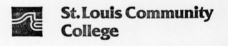

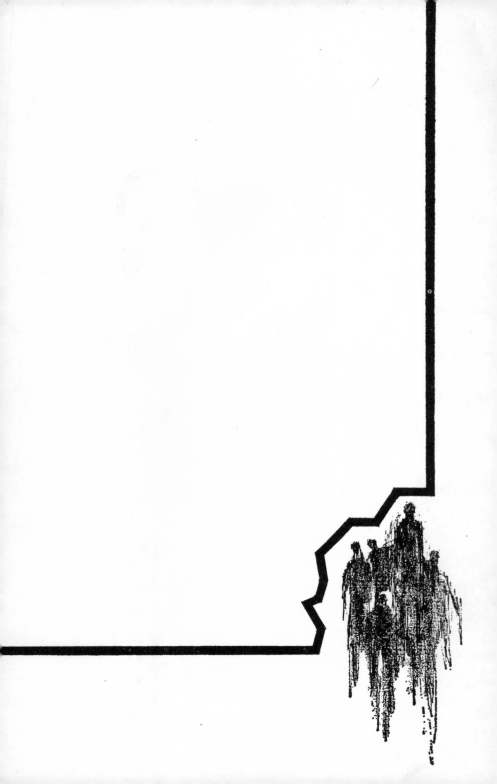

JIM CROW'S DEFENSE

ANTI-NEGRO THOUGHT IN AMERICA, 1900-1930

I. A. Newby

Louisiana State University Press / Baton Rouge

For My Family

ISBN 0-8071-0629-1 (cloth)
ISBN 0-8071-0132-X (paper)
Library of Congress Catalog Card Number 65-20297
Copyright © 1965 by Louisiana State University Press
Manufactured in the United States of America
1973 printing

Published with the assistance of a grant
from the Ford Foundation.

The real problem is not the negro,
but the white man's attitude toward the negro.

THOMAS PEARCE BAILEY (1914)

PREFACE

Recent Supreme Court decisions affecting civil rights and racial segregation have made the American people acutely aware of racial minorities and problems. Jolted by these decisions, Americans have been forced to reexamine both their treatment of and attitudes toward the Negro race. Made difficult by the moral and emotional nature of racial factors, this examination has been confused and complicated by the fact that racial attitudes have resulted from inheritance, environment, and prejudice, rather than from rational or philosophical conviction. Furthermore, as C. Vann Woodward's *Strange Career of Jim Crow* reminds us, these attitudes have frequently misconceived the history of race relations and misconstrued the evolution of racial attitudes and policies.

This is no wonder, however, because the development of anti-Negro thought—specifically, the body of ideas revolving around belief in the Negro's innate racial inferiority—has received little consideration from historians. Much has been written of the Negro in America and much has been made of racism as an element of American thought. Little attention, however, has been given to detailing basic ideas of anti-Negro racism, especially as those ideas have developed since 1865. This study undertakes to examine and recreate those ideas for one portion of the post-Civil War period, the first three decades of the twentieth century. Its object is to contribute to the white man's understanding of his attitudes toward and, thus, his treatment of the nation's largest racial minority.

Since race and race relations are emotional subjects which inevitably evoke "prejudice" one way or another, it seems pertinent at the outset to comment upon the approach of this study. As indicated, the chief purpose has been to develop the essentials of anti-Negro thought between 1900 and 1930 and to understand the meaning and implication of that thought. To accomplish this and to present a well-rounded picture of the subject, I have felt obligated to include a considerable amount of straight exposition of racist thinking. In so doing, I have adhered as closely as possible to the racists' writings and speeches. I have quoted them liberally, allowing them in this way to speak for themselves and at the same time preserving the colorfulness of expression which characterized much of their writings.

I have not attempted at every opportunity to flay or demolish the racists' thought or line of reasoning. The errors and distortions—and absurdities also—of their ideology are apparent and fall from their own weakness. Scientific, historical, and other scholarly researchers, it seems to me, have destroyed or refuted all major premises, tenets, and conclusions of anti-Negro thought of the early twentieth century. But despite this, I have attempted to treat the racists seriously as they developed and detailed their ideas. To dismiss them as crackpots, bigots, or uneducated simpletons is, I think, a mistake which friends of the Negro have too often made. An extensive reading of anti-Negro literature has convinced me that, whether intellectual or emotional in their approach, most racists were not hypocritical. They believed firmly and completely that Negroes were racially inferior, and they were concerned that racial policies reflect that belief. The fact that their efforts were misdirected and their beliefs rested upon prejudice, emotion, and ignorance did not make them any less real. They acted upon the assumption that they were correct, and their policies were justified by their premises.

Throughout this study, the term "racist" refers to those who held or voiced anti-Negro attitudes, including anyone who accepted the innate inequality of races and/or objected to social equality of whites and Negroes. Thus, broadly defined, it included the overwhelming majority of Americans in the early twentieth century and must be further defined to distinguish between moderates and extremists. Anti-Negro racism was an extremely complex phenomenon, and its complexity is intensified by the fact that it existed on various levels of intensity. First of all, several elements, referred to throughout the study as *extremists*, were openly hostile to the Negro. They were contemptuous of his racial characteristics, disdainful of his racial aspirations, and endorsed policies of a severely repressive nature. Secondly, those elements referred to as *moderates* were no less convinced of the Negro's innate inferiority, yet their approach to race problems was fundamentally sympathetic. Repelled by the extremism of the first group, they sought to apply "understanding" and "reason" to problems that were basically emotional. They were unimpressed by extremists who "proved" repeatedly that the Negro was inferior, for they assumed his inferiority to be self-evident. This assumption in turn led them to a callous disregard for the race and its longings for improvement, and they thus endorsed, directly or indirectly, policies of repression and discrimination. Included in this group were reputable scholars, scientists, politicians, and religious leaders who, despite their acceptance of or acquiescence in segregation and white supremacy, made substantial contributions in other fields of endeavor. Accordingly, no attempt has been made to assess their overall role in American history, and the reader must remember that they appear in these pages in their most vulnerable light. A general evaluation of the careers and writings of Howard W. Odum and Robert Penn Warren, for example, would absolve them of racist appellations. Yet, upon occasion in their early careers, both men expressed decidedly anti-Negro sentiments.

The third group of racists, whom I have called *reformers*, likewise accepted the Negro's racial inferiority, but they considered it as much a product of environment as heredity. Although siding with other racists on the crucial issue of social equality, they sought to apply fundamental and meaningful reforms to the race problem. Essentially paternalists, they would give the Negro both economic equality and the right to vote. They insisted, however, that political and social supremacy remain the white man's preserve.

Because this is a study of the formulation of anti-Negro ideas and only secondarily of the application given those ideas, I have dwelt upon the similarities rather than the differences of these three groups. On the printed page, there were frequently striking similarities in the ideas of different groups, for they wrote with similar assumptions. Yet the differences in policies which they proposed to implement were equally striking. The reader is cautioned to keep these differences in mind and not to read into the ideas of moderates and reformers more than is actually there. He is also cautioned to remember that the reforms they advocated would not substantially alter the white man's supremacy.

Broadly speaking, anti-Negro thought since Reconstruction has had a clear continuity, and breaking it into periods is arbitrary and artificial. However, its development has ebbed and flowed, and its relative importance has varied from time to time. In spite of overlappings and the absence of sharp breaks, there seem to be four distinguishable periods:

1 From the collapse of Radical Reconstruction to the late 1890's, perhaps to the Supreme Court's "separate but equal" decision of 1896. In this period Northerners dropped their concern for the Negro, and Southerners sought for the race a satisfactory "place" in the South.

2 From the late 1890's to the late 1920's. In this period the South, with Northern acquiescence, found and established the Negro's "place."

3 From the late 1920's to 1954. In this period the Negro's dissatisfaction with his "place" inspired efforts to improve his status, although the efforts were frustrated by Southern intransigence and Northern apathy.

4 From 1954, the year of the Supreme Court's decision against public school segregation, to the present. In this brief period there have occurred visible alterations in the Negro's "place," even in the South.

The years of this study, approximately 1900 to 1930, correspond to those of the second period. These were the years in which anti-Negro thought reached its zenith, the years which produced the greatest proliferation of anti-Negro literature, and the years in which that literature enjoyed its broadest appeal. Beginning with the South's formal disfranchisement and legal segregation of Negroes, this period lasted until the general decline of racist opinion among scientists, scholars, and other "authorities" in the middle and late 1920's. At its beginning came significant changes in policies toward the Negro; at its close came changes which were less obvious but no less important for future developments in race relations.

The anti-Negro ideas which enjoyed such popularity during this period were, of course, not new, but they were formulated with such intensity and in such detail that they merit the historian's attention. All but a few of them had been familiar to antebellum defenders of slavery, and they re-appeared now as a defense for disfranchisement, segregation, and other forms of discrimination. With them, the South justified or rationalized a new "place" for the Negro in the twentieth century.

For purposes of this study, anti-Negro thought has been divided into two parts: development of basic ideas (Chapters 1, 2, and 3), and application given those ideas, especially in the South (Chapters 4, 5, and 6). When I commenced the study, my intention was to include in Part II a chapter on the economic ideas by which racists justified their economic discriminations against the Negro. I discovered, however, that they rarely talked in economic terms and that they never developed a set of ideas to justify economic exploitation as they had done to justify social and political discrimination. This does not mean that racists opposed economic discriminations; it means instead that they justified their discrimination on grounds they found to be more appealing. The study is of *American* racism as well as *Southern* racism, for the two existed together. The one, in fact, complemented the other. Their difference at most was a matter of degree and consisted largely in the fact that Southerners lived among Negroes, were more immediately concerned with race problems, and were more inclined toward extremism. Southern attitudes were consequently more important and have been given greater attention.

Finally, a word about sources. Perhaps the chief difficulty in studying racist attitudes toward Negroes in the early twentieth century is the existence of mountains of readily available materials. Whatever the faults of racists of that period, they were not reticent about making their views public, and they obviously had no difficulty finding publication outlets. Large quantities of their writings were published by respectable and reputable Northern publishers, and anti-Negro opinions abounded in scholarly periodicals as well as popular and pulp magazines, in fiction as well as nonfiction. I have not attempted, therefore, to read all anti-Negro literature of the period. I have tried instead to study in detail representative types of that literature. The newspapers I have used are from extensive clipping collections in the libraries of Atlanta University and Tuskegee Institute, the latter being especially large and useful. In addition the Negro Collection of Atlanta University and the Booker T. Washington Collection at Tuskegee contain large amounts of anti-Negro literature, including many obscure books, pamphlets, and speeches not otherwise readily available. My intention has been to interrelate writings and authorities which influenced the development of racist thought with those which reflected the attitudes or emotions of popular opinion concerning the Negro.

I. A. NEWBY

ACKNOWLEDGMENTS

I wish to express my thanks to the library staffs at Atlanta University, Tuskegee Institute, and the University of California, Los Angeles, for making my research tasks easier; to the University of California, Los Angeles, for a fellowship which enabled me to complete this study; to Professor Theodore Saloutos of the University of California, Los Angeles, for his guidance and supervision of the study; and to my colleague Professor Jerald A. Combs of San Francisco State College, from whose constant criticisms both the study and I greatly benefited.

xiii

CONTENTS

JIM CROW'S DEFENSE

BACKGROUND TO REACTION

> Not many of the aspects of life in Alabama are untouched
> by the influence of racial attitudes. The Negro problem has
> given a distinct coloration to our judicial procedures, to
> our social attitudes, to our educational points of view and
> even to our artistic and scientific endeavors. Religion itself
> has not been immune to the influence.
>
> Birmingham *News* (January 12, 1934)

In 1928 historian Ulrich Bonnell Phillips suggested that the most significant facts of Southern history were the presence in the region of Negroes in large numbers and the resulting efforts of white men to maintain orderly government and "Caucasian civilization." "The white folk" of the South have "a common resolve indomitably maintained," he wrote, that their section "shall be and remain a white man's country. The consciousness of a function in these premises, whether expressed with the frenzy of a demagogue or maintained with a patrician's quietude, is the cardinal test of a Southerner and

3

the central theme of Southern history." [1] Though oversimplified, Phillips' statement is not without merit. "It cannot be denied," one of his most recent critics has written, "that a preoccupation with the issue of race, its mythology and its symbolism, has been one of the major themes of southern history, with innumerable ramifications into every aspect of southern life." [2]

The validity of this view is apparent. The summary of Southern attitudes published in 1914 by Dr. Thomas Pearce Bailey, Dean of the Department of Education and professor of psychology and education in the University of Mississippi, is illustrative. In one of the racists' best and most literate commentaries on Negroes and racial problems, *Race Orthodoxy in the South,* Bailey offered a succinct and comprehensive statement of his section's racial creed. Included were the following points: "blood will tell"; "the negro is inferior and will remain so"; "this is a white man's country"; "no social equality"; "no political equality"; "in matters of civil rights and legal adjustments give the white man, as opposed to the colored man, the benefit of the doubt, and under no circumstances interfere with the prestige of the white race"; "in educational policy let the negro have the crumbs that fall from the white man's table"; "let there be such industrial education of the negro as will best fit him to serve the white man"; "only Southerners understand the negro question"; "let the South settle the negro question"; "the status of peasantry is all the negro may hope for, if the races are to live together in peace"; "let the lowest white man count for more than the highest negro"; and "the above statements indicate the leanings of Providence." [3]

These ideas, stated above in their simplest form, constituted the core of anti-Negro thought in the South and motivated the Southerner's determination to preserve white supremacy. But, and this is equally important, *it was a core of ideas to which non-Southerners also generally subscribed.* Non-Southerners, of course, never gave the Negro as much attention as did Southerners, and they never so readily took action against the race. Yet they generally accepted the South's racial views, acquiesced in its racial policies, and shared its

---

1   Phillips, "The Central Theme of Southern History," in E. Merton Coulter (ed.), *The Course of the South to Secession* (New York, 1939), 152.
2   George B. Tindall, "The Central Theme Revisited," in Charles Grier Sellers, Jr. (ed.), *The Southerner as American* (Chapel Hill, 1960), 105.
3   Bailey, *Race Orthodoxy in the South, And Other Aspects of the Negro Question* (New York, 1914), 93.

determination that white supremacy be maintained. They also did much to develop, elucidate, and reinforce anti-Negro thought. Without this, the rigid subordination of Negroes could never have occurred or endured so tenaciously.

Belief in racial and ethnic inequality was a basic element of American thought in the late nineteenth and early twentieth centuries.[4] Pervading all levels of society and all sections of the country, this racism was manifested in a multitude of national policies. Its most important expression was probably the nativist movement which culminated in the restrictive immigration legislation of the 1920's. The triumph of this movement deprived racists of a primary source of energy and inspiration. Anglo-Saxonism, Aryanism, Teutonism, anti-Semitism, anti-Catholicism, and the "Yellow Peril" were other significant expressions, as were manifest destiny, imperialism, the white man's burden, and the racism upon which these were premised. In addition Anglo-Americans firmly believed that Latin Americans and American Indians were demonstrably poor racial stocks, although these aspects of racism remain largely unstudied by historians. Even the Protestantism of such men as Josiah Strong had racist overtones, as did much scientific, historical, and religious thought of the period.

To understand anti-Negro thought in the early twentieth century, the pervasiveness of American racism must be recognized. All facets of racist thinking were interrelated, and to isolate one from the others is to risk distortion. The psychology of racism was such that a belief in the innate inferiority of one race or ethnic stock was usually accompanied by a belief in the inferiority of all "strange" or alien groups. Yet racists generally concerned themselves with only one race or ethnic group and seldom gave serious systematic attention to others. This was especially true of Southerners concerned with proving or demonstrating the Negro's alleged inferiority.

As a part of American racism, therefore, anti-Negro thought had certain distinguishing characteristics. It was the most widely accepted of racist ideas, and national and Southern policies toward Negroes indicated that this race was considered the most inferior of all races. No other minority except the Indians fared so badly in America, yet no other minority was more important in national life

---

4 For a survey of racist ideas in American history see Thomas F. Gossett, *Race: The History of an Idea in America* (Dallas, 1963).

and thought. There was, however, an amazing diversity of opinion concerning the Negro. Americans rarely questioned his alleged inferiority, but they disagreed fundamentally concerning the correct or most desirable Negro policy. Although this disagreement was over alternatives which presupposed segregation and discrimination, it benefited the Negro by undermining the position of extremists.

Southern engrossment with the Negro around the turn of the century coincided with the belated achievement of political influence by poor whites. "The barriers of racial discrimination [in the South] mounted in direct ratio with the tide of political democracy among whites," C. Vann Woodward has noted. "In fact, an increase of Jim Crow laws upon the statute books of a state is almost an accurate index of the decline of reactionary regimes of the Redeemer and triumph of white democratic movements." [5] From this phenomenon (and Woodward's observation is correct), historians and racists have derived what is now regarded as a self-evident truth—that racial extremism in the South is largely the responsibility of poor whites. Conscious of its inferiority vis-à-vis the planter and aristocratic classes, the argument runs, this class vents its frustrations upon helpless Negroes. Upper-class Southerners, on the other hand, understand the Negro, sympathize with his aspirations, and desire to befriend his race. But poor whites now control Southern politics, and the upper class, alas, can do no more than moderate their wanton disregard for the elemental rights of Negroes.

For Southern Bourbons and their heirs such an attitude has obvious appeal. It not only removes from them all responsibility for deteriorating race relations after 1890, but it also credits them with the positive aspects of Southern race policies. At best, however, this view is an oversimplification. Perhaps it is also a distortion. Besides crediting poor whites with *de facto* control of Southern politics, it attributes to them the ability to prescribe racial attitudes and policies in the section. Yet one might suggest with equal truth that the poor whites' control of Southern politics was never absolute. More often than not, perhaps, their influence was channeled to benefit the self-interest of demagogues who had no fundamental quarrel with the middle-class, capitalist businessman. Is it legitimate to blame only poor whites for racial excesses which derived in no small part

---

5 Woodward, *Origins of the New South, 1877–1913* (Baton Rouge, 1951), 211.

from the troubled heritage of slavery and the violent tradition of Nathan Bedford Forrest's Ku Klux Klan? Is not racial unrest in the South after 1890 as well explained by attitudes inherited from slavery, Reconstruction, and "redemption," as by the enhanced political influence of poor whites? And who will say that the South's racial attitudes and policies before 1890 were prescribed by the poor whites? Were the excesses of segregation after 1890 more vicious and unendurable than those of slavery before 1865? Did spokesmen for the upper and middle classes after 1890 try as zealously to moderate mobs and demagogues as they did to divert populist, democratic attention from social and economic problems?

These questions have largely escaped the attention of historians, but since they are vital to an understanding of anti-Negro thought in the early twentieth century, they should be kept in mind. Perhaps the explanation for their neglect is related to the fact that historians, like racists, have emphasized *difference* in describing the attitudes of various groups and socioeconomic classes toward Negroes. Yet, to repeat, *similarity* was at least equally important and should be given equal emphasis. "All classes of white people," wrote a South Carolinian in 1902, "have the same feeling [toward Negroes]." Poor whites "simply come more into contact with the Negro," and their "position and feelings are [consequently] more emphasized." [6]

Whatever its background or nature, a sudden outpouring of anti-Negro literature inundated the South and the nation between the 1890's and 1920's. Paralleling Southern efforts to disfranchise and segregate the Negro, this inundation was a product of those efforts. "A comprehensive doctrine of race was essential to justify the developing patterns of segregation," Oscar Handlin has observed, and "reiteration of this argument was necessary through the whole nation. The white South was but a minority, and it needed to secure the acquiescence of the North in the abandonment of the rights guaranteed the Negro by the Thirteenth, Fourteenth, and Fifteenth Amendments." [7] The effort was facilitated by the respectability of racist thought in all sections of the country and, before running its course, produced more widely read anti-Negro literature than any other period in American history.

Anti-Negro attitudes of the late nineteenth and early twentieth

---

6   William P. Calhoun, *The Caucasian and the Negro in the United States* (Columbia, S. C., 1902), 126.
7   Handlin, *Race and Nationality in American Life* (Boston, 1957), 46–47.

centuries developed from several sources. More often than not they were simply the refurbished ideas of antebellum slavocrats whose defense of slavery had been a concoction of science, pseudoscience, and prejudice.[8] To this concoction after 1875 were added the ideas and myths of European science and race theory, and the natural and social sciences which blossomed between 1875 and 1925 provided the framework within which a new "science of race" matured.

In the decade before the Civil War, anti-Negro racism in America had been systematized by a host of scientific and pseudoscientific writers, most significant of whom was Josiah Nott, an Alabama physician. Nott's major work, *Types of Mankind,* was published in 1855 in collaboration with Egyptologist George R. Gliddon and is the chief monument to antebellum efforts to demonstrate the Negro's alleged inferiority. Synthesizing the researches of several disciplines, Nott sought to prove that Negroes are physically and mentally inferior to Caucasians, hoping thereby to show the necessity of racial purity and white supremacy.

The campaign which Nott's work climaxed elicited the services of leading men of science. The eminent Philadelphia craniologist Samuel G. Morton and the Harvard naturalist Louis Agassiz made contributions, as did such "sciences" as anthropology, Egyptology, craniology, phrenology, biblical criticism, ethnology, and anatomy.[9] Antebellum scientists agreed that Negroes were inferior to Caucasians. Some of them, including Nott himself, suggested that the races constituted separate species.

Scientific racism, which originated in Europe in the late eighteenth century, had thus flowered early in the United States. But because of rapid scientific advances the racism of 1860 was not acceptable in 1880 or 1900. It was necessary to restate the ideas of mid-century in more up-to-date scientific terminology.

This restatement was largely the task of Europeans, and their ideas seeped slowly into American science and opinion. Before the Spanish–American War, American interest in scientific racism lagged well behind that of Europeans. The preoccupation of racists with evolution and eugenics, which reached the proportions of

---

8 Guion Griffis Johnson, "The Ideology of White Supremacy, 1876–1910," in Fletcher Melvin Green (ed.), *Essays in Southern History* (Chapel Hill, 1949), 124–56.

9 See William Stanton, *The Leopard's Spots, Scientific Attitudes Toward Race in America, 1815–1859* (Chicago, 1960).

mania around 1900, was the handiwork of Europeans; and eugenics, especially, received little attention in this country before 1900. By that date, however, European influences dominated American racist thought. The chief of these influences as they affected attitudes toward the Negro resulted from research into the relative quality of races, the significance of their physical differences, and the consequences of their indiscriminate mixture. Although not specifically concerned with Negroes, the ideas and hypotheses of Europeans were readily applied to that race by Americans.

European racism achieved a new significance in 1853–55 with the publication of *The Inequality of Human Races* by the French aristocrat Count Arthur de Gobineau. The purpose of Gobineau's endeavors, which enjoyed considerable influence in America in the twentieth century, was to formulate a law which would adequately explain the rise and fall of civilizations. After examining the major civilizations of antiquity, he concluded that "all civilizations derive from the white race, that none can exist without its help, and that a society is great and brilliant only so far as it preserves the blood of the noble group that created it." Nations and civilizations, he discovered, "degenerate only in consequences of the various admixtures of blood which they undergo," and "their degeneration corresponds exactly to the quantity and quality of the new blood." [10] Convinced that a single race, the Aryans, had created all past civilizations, he presumed a correlation between racial characteristics and potential for civilization and further presumed that Aryans alone were capable of creating or maintaining civilizations in the future. The peculiar racial characteristics upon which he based this presumption were the Aryan's "reflective energy," "energetic intelligence," "feeling for utility," unusual perseverance, great physical power, extraordinary instinct for order, love of liberty and life, and hatred for that "strict despotism" which is the only way of governing the Negro.[11]

Gobineau's chief disciple was the Englishman-turned-German Houston Stewart Chamberlain. In 1899 Chamberlain published a tedious two-volume tome, *Foundations of the Nineteenth Century*, which was translated into English in 1913. Although enormously influential in Germany where for a time he was president of the

---

10   Gobineau, *The Inequality of Human Races* (London, 1915), 210.
11   *Ibid.*, 207. Gobineau was a confirmed believer in the racial inferiority of Negroes.

Gobineau *Vereinigung,* Chamberlain had little direct influence among Americans. His work, cited occasionally by such writers as Lothrop Stoddard and Madison Grant, was a study of world history whose object was to ascertain the sources of modern civilization. His appeal to American racists was due to his emphasis upon racial factors and to his acceptance of racist ideas then in vogue. Comparing racial differences to differences between breeds of animals, he preached the doctrine of Teutonic superiority. He made only passing reference to the Negro, whom he regarded as little better than human rubbish. Like Gobineau, he considered racial mixture a crime against nature and the source of racial decline. With him, race was the supreme reality of life.

Following the example of Gobineau and Chamberlain, other Europeans developed race theories which Americans found attractive. Ludwig Woltmann discovered that all great men in history were Teutons, and Carl Penka found that all Teutons were tall, blond, blue-eyed, and fair-skinned. Another German, Theodor Poesche, developed the relationship between religion and race. Protestantism, he declared, is the religious expression of Teutonic aggressiveness and love of liberty. Catholicism, on the other hand, expresses the natural submissiveness and obsequiousness of Mediterranean races. Among those who accepted these ideas were America's most influential race theorists, Madison Grant and Lothrop Stoddard. The same ideas appeared on a much lower level in the writings of Alfred P. Schultz, Ernest Sevier Cox, James Denson Sayers, and others.

A second European influence upon American racism, and one perhaps more lasting than that of the above race theorists, came from the researches and writings of Sir Francis Galton. In *Hereditary Genius* (1869) and other works, Galton made major contributions to the infant science of heredity. But while giving his theories general application, he fell into the trap which so often ensnares scientific pioneers: he read more into his theories than his researches justified. Individual and racial characteristics he found to be governed by the same laws of heredity. Both, he contended, were immutable products of evolution. In addition, they varied from race to race, as from individual to individual, and the result was innate, inherited inferiority in one race and superiority in another. Consequently, racial improvement was a matter of generations of genetic selectivity. The Negro, whom Galton considered the most primitive and inferior of races, was described as "childish, stupid, and simpleton like." There had never been a Negro genius, he declared flatly, for the race's intelligence was conspicuously below that of whites. The Negro was indeed poor eugenic material.[12]

Closely related to Galton's ideas, both in tone and content, were those of the French psychologist Gustave LeBon, who concerned himself with "the psychology of peoples." In an influential little volume by this title which he published in 1894, LeBon suggested that races are as different psychologically as they are physically. Each race, he declared, possessed "a mental constitution as unvarying as its anatomical constitution," and this mental constitution formed the "soul" of the race. As such, it represented "the synthesis of its entire past, the inheritance of all its ancestors, the motives of its conduct." Like Galton's racial characteristics, this soul was transmitted by inheritance and immune to education or environment. It was the source of racial culture and, thus, of civilization. Because of the abyss between the mental constitutions of different races, one race could not absorb the culture of another. Racial interbreeding, therefore, was objectionable, for it destroyed the soul of both races.[13]

The researches of German biologist August Weismann contributed a final hereditist influence upon American racism. Distinguishing between somatic (body) cells and reproductive (germ) cells, Weismann believed that the former were invariably controlled by the latter. Thus, germ cells were the sole determinants of individual character, but they were also isolated from body cells and immune to environment. The effect of Weismann's theory was to create the impression that individual and racial characteristics were fatally fixed in the germ plasm of an individual and that they emerged in each generation regardless of environmental factors.[14]

A third European influence upon American racism was a school of scientists who emphasized the importance of selection in determining racial characteristics. Members of this school, though recognizing the significance of heredity, were chiefly interested in measuring

---

12   Galton, *Hereditary Genius: An Inquiry into its Laws and Consequences* (London, 1950), 327–28.
13   LeBon, *The Psychology of Peoples* (New York, 1924), 5–6, 36, 29–30, 54.
14   See Weismann, *Essays upon Heredity and Kindred Biological Problems* (Oxford, 1891–92); and Weismann, *The Germ-plasm, A Theory of Heredity* (New York, 1902).

the racial effects of such factors as interbreeding, migrations, wars, and celibacy. Convinced that such effects were manifested in the physical characteristics of a race, they measured the physical features of European "races." Leaders of this school were the French anthropologist and biologist Vasher de Lapouge and the German anthropologist Otto Ammon. Upon the strength of researches in anthropometry and biology, Lapouge and Ammon concluded that the cephalic index [15] was the best measurement of racial composition. Building upon the theories of Gobineau and Chamberlain, they postulated a direct relationship between cephalic index on the one hand and social class and capacity for civilization on the other. The higher the social class, they maintained, the lower the cephalic index and the better the racial stock.[16]

A final European source of racist thought in America was Darwinism. Darwin himself was unconcerned with questions of racial superiority and inferiority, but by 1900 his evolutionary hypothesis was the chief scientific authority for racists in this country. His emphasis upon physical differences between races and his theory of natural selection—in fact the whole idea that racial characteristics result from evolution—became cornerstones of scientific racism. There was no doubt, Darwin wrote in *The Descent of Man*, that the races of man "differ much from each other—as in the texture of the hair, the relative proportions of all parts of the body, the capacity of the lungs, the form and capacity of the skull, and even in the convolutions of the brain." [17] This emphasis upon racial differences was appealing to racists, and it stimulated their efforts to measure racial features as a means of determining the extent of the Negro's inferiority. Social Darwinists, notably Herbert Spencer, also used the Darwinian ideas to defend racial inequality. As a matter of fact, after

15 The cephalic index "is simply the breadth of the head above the ears expressed in percentage of its length from forehead to back. Assuming that the length is 100, the width is expressed as a fraction of it. As the head becomes proportionately broader . . . this cephalic index increases." William Z. Ripley, *The Races of Europe, A Sociological Study* (New York, 1923), 37.

16 See Pitirim Sorokin, *Contemporary Sociological Theories* (New York, 1928), 233–34, 250–51. For selections from the writings of Europeans who agreed with Lapouge and Ammon, see Earl W. Count (ed.), *This is Race, An Anthology Selected from the International Literature on the Races of Man* (New York, 1950).

17 Charles Darwin, *The Descent of Man* (New York, 1874), 167. See also Darwin, "On the Races of Man," in Count (ed.), *This is Race*, 133–44.

1900 few popularizers of racist ideas quoted Darwin directly. Instead, they drew their Darwinism from Spencer, John Fiske, and other popularizers. But regardless of its source or accuracy, Darwinian influence upon American racism was pervasive.

The whole of European racist thought in the nineteenth century was synthesized for Americans by William Z. Ripley, a Massachusetts Institute of Technology sociologist and economist, who in 1899 published a massive and scholarly volume, *The Races of Europe*, which signaled the arrival of European racist thought in the United States. Ripley, however, was not consciously a racist and his work was rightly praised as a major accomplishment of science and scholarship. He rejected suggestions that Aryans had ever existed as a separate race, and in the opinion of racists he gave too much emphasis to environment as a molder of racial characteristics. Ironically, therefore, while racists frequently cited his volume, they found it only partially satisfying. Yet Ripley did accept many of the ideas of scientific racism, and by careful selection American racists found his work a storehouse of scientific support for their beliefs.

During the late nineteenth century the Negro's social, economic, and political status was determined by two interrelated factors: the abandonment of the race by Northern politicians and reformers and the triumph of Southern policies in race relations. The Fourteenth and Fifteenth Amendments were, of course, not repealed, and Republicans continued to harass Southern Democrats with force bills ostensibly intended to eliminate racial discrimination. In addition, individual Negroes and a scattering of Yankee philanthropists and Southern humanitarians made sustained efforts to protect the Negro's rights and promote the race's well-being. Yet the Negro was, for all practical purposes, at the mercy of Southern whites. The federal government had abandoned him, and, in spite of glowing campaign oratory to the contrary, the Republican party had done likewise.

Indeed, the tenor of the times was against the Negro. The psychology of exploitation which characterized the Gilded Age and the late nineteenth century sapped the energy of reform movements and channeled their interests into respectable and conventional protest. Before 1900 reform was associated in the popular mind with agrarianism, feminism, socialism, or other forms of radicalism and irresponsibility, and efforts to reform the race problem were similarly suspect. Reformers themselves, almost unanimously opposed to racial equality in social relations, found it difficult to espouse basic reforms. They were usually satisfied by the outward manifestations of reform and they rarely insisted upon substance. Racists were therefore able to hide a multitude of discriminations behind statements that their policies made no distinctions of race, and behind this fiction few reformers cared to look. As a result, separate-but-equal became a convenient rationalization for inaction and complacency among reformers, and a transparent camouflage for prostituting the American Constitution and elemental democratic processes.

Whatever their successes in other areas, reformers benefited Negroes hardly at all. Even populism, which occasionally championed the Negro,[18] intensified race prejudices by attempting to divide Southern whites politically and was probably detrimental to the Negro.[19] Likewise, Henry W. Grady's widely heralded "New South" offered the race nothing but hard work, menial opportunity, and a degraded "place." Whatever was new in Grady's plans related not to the Negro. "The whites shall have clear and unmistakable control of public affairs" in the New South, wrote Grady. "They are the superior race, and will not and cannot submit to the domination of an inferior race." [20]

Other Southern leaders of the period had similar ideas. Wade Hampton, governor and Senator of South Carolina and "redeemer" of his state from Radical Reconstruction, exemplified from the Negro's viewpoint the best of Southern Bourbonism.[21] A frequent champion of the freedmen against overzealous advocates of white supremacy, he sought to neutralize the harsher measures of repression and discrimination. Yet in 1890 he declared that "the constitution was violated when the negro was allowed to vote, and no greater crime against civilization, humanity, constitutional rights and Christianity was ever perpetuated under the guise of philanthropy." He urged the nation to rectify this evil by immediately revoking the Negro's citizenship and granting the white South full control of race problems.[22]

---

18   See for example Thomas E. Watson, "The Negro Question in the South," *Arena*, VI (October, 1892), 540–50.
19   See Woodward, *Origins of the New South, 1877–1913*, p. 258.
20   Grady, *The New South* (New York, 1890), 239–41. See also Grady, *The Race Problem* (Chicago, 1889).
21   See Hampton M. Jarrell, *Wade Hampton and the Negro, the Road Not Taken* (Columbia, S.C., 1950).
22   Wade Hampton, "The Race Problem," *Arena*, II (July, 1890), 135–38.

The anti-Negro views expressed by Grady and Hampton were products of a peculiarly Southern dilemma. Both men were paternalistic and generous in their attitudes toward Negroes, and neither was interested in making political capital out of race problems. Hampton was himself a victim of Ben Tillman's exploitation of the race issue, and Grady, as an advocate of reform and innovation, was well aware of the threat of demagoguery. Thus, they both felt it necessary to appear thoroughly orthodox on the Negro question, and both went to great lengths to reassure Southerners on this point. In effect they were ostensibly anti-Negro in order to be able to continue public careers from which Negroes as well as whites derived substantial benefits. This dilemma confronted every moderate in Southern politics, and many of them after 1900 emerged from it more tarnished than did Grady and Hampton.

The nation's imperialistic adventures around the turn of the century also reverberated against Negroes. By acquiring overseas dependencies inhabited by "our Brown brothers," the United States not only shouldered a share of the white man's burden, but thereby endorsed the racism which had created and sustained that burden. As imperialism permeated national thinking, Northerners became noticeably less antagonistic toward Southern race policies. The force-bill psychology, endorsing federal action to protect the Negro, was replaced by an exaggerated emphasis on nationalism, reunion, and the superior ability of Southerners to understand and solve their own problems. Republicans, who had traditionally advocated an expanded political role for Southern Negroes, now denied Filipinos, Hawaiians, and Puerto Ricans participation in their own governments. To Southerners this was both paradoxical and hypocritical and indicated the insincerity of Republican preachments on race questions.[23] In response to this criticism Republicans chose to desert the Negro (where they were not already ignoring him) rather than forego the fruits of imperialism.

In this milieu the Negro faced the new century. Ignored by reformers, forgotten by friends, sacrificed along the road to reunion, his prospects were never lower. The masses of the race had been brain-washed into believing that they *were* inferior to whites and had no hope for a better life. Even their leaders—except the perennially optimistic Booker T. Washington—despaired. Unable now to

---

23 See for example B. R. Tillman, "Causes of Southern Opposition to Imperialism," *North American Review,* CLXXI (September, 1900), 439–46.

moderate the outbursts of extremists and without legal or political recourse, the Negro had no alternative but sullen acquiescence, resignation, or sycophancy. This reinforced anti-Negro stereotypes and profoundly affected racist attitudes toward Negroes. It intensified the racists' arrogance, reinforced their contempt for the Negro, strengthened their self-righteousness, and reaffirmed scientific, historical, and religious "proof" of the Negro's inferiority. In examining and evaluating racist thought during the early twentieth century, the lowly status of the Negro must be borne constantly in mind. There was little to indicate in 1900 that within a few decades traditional attitudes toward Negroes would be seriously questioned and the basis laid for a revolution in race relations in the South as well as in the North.

In the three decades following the Spanish–American War, anti-Negro racism developed on two rather ill-defined and overlapping levels. The first consisted of systematic ideas developed by scientists, social scientists, historians, and religious leaders—groups who endeavored to create a racist ideology supported by scientific, historical, and/or religious authority. The second consisted of popular attitudes formulated and expounded by journalists, politicians, and popularizers—groups concerned with molding or reflecting popular opinion. The two groups differed materially in their mode of expression, the nature of evidence each offered to support its allegations, and the practical application each sought to give its ideas. In other respects, however, they were strikingly similar, for the ideas of the second were often derived from the researches of the first. Both were based upon a mixture of truth, half-truth, and untruth; prejudice, fancy, and wishful thinking; misconception, misinformation, and ignorance. Both contained much that was inexact, illogical, and inconsistent. Both were reflected in national and sectional policies toward the Negro. It is impossible therefore to understand those policies without also understanding the ideas from which they were derived. It matters little that those ideas were often false or incorrect. What the white man thought about the Negro was, in the short run at least, much more important than whether it happened also to be true.

Part I

DEVELOPMENT
OF ANTI-NEGRO THOUGHT

1

THE CONTRIBUTIONS
OF SCIENCE AND SOCIAL SCIENCE

> The theories of scientists are of no more value than those of
> other men. What we look to them for is facts, and from ad-
> mitted truth others can argue as well or better than they;
> for they are by no means the best logicians.
>
> "Caucasian," *Anthropology for the People* (1891)

In formulating and disseminating their ideology, anti-Negro writers
unconscionably exploited science and social science. Drawing heavily upon the theories and researches, as they interpreted them, of
eugenics, genetics, ethnology, biology, psychology, physiology, anthropology, sociology, and geography, they assembled a formidable
array of scientific and pseudoscientific evidence to support their
cause. Their efforts, moreover, were facilitated by reputable scientists in all disciplines who accepted the contentions that races are
unequal and that Negroes are inferior to other basic stocks. Thus
fortified by respectable scientific authority, they developed in detail

the "science of race." They often disagreed among themselves upon details and the implications of basic concepts, but they generally agreed upon fundamentals. In this manner they gave coherence to a body of thought that was in other respects amorphous and disorganized.

The twentieth century is an age of science, and racists, like other Americans, have felt compelled to give their ideas an elaborate scientific rationale. Indeed, between 1900 and 1930 this was their primary concern, and during these years they made science the chief bulwark of their ideas. As was the case throughout the nineteenth century, academic and scientific opinion continued in the new century to be against the Negro. Since this opinion seemed to explain his inferior position in society and to justify the prejudice which kept him there, it appealed to the popular mind. To the latter the Negro's inferiority was obvious. Was not the Negro immoral, criminal, ignorant, and impoverished, but withal contented? Surely he was. The achievement of scientific racism was to strengthen this popular prejudice by clothing it in a mantle of academic and scholarly authority. To no small extent this achievement was made possible by several newly developed branches of science and social science.

The nineteenth century had been an important one for American science. New discoveries and techniques had brought phenomenal advancements in the pure sciences as well as the rise of new sciences relating to man and society. Disciplines which a few decades before 1900 had been nonexistent or in their infancy now emerged to rival older ones in interest and importance. Concerning themselves with the discovery of universal laws through experimentation, observation, and statistics, the new disciplines prided themselves upon their scientific methodology. In the twentieth century they would make valuable contributions to American science and society, but in 1900 they still suffered from the overenthusiasm of youth. New hypotheses and exciting speculations often led sociologists, psychologists, biologists, anthropologists, and others to conclusions and inferences which later and calmer researchers disproved.

Members of these newer disciplines often failed to dissociate themselves from the preconceptions with which they approached their study; as a result they made no distinction between superficial observation and scientific evidence. They also had a disconcerting propensity to equate their techniques, however hit or miss, with scientific objectivity. For these reasons they were usually untroubled by exceptions to their generalizations, and they seldom withheld judgment because of inconclusive evidence. Important leaders of each discipline readily acknowledged these signs of immaturity and were chagrined by the racists' misuse of science, but they were not always heard by the public. The immaturity, therefore, not only was a source of embarrassment to conservative elements in the sciences but became a valuable boon to racists as well. They were enabled thereby to affix upon the Negro a stigma of inferiority more humiliating in many respects than that of slavery, and from which he has not yet fully recovered. Yet the capitulation of science to racism would not long survive in the twentieth century. By 1920 scientists were taking the lead in overturning racist concepts and within a decade had delivered the *coup de grâce* to racism as a respectable idea.

The science of race which developed in this country in the early twentieth century was all inclusive, especially as it applied to the Negro. It commenced by affirming that his inferiority began with the racial differentiation of mankind, and it concluded with scientific justification for Southern race policies and prejudices. It started, therefore, with ethnology and anthropology—sciences which study the origin of man, his division into races, and his distribution over the earth. It was necessary to begin with the origin of man, noted Edward Eggleston (a Virginia planter who is not to be confused with the Hoosier novelist of the same name), in order to appreciate fully the real deficiency of the Negro and the menace of his presence to the white population. Yet of all the disciplines which racists raided, they received least satisfaction from ethnology and anthropology. Perhaps because the origin of races was a matter of speculation anyway, anthropologists and ethnologists were wary of the pitfalls of overenthusiasm. By the same token, however, those who were inclined to do so had wide leeway for their speculating, and they developed an infinite number of interesting and ingenious theories concerning the origin of man and his separation into unequal races.

Those of Eggleston himself were illustrative. Without formal training in ethnology or anthropology, Eggleston had read widely in both, and by borrowing liberally from the speculations of others he was able to write "authoritatively" on the origin of man. In his view man began in Java as *Pithecanthropus Erectus,* and while still in an apelike state spread over the earth. After an almost inconceivably long time of evolution in different environments, he emerged in four basic races: Caucasian, Mongolian, American Indian, and Negro. Those in invigorating climates had their minds whetted and developed superior qualities. Those in less challenging surroundings retained the generalized and primitive qualities of their simian ancestors. All races had begun in an apelike form and on an equal footing, but natural law had so favored one as to cause it to develop out of all proportion to the other. The modern European, with his "superior mental attainment," was thousands if not millions of years ahead of his "laggard black brother." The conclusion was unavoidable: "Modern ethnologists have thoroughly established the fact that in all essential qualities the [Negro] race seems to be totally incapable of development in any marked degree." [1]

A multitude of other writers, some with impressive scientific credentials shared Eggleston's views on the relationship between evolution and racial inequality. Psychologist Marion J. Mayo, for example, used "the teachings of present-day anthropology" to prove that all races had descended from a common ancestral stock. But in accordance with the laws of heredity, he added, they had departed from this ancestral stock "more or less widely under the influence of environment and the principles of survival." The result was mental and physical superiority in Caucasians and stagnation in Negroes. The British-born Harvard psychologist William McDougall likewise believed that Europeans were "innately superior" to Negroes and that their superiority was "produced in the course of the immensely long ages of human life that preceded the dawn of civilization." [2] In the 1920's McDougall was one of the country's most influential and respected social psychologists. His *The Group Mind* was a minor classic in its field. Yet, like his other writings, it contained frequent illustrations of his conviction that Negroes are grossly inferior to whites. In two works published in the twenties, *Is America Safe For Democracy* (1921) and *The Indestructible Union* (1925), he succumbed completely to racism and nativism.

Henry Fairfield Osborn, eminent paleontologist and naturalist, was another giant of American science who endorsed the ideas of

---

1   Eggleston, *The Ultimate Solution of the American Negro Problem* (Boston, 1913), 27, 55.
2   Mayo, *The Mental Capacity of the American Negro* (New York, 1913), 51; and McDougall, *The Group Mind* (New York, 1920), 167.

Eggleston. Advancing the theory that racial stocks had separated before the Pleistocene period, Osborn suggested that "Negroid stock" was older and more primitive than others. It had evolved earlier than Caucasian or Mongolian stock and, therefore, more closely resembled its anthropoid ancestors. As a result, the Negro today was both physically and mentally retarded. His intelligence rarely exceeded "that of the eleven-year-old youth of the species Homo sapiens," and his wisdom teeth erupted eight to seventeen years earlier. In this casual fashion Osborn accepted one of the racists' most extreme contentions—that the races of man constitute separate biological species. By so doing, he added significantly to the authority of that contention and incidentally illustrated the connection between scholarly racism and its popularizers. It was from such writers as Osborn that Madison Grant and other propagandists drew their scientific authority. Grant, who is discussed later in more detail, could therefore think it old-fashioned to group the races into a single species, and by the same token he could advocate a classification system for man similar to that used for lower animals. He was certain that the physical differences between Nordics and Negroes, Australoids and Mongols, if found among lower mammals, "would be much more than sufficient to constitute not only separate species, but even subgenera." [3]

As the above reference to Osborn indicates, racists often pondered questions concerning the relative ages of races. To those who sought scientific explanations of racial inequality the evolutionary hypothesis was especially appealing. Yet in its simplest form, which Eggleston had expressed, it ignored major questions. Many of these were eventually solved by further development of the relationship between evolution and physical environment, which is discussed below. But other questions were also involved. Were Negroes at the same evolutionary stage as whites, but evolving along a different path? Or were they a "child race" following the same path thousands of years behind? Although the two questions involved contradictory ideas, both received substantial support among racists. The one, however, was bluntly rejected by proponents of the other.

The varieties of opinion regarding these questions illustrate the amorphousness of scientific racism and the dissimilarity of persons it

---

3 Osborn, "The Evolution of Human Races," *Natural History*, XXVI (January, 1926), 5; and Grant, *The Conquest of a Continent, or the Expansion of Races in America* (New York, 1933), 20.

appealed to. Glenn Frank, associate editor of *Century Magazine* and later president of the University of Wisconsin, declared in 1919 that "the Negro is not a white man with a black skin." He is instead "a different race at a different stage of racial evolution." Emory Q. Hawk, an economist from Birmingham Southern College and author of a widely used textbook, *Economic History of the South,* noted in one of his few references to the race that the Negro "unlike the Anglo-Saxon, has not yet passed through a long process of evolution in an environment requiring initiative and creative imagination." Seth K. Humphrey, a Massachusetts author of middling influence among nativists and anti-Negro racists, was convinced that there was no basis for the belief that non-Aryan races were "following, ages behind, in the footsteps of the White and destined for later emergence. They are contemporary races following different courses because of different inheritances." It mattered not that they readily adopted the ideas or products of Aryan civilization. The true test was their ability to contribute to that civilization. The Negro, he declared, was a million years from creating a telephone or gun. Convinced by such authorities as Frank, Hawk, and Humphrey, William Joseph Simmons, Imperial Wizard of the Ku Klux Klan, felt the Klan's treatment of the Negro to be fully justified. The race's "state of biological evolution," he stated, made Negroes "physically, and hence morally" unfit for democratic responsibilities. "The cause is biological." [4]

But the impression should not be given that such statements were the only responses to questions concerning the Negro's age and racial evolution. An entirely different response, and one of racism's most ingenious theories, came from the pen of Henry F. Suksdorf, a popularizer of racial ideas who appears to have had little scientific training. Endorsed by such writers as the prolific and prolix Californian Joseph P. Widney, whose writings mirror the spectrum of racist theory between 1900 and 1940, Suksdorf's thesis was that races, like individuals, have infancy, childhood, youth, maturity, old age, and dotage and that this fact explains the rise and fall of civilizations. When a people matured, he theorized, they became the world's superior race and created an advanced civilization. After a maturity

4   Glenn Frank, "The Clash of Color," *Century Magazine,* XCIX (November, 1919), 95; Emory Q. Hawk, *Economic History of the South* (New York, 1934), 511; Seth K. Humphrey, *The Racial Prospect* (New York, 1920), 119; William Joseph Simmons, *The Klan Unmasked* (Atlanta, 1924), 149.

of uncertain duration, however, due to inexorable natural forces, the race became old, and eventually passed into dotage. Its civilization then stagnated, and presently disintegrated. American Indians, for example, had reached their prime in the Aztec and Inca civilizations and had since fallen into the senility which accompanies racial dotage. The Australian aborigines were also now in their dotage, whereas most south and east Europeans and Asiatics, except Japanese, were in old age. Italians, Spaniards, and Portuguese were likewise past prime and declining, but Frenchmen, Anglo-Saxons, Germans, Dutch, Scandinavians, and Japanese were in full maturity. Negroes and Malayans were in childhood or infancy.[5]

It becomes apparent upon examining this hierarchy that Suksdorf was writing before World War I. He published his volume *Our Race Problems* in 1911 when Europeans still ruled the world, and his list conforms to the world power structure of that time. He illustrates, therefore, in a remarkable way, one of the principal characteristics of American racists, a characteristic which they incidentally shared with many scientists, social scientists, and historians. They pronounced general laws and universal theories, but they invariably reflected the time and place in which they wrote. Their attitude toward races and nationalities always coincided with the realities of world politics and economics, for they equated racial capacity with political power and technological advancement. Thus, Europeans were always superior to non-Europeans, but those who were most advanced industrially and technologically were more superior than others. Non-Europeans who had embraced the industrial revolution, e.g., the Japanese, were likewise superior to those who had not, such as the Chinese. Suksdorf, like most racists, including some who took pride in their scientific preciseness, paid little attention to distinctions between race and nationality. This of course created much confusion in their minds and was a source of much of the vagueness of scientific racism.

Speculating upon the Negro's evolutionary development, some

---

5 Suksdorf, *Our Race Problems* (New York, 1911), 316; and Widney, *The New World,* Volume II of *Race Life of the Aryan Peoples* (New York, 1907), 184, 238. On a much more sophisticated and plausible level, the cyclical theory of racial history toward which Suksdorf is groping was endorsed by such reputable writers as Australian geographer Griffith Taylor, a frequent contributor to various American journals. See his "The Evolution and Distribution of Race, Culture, and Language," *Geographical Review,* XI (January, 1921), 56.

racists eventually concluded that the race was a freak, an anachronism of nature, or in the words of William Hannibal Thomas, "the most unique feature in universal anthropology." Thomas, himself a mulatto, was one of the most singular authors in the annals of anti-Negro literature. Descended from a family which had been mulatto, free, and Northern for three or four generations, he had little in common with the mass of Southern Negroes. Apparently well educated and well read in subjects relating to Negroes and their history, he had been caught in the wave of idealism which swept pro-Negro elements in the North after the Civil War. Intent upon remaking the Negro in the white man's social, economic, and political image and raising him to the white man's level in education and middle-class morality, he had joined the ranks of carpetbagger idealists in the South. He served for a time in the South Carolina legislature as an outspoken champion of reforms in the Negro's interest, but as a result of his experiences there he became disillusioned with the Negro and convinced that the race was hopelessly degraded and vicious. Eventually he reached the racists' conclusion that the Negroes were in fact innately inferior to whites. In 1901 as a final expression of his despair, he published *The American Negro, What He Was, What He Is, and What He May Become*—a work more notable for its pomposity and flamboyance that its insight into racial problems.[6]

Thomas' observation that the Negro was an anthropological freak was reiterated by T. T. Waterman, an ethnologist from California State College at Fresno. Writing in the *American Anthropologist* in 1924 as a "disinterested" and "detached" spokesman on racial questions, Waterman endorsed the hypothesis that Negroes were "an earlier type" which had evolved prior to other basic stocks. In the earliest stages of evolution, he suggested, the Negro had occupied most of the world's land area, excluding America. With the appearance of more advanced human types, however, he was gradually forced out of the more desirable areas and eventually was shunted into Africa and Australia. His earlier and more primitive development had prevented him from competing with other races, a deficiency from which he still suffered. He could expect, therefore,

---

6   "There is a common agreement in the public mind," he wrote, "that the negro represents an accentuated type of human degradation." Thomas, *The American Negro, What He Was, What He Is, and What He May Become* (New York, 1901), 106.

"to disappear in time from off the face of the earth." But before this happened, Waterman urged the nation to "save out a few good Negro types" and prevent their extinction. Perhaps a conservation policy like that adopted for the buffalo was what he had in mind. The Negro was "'out of it,'" he declared. The whole race was "an anachronism, like the kangaroo and the ornithorhynchus."[7]

As indicated previously, scientific racists relied heavily upon the race-climate hypothesis to prove that evolution was the source of racial inequality. Few hypotheses received greater attention from racists or were developed in more detail. They arrogated to themselves the theory, long supported by many geographers, that racial characteristics represented adaptations to the physical environment in which evolution had occurred. For racist purposes this idea was as plausible as it was ingenious. The hot and stultifying climate of tropical Africa, its dense and humid jungles, had halted the Negro's evolutionary development at primitive, generalized levels. The invigorating and exacting climate of the north temperate zone, however, had stimulated the Caucasian's development into advanced and specialized channels. The result was a fundamental difference in physical appearance, emotional stability, and mental capability.

The influence of climate upon race was not merely presumed, however. Like other tenets of scientific racism it too was buttressed by reputable scientific authority. Especially valuable to racists in this connection were the writings and theories of Ellen Churchill Semple. Miss Semple, the chief American disciple of German anthropogeographer Friederick Ratzel, was widely esteemed in American geographic circles. Her researches into the relationship between physical environment and the characteristics of race and nationality were landmarks in the history of geographic theory. Hers was a supple scientific mind, with a remarkable ability to synthesize diverse fields of knowledge. Yet like many of her contemporaries she wrote with definite racist and nativist overtones. She repeatedly referred to non-Europeans as inferior races, and she assigned to Anglo-Saxons a monopoly on such racial characteristics as "energy, initiative, adaptability, and receptivity to new ideas."[8] Her racism,

---

7 Waterman, "The Subdivisions of the Human Race and their Distribution," *American Anthropologist*, XXVI (October, 1924), 474–90.

8 Semple, *Influences of Geographic Environment on the Basis of Ratzel's System of Anthropo-Geography* (New York, 1911), 620.

however, was a product of her scientific imagination and she did not intend it as a justification for policies of repression or discrimination. But it was made to order for proponents of such policies.

Miss Semple's theses were developed in her most significant work *Influences of Geographic Environment,* which she published in 1911. She contended that over the centuries geographic factors such as mountains, rivers, oceans, jungles, humidity, and temperature had produced special characteristics in local populations which subsequently had become fixed and inherited. Although this process had begun as one of individual adaptation to environment, it had eventually created the racial and subracial divisions of mankind. It had generally been so gradual as to be imperceptible, but some aspects of it were now obvious. The influence of climate and altitude upon pigmentation, for example, was apparent—high altitude and high latitude induced blondness. There was also a correlation between temperament and climate. North Europeans were "energetic, provident, serious, thoughtful," whereas south Europeans were "easygoing, improvident, . . . gay, emotional, imaginative." In addition, she observed that "among Negroes of the equatorial belt," the qualities of south Europeans "degenerate into grave racial faults." [9]

Utilizing the theories of Miss Semple, racists detailed the relationship between Africa's climate and the Negro's racial characteristics. Among many of them this subject became a fetish. Tropical life, they insisted, was too simple to stimulate inquisitiveness and curiosity. The climate there encouraged sloth on all sides. Food was abundantly supplied by nature, as were shelter and clothing when they were needed at all. Consequently, there was no struggle for existence and, hence, no inducement to rapid and varied selection. Social organization was monotonously simple, whereas intellectual and spiritual development was stagnant. As a result, the Negro was a victim of arrested development and of "deeply ingrained race traits, in which the instinctive and the impulsive predominate over the rational." [10]

An interesting aspect of this phase of anti-Negro thought was its acceptance by persons who were little interested in the Negro or

9   *Ibid.,* 120, 22.
10   These and similar ideas were developed in Osborn, "The Evolution of Human Races," *Natural History* XXVI (January, 1926), 3–13; John Moffatt Mecklin, *Democracy and Race Friction, A Study in Social Ethics* (New York, 1921), 25–26; and Edward A. Ross, "The Causes of Race Superiority," *The Annals,* CXVIII (July, 1901), 67–89.

what racists called "the Negro problem," and even less interested in the popular extremism which that problem generated. Henry Fairfield Osborn again, the distinguished sociologist E. A. Ross, the renown and influential psychologist G. Stanley Hall, the eminent and scholarly economist John R. Commons—each a pioneering giant in his own field—were examples of authorities who endorsed this idea, often as casually as they endorsed any obvious and generally held truth. Thus, widely did it pervade American thought! Hall, for example, referred to the Negro's "tropical imagination," and Commons believed that the race was "indolent and fickle" because of its development under a tropical sun. Other writers alluded to the Negro's "heat-loving body," his "tropical exuberance of temperament," and described him as the "son of a wild and tropical race content for thousands of years to roam the jungles of Africa." It was this long sojourn in the tropics which had also produced the race's skin color, hair texture, nose configurations, "intense sexual passions," and "hereditary distaste for exertion of any kind." Albert A. Hopkins, associate editor of *Scientific American,* wrote in 1925, "In the sunlit tropics the human skin grows darker and the hair apparently grows short and kinky. . . . Nobody knows why this happens but it does." [11]

The uses to which racists put these ideas revealed the manner of their exploitation of science. There was, of course, nothing innately racist in asserting that the Negro had evolved in Africa, or that his racial characteristics were adaptations to the African environment. Such ideas were often advanced by scientists who were in no sense racists, by Harvard anthropologist Roland B. Dixon in *The Racial History of Man,* for example, and by anthropologist Carleton S. Coon in *The Story of Man* and *The Origin of Races.*[12] What racists

11 See note 10, p. 28. See also G. Stanley Hall, "The Negro in Africa and America," *Pedagogical Seminary,* XII (September, 1905), 355; John R. Commons, *Races and Immigrants in America* (New York, 1915), 136; and Albert A. Hopkins, "Which Races Are Best?" *Scientific American,* CXXXII (February, 1925), 78.

12 Coon, *The Story of Man* (2nd. ed. rev.; New York, 1962); Coon, *The Origin of Races* (New York, 1962). It is interesting to note that Dr. Coon's latest works have already been cited as a support for anti-Negro racism. See for example, Carleton Putnam, "Evolution and Race: New Evidence," *The Citizen,* VI (July–August, 1962), 7–10. (*The Citizen* is the official journal of the Citizens Councils of America.) Dr. Coon's works are conveniently summarized by him in "New Findings on the Origin of Races," *Harper's,* CCXXV (December, 1962), 66–74.

did was to label as inferior all characteristics which allegedly resulted from the Negro's evolution in Africa. It was not their efforts to
account for his black skin that were racist. It was instead their
attempt to make that black skin an innately inferior characteristic.
As will be shown in more detail later, they made Caucasian characteristics their standard of excellence and insofar as the Negro diverged from them he was held to be inferior. If his inferiority sprang
ultimately from evolution and if his evolution occurred in Africa,
Africa was *ergo* the source of inferiority.

Impelled by their own logic, racists eventually concluded that
evolution had adapted each race to a unique natural habitat. Charles
E. Woodruff, a peddler of scientific racism in its most annoying form,
was especially attracted to this idea. As an army surgeon, Woodruff
had spent several years in the Philippines where he became interested in the effects upon American servicemen of long exposure to
the Philippine climate. Frequently, he noticed, whites had difficulty
adjusting to the heat and humidity, and continued activity there
often produced general debilitation. He noticed no such reaction
among Negroes, however, and concluded that as a race Caucasians
were ill adapted to the Philippine climate. The glaring sunlight and
ubiquitous heat of the tropics were too radical a departure from the
cold, foggy northland in which the race had evolved.

Woodruff developed these ideas in *The Effects of Tropical Light
on White Men* (1905), a ponderous and preposterous volume which
he revised and reissued a decade later under the title *Medical
Ethnology*. His object was to formulate a general anthropological
law to explain the relationship between race and climate which he
had observed in the Philippines. To do this he simply postulated a
correlation between skin color and racial habitat and concluded that
the darker a race the nearer it belonged to the equator. Therefore,
Negroes thrived only between 30 degrees north and 30 degrees south
latitude, brown races between 30 and 35 degrees, "olive peoples"
between 35 and 45, and blonds between 55 and 60.

Elsewhere each group lost its vitality and slowly declined. This
meant of course that the United States was too far south to preserve
the racial vigor of blonds and was best suited to the mediocre stocks
of central and southern Europe. Indeed the area between 30 and 35
degrees north latitude, which includes Atlanta, Little Rock, Dallas,
Phoenix, and Los Angeles, was unsuitable for whites of any complex-
ion. Unless the whites of that zone migrate north every summer, he

wrote, they will become enfeebled. Eventually degeneration will commence and extinction will follow. At the same time, however, the United States was also unsuitable for blacks. Winters there were "too cold for the open nostrils of the Negro," and Woodruff predicted the race's "probable extinction in America." He also informed Americans of superior stocks, such as Nordics and blonds, that the only way to preserve their racial vigor was to wear heavy clothing, avoid sunlight, and live in darkened homes. Otherwise, he warned, the best racial stocks would disappear from this country, except possibly from the Pacific Northwest.[13]

Woodruff's theories were applied in the most literal manner to Negroes in America. Racists agreed that anyone from the "damp, steaming tropics" faced serious problems in the "comparative chill" of this country. The Negro's indolence, sexual promiscuity, lack of foresight, and dependence had served him well in the tropics, but these were liabilities in the temperate zone. Here the struggle for existence was between well-equipped whites and ill-equipped blacks, and this was why Woodruff had predicted the race's extinction in America. "When any people," wrote anatomist Robert Bennett Bean of the University of Virginia, "have been relocated in an environment utterly alien to that in which they have evolved and lived in for thousands of years they have almost invariably disappeared." [14]

Different and more optimistic conclusions were sometimes drawn from this by popularizers of scientific racism. Going a step beyond Bean or Woodruff, both of whom were scientists and wrote as such, other writers felt that environmental forces in the temperate zone would react upon the Negro just as they had upon whites. This reverse side of the race-climate hypothesis elicited virtually no attention from scientists, although a contributor to *Scientific American* in 1910 did venture the opinion that "the same causes and elements of nature [in the temperate zone] that have depigmentized the skin

13 Charles E. Woodruff, *The Effects of Tropical Light on White Men* (New York, 1905), 271, 276. Similar ideas were endorsed by James Bryce and Dean N. S. Shaler of Harvard's Lawrence Scientific School. "Statistics show," Bryce wrote, "that the Negro race increases comparatively slowly in the north of latitude 40°," in *The American Commonwealth* (New York, 1908), II, 813. And see N. S. Shaler, *The Neighbor, The Natural History of Human Contacts* (Boston, 1904), 132.
14 Bean, *The Races of Man, Differentiation and Dispersal of Man* (New York, 1932), 53.

and straightened the hair of 'Homo Caucasius' will, in time, produce the same results on the Afro-American's skin and its appendages." [15] Other racists, however, were even less sophisticated. "It is a scientific fact that the pure black characterizing the skin of the natives of tropical Africa cannot for very many centuries show on the skin of successive generations of inhabitants in a temperate climate," wrote one of them. "It is only a question of some more generations through some more centuries, when nature, through the inevitable working of the laws of human proximity, and through temperate and colder climates, will eventually obliterate the line of demarkation between the so-called white and black races in the United States." The process, moreover, was well under way, for American Negroes were already "much changed in cranial formation and facial contour from their benighted ancestors." [16] They could ultimately expect to become Caucasians, for while their skin grows lighter, their "tropical indolence" will evolve into "northern activity," and their "sluggish African blood . . . [will] quicken in its flow." [17]

The fallacies of the race-climate hypothesis as here developed seem not to have troubled its advocates, although they never applied it to other races or locales. They never considered its implications for whites in Africa, for example, or for the European immigrants then flooding into America. More important still, they ignored its implications for American Indians. Few of the writers obsessed with this hypothesis were bothered by the fact that the oldest Americans were not Nordics at all, but Indians, members of an "inferior" colored race and a silent refutation of their entire theory. Indians in tropical America were not black, just as those in cold and foggy areas were not white. But perhaps, as racists insisted, their stay in America had been too brief. And—it must be admitted—the climate hypothesis

---

15   J. M. Boddy, "The 'Kinks' in the Negro's Hair," *Scientific American,* CII (April 30, 1910), 359.

16   These were the opinions of John Louis Hill of Tennessee, a fundamentalist protestant minister. See his *Negro, National Asset or Liability?* (New York, 1930), 66, 69–70. Ray Stannard Baker, who muckraked the American race problem and who reflected enlightened Northern opinion, likewise felt that it was "certainly in accord with the best scientific beliefs" that "Negroes even without the admixture of white blood were gradually growing lighter" in the United States. See his "The Tragedy of the Mulatto," *American Magazine,* LXV (April, 1908), 585.

17   Joseph Alexander Tillinghast, "The Negro in Africa and America," *Publications of the American Economic Association,* 3rd Ser., III, No. 2 (1902), 171.

was much more plausible when applied to Negroes than to Indians or other races.

Convinced now that evolution was the source of racial inequality, racists turned their attention to heredity, the process through which they believed this inequality to be perpetuated. They were convinced that this was the real function of the laws of heredity, and not until the twentieth century did they take the trouble to explain fully the scientific mechanisms by which those laws operated. Beginning about 1900 this emphasis on heredity—on genetics and eugenics— formed the most significant new element in racist thought in the. twentieth century. For the first quarter of the century, indeed, eugenics and genetics constituted the single most important authority of scientific racists. So completely were these sciences permeated by racism that Harvard anthropologist E. A. Hooten complained as late as 1937 that eugenics was little more than "a lay form of ancestor worship" clothed in "Ku Klux Klan regalia." [18]

The sources of eugenic racism were two. One, Sir Francis Galton's science of heredity, was discussed earlier. The other, the application of genetics to plant and animal breeding, must also be noted. Long before racists became interested in heredity, the principles of genetics had been known and practiced by American plant and animal breeders, and the results had sometimes been phenomenal. They eliminated undesirable strains and unhealthy characteristics, developing new and heartier breeds of animals as well as plants. Was it not reasonable that an application of similar principles to mankind would create a new race of human thoroughbreds?

The ideas of Luther Burbank and W. E. D. Stokes are representative of this point of view. Burbank, the nation's most successful and widely known horticulturist, had worked miracles in his experiments with plant genetics and hybridization. Almost singlehandedly he had made the nation conscious of the possibilities of such experimentation. A conscientious scientist engrossed in his work and enthusiastic over the possibilities which he thought it held for mankind, he became convinced that man should adopt the principles which he had used so successfully upon plants. Only in this way, he felt, could a stronger and better race, a superior "human plant," be evolved. Burbank, of course, had no interest in demonstrating the Negro's alleged inferiority, yet his ideas had obvious appeal to

---

18   Ernest Albert Hooten, *Apes, Men, and Morons* (New York, 1937), 231.

racists. "If a race has not acquired and stored among its hereditary tendencies sufficient perseverance and adaptability to meet all the changes to which it must always be subjected by its ever-changing environment," he wrote in language strikingly similar to the racists, "it will be left behind and finally destroyed, outstripped by races better equipped for the fray." [19]

W. E. D. Stokes, owner of Patchen Wilkes Stock Farm at Lexington, Kentucky, was one of the nation's leading horse breeders. Like Burbank, Stokes conducted numerous experiments in selective breeding, and he studied the results through generations of race horses. Impressed by his success in manipulating the characteristics of horses, he too became convinced that mankind could benefit from eugenic breeding. Among all elements of the population, he observed, human breeding was a haphazard affair which often as not had undesirable consequences. Its immediate result was an appalling wastage of human resources. Its ultimate effect, and the source of Stokes's alarm, would be national disaster. He sought, therefore, to arouse the public, and toward that end he wrote one of the most remarkable items in the literature of scientific racism, *The Right to be Well Born, or Horse Breeding in its Relation to Eugenics* (1917). National decay was so far advanced, he lamented, that not more than four thousand men now possessed the physical and mental force necessary to "improve the breeding of our human family." This choice stock must be located at once, and for that purpose the pedigree of every American should be investigated and made a matter of public record. On the basis of knowledge so accumulated, like would be mated with like, and a brave new world would emerge in which individuals were bred to their occupation and locality. "Why, there is no trouble to breed any kind of men you like," he wrote, "4 feet men or 7 feet men—or, for instance all to weigh 60 or 400 pounds, just like we breed horses. It only takes a longer time and more patience." Like most Americans of his generation Stokes accepted the idea of racial inequality, and he declared emphatically that Negroes were eugenically undesirable. He did feel, however, that an adequate program of selective breeding could remake the race into a satisfactory servant class.[20]

Stokes expressed rather crudely the attitude of a large element of

---

19   Luther Burbank, *The Training of the Human Plant* (New York, 1908), 80.
20   W. E. D. Stokes, *The Right to be Well Born, or Horse Breeding in its Relation to Eugenics* (New York, 1917), 49, 81–83, 101, 169.

American science, an attitude which crystallized between 1915 and 1925 in a flood of literature on eugenics, genetics, and heredity. Although primarily concerned with immigration restriction, this literature discussed the "Negro question" in detail, for Negroes, of course, were "inferior" to all southern and eastern Europeans. Typical of this literature were the works of Seth K. Humphrey, the Massachusetts nativist mentioned above. A writer of considerable facility and persuasiveness, Humphrey was active in the campaign to educate Americans on the "racial dangers" of unselective European immigration. His chief work *Mankind, Racial Values and the Racial Prospect* (1917) was so successful that he revised and reissued it three years later as *The Racial Prospect*. Writing for "the lay reader who is willing to think, but not ready to go into the depth of a new science," Humphrey illustrated the chief characteristics of writers on eugenics. They wrote for the popular reader and to influence public policy. Like Stokes, but on a more sophisticated and rational level, they urged the adoption of public policies to increase the birth rate among racially desirable elements and to reduce it among the undesirable. They agreed with New York journalist and amateur eugenicist Albert Edward Wiggam that environmental factors were futile in checking racial decline. The golden rule without eugenic safeguards, warned Wiggam in *The New Decalogue of Science,* only hastens the decline. A member of the advisory board of the American Eugenics Society and the editorial board of *Eugenics Magazine,* Wiggam expressed the eugenicists' fear that Nordics and other "superior" stocks were committing suicide by their alarmingly low birth rate.[21]

The ideas of Wiggam, Humphrey, and others were summarized by Paul Popenoe, editor of the *Journal of Heredity,* and Roswell Hill Johnson, of the University of Pittsburgh, in their popular and influential textbook *Applied Eugenics.* Surveying the history and present state of eugenics, Popenoe and Johnson illustrated the remarkable confluence of scientific and racist thought on this subject. Relying upon such authorities as John Moffatt Mecklin's *Democracy and Race Friction* (1921), they endorsed racial segregation as "a social adaptation with survival value." It was necessary because the

---

21   See Wiggam's *The New Decalogue of Science* (Indianapolis, 1922), 37, 54; and *The Fruit of the Family Tree* (Indianapolis, 1924). For similar ideas see two works by William McDougall, *Is America Safe for Democracy?* (New York, 1921); and *The Indestructible Union* (Boston, 1925).

mental development and group traits of Negroes are more primitive than those of whites. "We feel justified in concluding," they wrote, "that the Negro race differs greatly from the white race, mentally as well as physically, and that in many respects it may be said to be inferior when tested by the requirements of modern civilization and progress, with particular reference to North America." Specifically, "the Negro lacks in his germ plasm excellence of some qualities which the white races possess, and which are essential for success in competition with the civilizations of the white races of the present day." He is, therefore, not only different from the white but in large measure eugenically inferior as well. Thus, "if eugenics is to be thought of solely in terms of the white race, there can be no hesitation about rendering a verdict. We must unhesitatingly condemn miscegenation." [22]

The average American had difficulty in distinguishing between these ideas and the endorsement of "deep-going eugenic reform" by Madison Grant, Lothrop Stoddard, and—ultimately—by Hiram Wesley Evans of the Ku Klux Klan.[23] The distinction between science and racism had been blurred.

While racist ideas pervaded the study of eugenics, American scientists pondered the role of heredity and environment in determining individual and group characteristics. Jukeses and Edwardses and other families were carefully studied for evidence of persistence and discontinuity in individual and family traits. After long and painstaking research, there was a general consensus among scientists that heredity predominated. "Experimentally and statistically," declared biologist Frederick Adams Woods, who made intensive studies of European royalty and other great families, "there is not a grain of proof that ordinary environment can alter the salient mental and moral traits in any measurable degree from what they were predetermined to be through innate influences." Such an idea had obvious appeal to spokesmen for "superior" races, who drew from it inferences which Woods perhaps had not intended. It became at

22   Paul Popenoe and Roswell Hill Johnson, *Applied Eugenics* (New York, 1918), 280–85, 291–92.
23   Stoddard, *The Revolt Against Civilization, The Menace of the Under Man* (New York, 1923), 84; Grant, *The Passing of the Great Race, or The Racial Basis of European History* (New York, 1921), 48; and Evans, "Where Do We Go From Here?" *Papers Read at the Meeting of Grand Dragons, Knights of the Ku Klux Klan at Their First Annual Meeting . . . July 1923* (Asheville, 1923), 7–13.

once a justification for racial separateness and social exclusiveness and as such filtered down to popular racists. "The one clear message that biological investigation has brought as its gift to the thought of the twentieth century," University of Virginia biologist Ivey F. Lewis told members of the university's race-conscious Anglo-Saxon club in 1923, "is that the idea of environment moulding something out of nothing is sheer nonsense. What goes into the hereditary mill is what comes out of it." [24]

Again the distinction between science and racism was blurred, and the American layman readily accepted an idea that seemed so obviously correct. Racists had, he felt, convincingly demonstrated the great lesson of the science of race—that "somatological or bodily characters" and "physical predispositions and impulses" are immutable. The Negro's inferiority, as they had long insisted, *was* innate, inborn, ingrained—in a word, inherited.

Interwoven in these discussions of evolution and heredity was another subject of equal concern to racists—the physical, intellectual, and emotional qualities of Negroes which reflected the race's alleged inferiority. Here as elsewhere the white man's characteristics, as racists described them, were the standard of excellence and to the extent that Negroes diverged from them the Negroes were inferior. This divergence, however, was often less apparent than real and, as a result, susceptible to misunderstanding. Consequently, racists assumed the considerable task of measuring and describing the physical characteristics of both races, and so zealously did they perform the task that it became in their view an exact science.

Measuring physical features, however, was considerably less difficult than measuring emotional or intellectual traits. For the latter, racists studied the Negro's mentality, behavior patterns, and physiological characteristics and from them deduced his emotional and intellectual traits. In either case it was *difference* which impressed racists. They interpreted minute variations in racial averages as profoundly significant but dismissed extensive overlappings as inconsequential. Typically, they dwelt exclusively upon data which supported their premise, but in this process, it should be noted, excepting only their researches into the Negro's brain and mental

---

24 The quotation from Woods is in Stoddard, *The Revolt Against Civilization*, 48; the Lewis quotation is from the Asheville (N.C.) *Citizen*, April 6, 1924.

capacity, they received little assistance from reputable scholars after 1900. They were able, however, to appeal to older scientific authorities and to interpret to their advantage the scholarship of others. Largely an activity of popularizers, it nevertheless had sufficient scientific endorsement to win general public acceptance.

The success of any attempt to prove the Negro's alleged physical, mental, and emotional inferiority depended upon proof that his brain was inferior to that of other races. Racial differences in the brain were not apparent to the untrained observer, and this fact complicated the racists' problem. One could readily see, for example, that the Negro's hair was more "kinky" than the Caucasian's; therefore racists had merely to show the inferiority of kinkiness. Not so with the brain, however. Yet races undoubtedly differed as much in brain capacity as they did in other ways. Evolution had produced variations in hair texture, skin color, and head shape. Was it not logical that it had also produced "correspondingly important neural differences"? To ask the question was to answer it. The inferiority of the Negro's brain was therefore assumed, and racists concentrated their attention upon isolating and describing features which demonstrated that fact.[25]

They began with the premise that a direct correlation existed between brain size and mental capacity. From this they inferred that the average Negro brain was significantly smaller than the average white brain, an inference which they substantiated by a multitude of studies on the relative cranial capacity and brain weight of different races. Drawn largely from studies made by Europeans in the nineteenth century, these studies were particularly attractive because they corresponded invariably to the racists' hierarchical ranking of races. According to figures offered by sociologist John Moffatt Mecklin, the cranial capacity of the average Caucasian male was 1,500 to 1,600 cubic centimeters, of the Mongolian 1,500 to 1,580, of the Negro 1,388, of the Australian aborigine 1,245.[26]

In the opinion of racists no more graphic illustration of the Negro's mental inferiority could be given, although other factors could and

---

25   George Oscar Ferguson, "The Mental Status of the American Negro," *Scientific Monthly,* XII (June, 1921), 534; and Mayo, *The Mental Capacity of the American Negro,* 61.

26   Mecklin, *Democracy and Race Friction,* 32. Other representative listings are in Tillinghast, "The Negro in Africa and America," 92; and R. W. Shufeldt, *America's Greatest Problem: The Negro* (Philadelphia, 1915), 30.

did supplement its authority. Among these the most important were the relatively smooth surface of the Negro's brain and the angular shape of his head. The former was a result of fewer and less complex convolutions and shallower fissures and significantly reduced the cerebral surface. The latter resulted from underdevelopment of the brain's frontal lobes and overdevelopment of those in the rear. This, of course, was profoundly significant. Underdevelopment of the frontal lobes meant underdevelopment of the anterior association center which controlled the higher mental processes. This in turn caused a lack of self-control, an absence of subjectivity, and an incapacity for ethical and esthetic judgment. Among persons so affected sudden "sexual excitement, anger, or vexation" could cause a loss of self-control and a disregard for custom and good taste.[27]

Perhaps the most influential exponent of these ideas during the early twentieth century was Robert Bennett Bean, physician, anthropologist, and professor of anatomy in the University of Virginia medical school. Possessing a broad knowledge of human anatomy and physiology, Bean buttressed his writings with an imposing array of scientific and pseudoscientific authority. At the same time, however, he was interested in influencing popular opinion, and he wrote in a straightforward, though somewhat turgid, style. A rather productive writer on the subjects of race and the Negro, he had considerable influence among popular racists, who frequently cited his works.[28]

Racists explained the physiological deficiencies of the Negro's brain by theorizing that its physical growth halted abruptly at puberty. At this time the sutures of the skull were said to knit firmly together, preventing further enlargement of the brain. Puberty was, of course, an especially inopportune time for the cessation of mental development. Prior to this age brain activity involved only such

---

27 Bean, *The Races of Man*, 94–95; Bean, "The Negro Brain," *Century Magazine*, LXXII (October, 1906), 783–84; Bean, "Some Racial Peculiarities of the Negro Brain," *American Journal of Anatomy*, V (September, 1906), 353–432.

28 It is interesting to note that Bean is cited several times in the most important recent example of biological racism, *The Biology of the Race Problem* (n.p., 1962), by Wesley Critz George, emeritus professor of histology and embryology and formerly head of the department of anatomy of the University of North Carolina medical school. George's report was prepared by commission of the governor of Alabama, and is circulated by the Citizens Councils of Mississippi.

processes as perception, memory, and motor responses. Not until later did it broaden into abstraction, critical thinking, comprehension of complex and subtle relationships, and "ability to appreciate logical, aesthetic and moral situations." But even though the Negro's mental development ceased at puberty, his animal and sexual development continued unabated. The adult Negro was, thus, physically and sexually mature, but lacking in the restraints of mental maturity. He was a boy with a man's passions but a deadened intellect. He could never escape from mental and consequently moral retardation.[29]

Confidence in this conviction was enhanced between 1910 and 1925 by a flood of new evidence from psychologists and educators. Eager to understand a new psychological phenomenon, the intelligence quotient, and to experiment with tests which purported to measure it, psychologists and educators during those years rushed into large-scale testing programs which often sacrificed scientific standards to overenthusiasm. Large groups and small, white groups and Negro, young groups and old were tested and sometimes retested, and the results carefully reported and analyzed. Occasionally whites and Negroes were tested with the specific purpose of comparing racial intelligence. Sometimes whites were separated into nationality groups for the same purpose, and Negroes were divided into "pure" Negroes and mulattoes to determine the effects of racial intermixture. More often, however, the object of testing was simply to determine the intelligence of the group tested. Soon the results were being collected and compared by psychologists, some of whom were especially interested in demonstrating the Negro's mental inferiority. The test results varied somewhat, of course, but the variation was within a larger area of agreement. Whites invariably scored substantially higher than Negroes, and northern and western Europeans and old American stocks scored higher than other whites.

---

29   George Oscar Ferguson, *The Psychology of the Negro, An Experimental Study* (New York, 1916), 123–24; and Mayo, *The Mental Capacity of the American Negro*, 58. This idea was also endorsed by H. L. Mencken, the Baltimore sage, and Albert Bushnell Hart, the historian. "His [the Negro's] brain is not fitted for the higher forms of mental effort," wrote Mencken. "That mind is unable to grasp any but the most elemental concepts," he continued. "The theory that the Negro mind ceases to develop after adolescence perhaps has something in it," agreed Hart. *Men Versus the Man, A Correspondence Between Robert Rives LaMonte, Socialist, and H. L. Mencken, Individualist* (New York, 1910), 110, 116; and Hart, *The Southern South* (New York, 1912), 104.

Collectively, the results were so comprehensive and overwhelming that neither scientist nor layman cared to challenge them.[30]

The racist uses of intelligence tests were typified by the studies of George Oscar Ferguson and Carl C. Brigham. Both Ferguson and Brigham were reputable professional psychologists, and both had distinguished academic careers, Ferguson at the University of Virginia and Brigham at Princeton. Both were convinced that intelligence tests proved the inequality of races, but they were concerned with different races. Ferguson shared the Southerners' preoccupation with Negroes, and among academic psychologists he was by 1920 the most authoritative voice "proving" the Negro's inferiority by intelligence tests. Brigham, on the contrary, reflected the Easterners' concern with European immigrants.

Ferguson administered tests to hundreds of Negroes and whites, and reported the results in *The Psychology of the Negro, An Experimental Study*. The average IQ of whites, he found, was one hundred, and that of Negroes only seventy-five. His tests revealed considerable overlapping, since many Negroes scored above the white average and a few were in the highest categories. He accounted for this by chance—he never denied that an occasional Negro could be intellectually gifted—and by the intermixture of white blood. The latter was so important, he felt, that he undertook to determine scientifically the effect of race mixture on intelligence. To do this he divided his testees according to the amount of racial intermixture, which he determined by the color of their skin. The results were exactly as he expected. "The percentage of success for Negroes compared to whites on the test were 69.27% for pure Negroes; 73.2% for ¾ Negroes; 81.2% for mulattoes (half-whites); 98.7% for quadroons." [31]

Unlike Ferguson, Brigham did not himself administer large numbers of intelligence tests. Instead, he analyzed tests administered to thousands of army inductees during World War I. The product of his endeavors, *A Study of American Intelligence*, was impressive at first sight for the large number of subjects tested and the ostensible

---

30 For a summary of the literature on these tests see Morris S. Viteles, "The Mental Status of the Negro," *The Annals*, CXL (November, 1928), 166–77; and James L. Graham, "A Quantitative Comparison of Rational Responses of Negro and White College Students," *Journal of Social Psychology*, I (February, 1930), 97–121.

31 Ferguson, "The Mental Status of the American Negro," 533–43; and Ferguson, *The Psychology of the Negro*.

objectivity of its author. Here at last seemed to be a disinterested scientific study of comparative racial intelligence, and it was so accepted by the American public. A second and closer look, however, revealed Brigham's kinship with the racists. His bias against south and east Europeans and Negroes, although couched in scientific terminology, was present throughout the study and noticeably influenced his conclusions. He completely ignored environmental factors and further weakened his case by citing Madison Grant, Charles W. Gould, and the now superseded William Z. Ripley as authorities on "the race hypothesis." He found that only 13.13 percent of Negro draftees equaled the average white draftee in intelligence. Dividing Negroes into Northern and Southern groups, he noted that the former did considerably better than the latter, but he explained this by assuming that Negroes who migrated north were more intelligent than those who remained in the South. Like Ferguson he concluded that racial differences in intelligence were innate, and in so doing he offered formidable scientific authority for a major racist idea.[32]

But the Negro's inferiority was not manifested by his low intelligence and deficient brain alone. The whole gamut of his physical features, from the top of his frizzled head to the bottom of his prehensile big toe, likewise attested his inferiority. His features, insisted racists, were generalized and primitive and much nearer to those of anthropoids than those of Caucasians. One of the oldest of racist beliefs,[33] this idea has been reinforced by Darwinism, and it persisted among extremists in the twentieth century. "The anatomy of the Negro exhibits a much closer approach to the anthropoid apes than does any other race," wrote one of the most immoderate racists, the physician R. W. Shufeldt. "Many vestigial or rudimentary organs and structures" which are constant in animals below man appear far more frequently in the Negro than in the white race. Even the scholarly and influential sociologist Franklin Henry Giddings, who

---

32 Carl C. Brigham, *A Study of American Intelligence* (Princeton, 1923), xvii–xviii, 82. For another example of the use of these army tests to prove the Negro's inferiority see Robert M. Yerkes, "Testing the Human Mind," *Atlantic Monthly*, CXXXI (March, 1923), 358. Yerkes, director of psychological testing for the army in World War I, was editor of the *Journal of Comparative Psychology*.

33 Gobineau for example had been "involuntarily reminded of the structure of the monkey" while observing Negroes in Africa. Gobineau, *The Inequality of Human Races*, 107.

gave little attention to the Negro or to questions of racial inequality, noticed "a large number of simian survivals" in the average Negro's anatomy.[34]

In describing those features which made the Negro a "better animal" than the white man, racists began with the "exceeding thickness" of his skull, a thickness so great that it made his head a battering ram.[35] From there they proceeded to his "decidedly prognathous" facial angle which unduly projected his lower face forward.[36] His eyes, they continued, were large and black and the sclerotic coat was tinged with yellow. His lips were "thick and brutal," indicating passion. His mouth was "projecting," his forehead "low and compressed." His lips, covering teeth slantingly implanted in blue gums, were often everted, displaying the red mucous membrane of the mouth. His broad and flat nose, with dilated nostrils and concaved ridge, also exposed the red inner surface of the mucous membrane. His facial muscles were less finely differentiated than those of whites, and he was unable to register a great range of varied expressions.[37] Overall, his face gave the appearance of a muzzle, with his mouth, "the organ of gluttony," its central character.

The Negro's hair, which was not hair at all, was elliptical and

---

34   Shufeldt, *America's Greatest Problem: The Negro*, 31–36; and Giddings, *The Principles of Sociology* (New York, 1896), 235.

35   This discussion of the Negro's physical features is taken from a general reading of racist literature. Representative discussions of these characteristics are found in Charles H. McCord, *The American Negro as a Dependent, Defective and Delinquent* (Nashville, 1914), 25–27; Frederick L. Hoffman, "Race Traits and Tendencies of the American Negro," *Publications of the American Economic Association*, XI (August, 1896); William B. Smith, *The Color Line, A Brief in Behalf of the Unborn* (New York, 1905), 45–48; and E. H. Randle, *Characteristics of the Southern Negro* (New York, 1910).

36   This characteristic was considered so important that William Archer, an English commentator on the Southern race problem, asked, "Does any one really believe that the genius of Caesar and Napoleon, of Milton and Goethe, had nothing to do with their facial angle, and could have found an equally convenient habitation behind thick lips and under woolly skulls?" *Through Afro-America, An English Reading of the Race Problem* (London, 1910), 233.

37   In this connection, Robert Bennett Bean's description of a Negro's smile is revealing. "The neuro-muscular mechanism in the Black Race is less controlled, and when the nerve impulses, not so finely graded as in the White Race, reach the mimetic muscles, the latter are set into sudden, strong contractions of a primitive type. The bulky lips are pulled upward and outward, the large white teeth are exposed in contrast with the black face, and instead of a graded smile or laugh we notice the broad grin characteristic of the Black Race." *The Races of Man*, 37–38.

flattened. Therefore, it grew spirally and had a "distinctly woolly" and not merely frizzly appearance. His thick skin was "cool, soft, and velvety to the touch" and emitted "a peculiar rancid odor" comparable to that of the buck goat. The emanation from "certain overabundant sudorific glands," this odor was especially strong under heat and excitement, so strong in fact that white persons were "brought almost to the stage of emesis when compelled to inhale it for any length of time." [38]

Indicating his proximity to anthropoids, the Negro's arms and legs were longer and slimmer than the white man's; his feet were sometimes used as hands; his ears were small and "conspicuously pointed at their upper margins." As evidence of his physical inferiority, his stature was shorter than the white man's, his shoulders and lifting strength less powerful, his lung capacity and chest circumference smaller, his muscular and nervous systems less developed, and his blood circulation slower. Finally, he had a shorter and thicker neck (which gave strength in carrying burdens), a narrower and more pointed pelvis, "larger and grosser sexual organs," and such thick skin on the soles of his feet and palms of his hands that he was virtually insensible to pain. He was, in short, "something between a child, a dotard, and a beast," so grossly different from Caucasians that the races required different hygienes and regimens. Physicians who treat one race, said G. Stanley Hall in one of his more irrational moments, are impaired in their treatment of the other. Treatment of the two races, he said, was as different "as the application of veterinary medicine for horses is from that applied to oxen." [39]

Despite this attention to the Negro's physical features, anti-Negro writers had greater interest in other, more basic features of the race. Racial differences, they felt, were more fundamental than the dissimilarity of curly blond hair and kinky black wool. The real differ-

---

38 This idea was part of a general law which gave a peculiar odor to all races. Stephen Graham, for example, an English observer of the South's race problem, who described the "pungent and sickening odor" of the Negro, reported that whites also had a racial odor, which came from "the animal in us." Negroes, who had more "animal" in them, thus had the strongest racial odor, a fact which was proven by the ease with which bloodhounds followed their trail. Racial odors were described by Robert Bennett Bean as "pungent" in the Negro, "acrid" in the white, and varied in the Yellow-Brown. See Graham, *The Soul of John Brown* (New York, 1920), 33–34; and Bean, *The Races of Man*, 51.

39 Hall, "The Negro in Africa and America," 360.

ence lay in race psychology, in those innate traits, instincts, and aptitudes which formed the psyche or soul of a race. The intrinsic superiority of the Caucasian consisted of the characteristics and accomplishments which derived from this soul. "There are peculiarities in the function of [the Negro's] instincts, impulses, emotions, and modes of response to external stimuli fundamentally different from those of the white," concluded American racists, drawing upon the ideas of Gustave LeBon. His "racial mental-set, racial ways of thinking, and racial reactions to the influences of ideas are as characteristic and as recognizable as [his] racial skin-color and skull-conformation." [40]

From this idea racists drew far-reaching conclusions. Differences in racial psychology, they declared, are reflected in the political, social, cultural, and religious institutions created by each race, and the institutions of one race cannot be comprehended or assimilated by another. Similarly, all races, especially superior ones, instinctively recognize these racial differences and consciously or unconsciously protect themselves through racial pride or prejudice.

The idea that societal institutions expressed racial genius or lack of genius was especially popular in the decades around 1900. It was one facet of the nativist movement then coalescing in the East, and it closely paralleled the racism of American imperialists. In many respects nativism, imperialism, and the ideas of racial psychology sprang from the same sources. All three accepted the "superiority" of northwestern Europeans and old American stocks, and each justified the callous disregard for "inferior" races which accompanied imperialism, racial segregation, and immigration restriction. The intellectual milieu which encouraged one of these movements was equally propitious for the other.

The ideas of racial psychology were best expressed by writers such as Lothrop Stoddard, James K. Hosmer, and John W. Burgess. America, felt Stoddard, was a white nation, "founded by White men who evolved institutions, ideals, and cultural manifestations which were spontaneous expressions of their racial temperament and tendencies." The country, therefore, could retain its greatness and the inviolability of its institutions only so long as it maintained its

---

40 Mecklin, *Democracy and Race Friction*, 30; and James Bardin, "The Psychological Factor in Southern Race Problems," *Popular Science Monthly*, LXXXIII (October, 1913), 372.

historical racial composition,[41] which was now threatened, chiefly by European immigration and secondarily by advocates of social and political equality for Negroes. Protestant Christianity, for example, with its "single, unlocalized Deity, whose attributes express the loftiest ideals attained by the white race," could never survive among Negroes. Nor could the purity of the English language. Each word in a language, explained a contributor to *Popular Science Monthly* in 1897, is a generalization based upon "traditions, customs, experiences, sentiments, and ideas" which form the heritage of a race. Because the Negro's racial heritage was radically different from that of Englishmen, he was at a peculiar disadvantage in the use of English, a fact which helped explain his incapacity in the power of abstraction, judgment, and analysis.[42]

These, of course, were the ideas of racial psychology as expressed by popular and naïve writers. They were not, however, much corrupted from the form in which they were originated by such scholars as James K. Hosmer, historian, and John W. Burgess, political scientist. Principally interested in the political implications of race psychology, Hosmer and Burgess believed that Aryans or Teutons, including Anglo-Saxons, possessed a unique genius for political democracy, constitutional government, and economic individualism. The United States Constitution, they declared, was the modern expression of Anglo-Saxon–Teutonic political genius—a genius which had originated in the black forests of Germany, spread through England and North America, and expressed itself in the Magna Carta, the Glorious Revolution, and the American Revolution. A race which had not experienced this evolution was incapable of appreciating liberty or constitutional democracy, for the capacity to do so came down in the blood. Consequently, American Negroes were a "hostile" racial element which deserved no voice in local,

41   Cf., the following statement by sociologist John Moffatt Mecklin of Dartmouth and the University of Pittsburgh: "In view of the intimate and organic relations between the child of Anglo-Saxon ancestry and the democratic institutions to which he falls heir at birth it would seem at least plausible that his social instincts would further a more immediate and thorough sympathy with those institutions than is possible in the case of the . . . negro child which inherits race instincts shaped by a totally different race history." *Democracy and Race Friction*, 9.

42   Lothrop Stoddard, "The Impasse at the Color-Line," *Forum*, LXXVIII (October, 1927), 513; Tillinghast, "The Negro in Africa and America," 150; and Anna Tolman Smith, "A Study in Race Psychology," *Popular Science Monthly*, L (January–March, 1897), 359–60.

state, or national affairs. Indeed, declared Burgess, a nation cannot exist without ethnic homogeneity. It might, therefore, "righteously deport the ethnically hostile element in order to shield the vitals of the state from the forces of dissolution, and in order to create the necessary room for a population sufficient in numbers, in loyalty, and capacity to administer the empire and protect it against foreign powers." [43]

Race psychology explained the significance of racial differences, the impossibility of racial equality, and the horror of racial mixture. It was fortunate, therefore, that each race recognized its distinctiveness and was repelled by the idea of equality and intermixture. Among individuals of every race there was a "consciousness of kind," a "call of race," a "call of the blood," which generated a spontaneous gregariousness toward one's own kind and an instinctive aversion for strangers. It was also fortunate that such feelings were much stronger in "superior" races than "inferior" ones.

A scientific explanation for this theory was offered by University of Chicago sociologist William I. Thomas, whose interest in race psychology was purely scientific and whose concern for popular racism seems to have been nonexistent. Exploring the psychology of race prejudice for readers of the *American Journal of Sociology*,[44] Thomas sought to determine if there were "any conditions arising in the course of the biological development of a species which . . . lead to a predilection for those of one's own kind [and] a prejudice against organically different groups." He concluded that "we do, in fact, find such conditions." The instinct toward one's own kind he found to be an expression in man of a similar instinct existing in all forms of animal life. It was expressed by emotions

---

43 John W. Burgess, *Sovereignty and Liberty* (Boston, 1913), 42–44, Volume I of *Political Science and Comparative Constitutional Law;* and James K. Hosmer, *A Short History of Anglo-Saxon Freedom, The Polity of the English-Speaking Race* (New York, 1890), 272. Cf., the following statement made by W. J. Simmons, Imperial Wizard of the Ku Klux Klan: "During the last 5,000 years 'something inherent' in the Anglo-Saxon has pushed its way up into the consciousness of the individual until it found expression in constitutional government, in freedom of thought and speech, and in all the elements of political and religious liberty." Because it protected Anglo-Saxons against aliens and Negroes, the Klan was, said Simmons, a manifestation "of the genius and mission of the Anglo-Saxon." *The Klan Unmasked*, 51, 27.

44 Thomas, "The Psychology of Race Prejudice," *American Journal of Sociology*, IX (March, 1904), 593–611.

which unfavorably predisposed an individual to whatever was strange or different. The habitual recurrence of this reaction produced an instinct by which the individual identified himself with his own racial group and was repelled by association with others. At first subconscious, this repulsion was evoked and strengthened by the physical features which differentiated racial groups. Eventually, the mere sight of those features provoked a reflex which generated feelings of dislike.

The emotion of prejudice thus produced was complex, although easily diagnosed. "Intense and immediate," it was beyond reason "because, like the other instincts, it originated before deliberative brain centers were developed." It had "a persistence and a certain automatism appropriate to a type of reaction valuable in the organic scheme but not under the control of the deliberative centers." Race prejudice, Thomas concluded, "is an instinct originating in the tribal stage of society, when solidarity in feeling and action were essential to the preservation of the group. It, or some analogue of it, will probably never disappear completely."

With no intention of doing so, Thomas had provided rational and scientific justification for racial discrimination and segregation. He had made more plausible the assertion that Southern race policies were expressions of biological law and racial instinct rather than bigotry and prejudice. As a consequence, Representative Hatton W. Sumners of Texas could declare with perfect aplomb that mobs who lynched Negro rapists were merely answering the call of the race. Sociologist Lester Frank Ward, as generous and warmhearted as any man in his generation, could also declare in one of his rare references to the race that Negro men raped white women because of the "biological imperative" to improve their offspring and that Negro women submitted to white men for the same reason. But alas, Ward continued, "impelled . . . by the biological law of self-preservation," indignant whites invariably lynched the Negro rapist forthwith. Even Edgar Gardner Murphy, one of the most conscientious and sincere friends of the Negro in the South, thought that race prejudice was "beneficent" insofar as it "served through the force of inherent and natural antipathies to prevent the mixture of blood and to preserve the purity of each racial stock." [45] This, indeed, was the

45   *Congressional Record*, 66th Congress, 1st Session (November 15, 1919), 8577; Lester F. Ward, *Pure Sociology, A Treatise on the Origin and Spontaneous Development of Society* (New York, 1907), 359; and Edgar

ultimate use of prejudice. It benefited the Negro, preserved him as a separate race, and protected him from the white man.

In assessing the scientists' contribution to racism, two questions are important: To what extent did scientists in general believe that Negroes were innately inferior to other races? And to what extent did they consciously support the anti-Negro policies which that belief justified? Of course such questions admit no precise answers, but certain conclusions seem obvious from the above summary. It seems apparent that scientists—and social scientists, too—endorsed the idea of racial inequality and its corollary that Negroes are inferior to Caucasians and Mongolians. Indeed such a statement hardly needs documentation. Prominent scientists in all disciplines often expressed such views and had no qualms in doing so. Nor were they quacks and second-raters. They held academic positions in the East and Midwest as well as in the South. Frequently, they were among the pioneering giants of their discipline. They published voluminously, and their easy access to scholarly journals further indicates the racist permeation of the sciences. Journals which appealed only to scientists and social scientists contained numerous articles which incidentally accepted or intentionally developed anti-Negro ideas. And the same was true of such popular periodicals as *Science, Scientific Monthly,* and *Popular Science Monthly.* The anti-Negro bias of many textbooks and general works indicates that such ideas were not offensive to publishers and college professors. Conversely, between 1900 and 1930 an exceedingly small number of scientists were willing to dispute the alleged superiority of Caucasians.

Concerning the second question, the evidence is less conclusive. Scientists were, of course, aware that they and their ideas were used to justify discriminatory policies against Negroes. In fact, many scientists themselves endorsed such policies. Sociologist John Moffatt Mecklin was convinced that segregation was necessary to preserve white civilization in the South. Howard Odum felt that Negroes did not deserve to be enfranchised because of their inability to vote intelligently or to understand public policies. Princeton biologist Edwin Grant Conklin believed that "every consideration

---

Gardner Murphy, "The Task of the Leader," *Sewanee Review,* XV (January, 1907), 20.

should lead those who believe in the superiority of the white race to strive to preserve its purity and to establish and maintain the segregation of the races." [46]

Such evidence, however, can be easily misinterpreted. Racists themselves, in fact, did misinterpret it. In general, the scientists' preoccupation with and endorsement of racial inequality differed considerably from that of extremists. During the first twenty-five years of this century racism was a general tenet of American thought and scientists like other Americans accepted it without protest. A few of them, notably in eugenics and psychology, did extensive research to prove its validity, and the evidence they collected was impressive, especially to unsophisticated laymen and designing racists. But the *mesalliance* between science and racism was largely due to other factors, to the errors of judgment and scientific shortcomings of scientists themselves, which led them to endorse the "obvious" fact of racial inequality without adequate empirical proof. In addition, they often conducted their experiments and reported their findings in the isolated atmosphere of the laboratory, with little concern for the social or political implications of their data. Thus, researchers such as George Oscar Ferguson, Robert Bennett Bean, Henry Fairfield Osborn, or Paul Popenoe could accept the "fact" of Negro inferiority and urge that whites and Negroes be socially segregated in order to remain biologically separated. But they did not endorse or condone the extremism of Ben Tillman, James K. Vardaman, Cole Blease, or Tom Heflin. The scientists wanted only segregation, and a benevolent segregation at that, which was not to them inconsistent with interracial harmony and improvement of the Negro. They never understood that the demagogue's excesses, like his successes, were inevitable results of the segregation they were urging. More often than not, the product of their endeavors was the demagogue's extremism rather than the reforms sought by committees on interracial cooperation.

By 1925 a marked change was occurring in the attitude of scientific circles toward the subject of race. Before that date science had furnished more authoritative "proof" of Negro inferiority than all other branches of knowledge combined. Henceforth, however, the weight of scientific evidence would be against dogmatic asser-

---

46   Mecklin, *Democracy and Race Friction,* 220, 244–45; Howard Odum, *Social and Mental Traits of the Negro* (New York, 1910), 286; and Edwin Grant Conklin, *The Direction of Human Evolution* (New York, 1922), 53.

tions of racial inequality. Higher standards were now demanded of students of race,[47] and scientists were increasingly critical of what biologist W. E. Castle called "ethnomaniacs," that is, writers who overemphasize race. As the Negro improved his position in American society, the neglected researches of Franz Boas [48] and others began at last to fructify. Within a short time Boas became the most authoritative spokesman on race in the country, and together with a number of his influential students and colleagues at Columbia University—Ruth Benedict, Gene Weltfish, Howard Odum,[49] Ashley Montagu, Margaret Mead, Otto Klineberg, Melville Herskovits— he succeeded in eradicating the racist ideas of American scientists.[50] By 1930 the amount of scientific literature purporting to prove the Negro's alleged inferiority had precipitously declined. During the next decade the amount of popular anti-Negro literature was likewise conspicuously reduced. The change signalized a reinterpretation of basic assumptions. Science and scientists had changed their minds about the Negro.

47 See for example E. A. Hooten, "Methods of Racial Analysis," *Science,* LXIII (January 22, 1926), 75–81; and Robert J. Terry, "The American Negro," *Science,* LXIX (March 29, 1929), 337–41.
48 See, for example, Boas, *The Mind of Primitive Man* (New York, 1911).
49 Odum's early work, for example, *Social and Mental Traits of the Negro* and "Negro Children in the Public Schools of Philadelphia," *The Annals,* XLIX (September, 1913), 186–206, was decidedly anti-Negro. He later renounced this view, however, and became a dedicated champion of the race. See for example his *Race and Rumors of Race* (Chapel Hill, 1943).
50 It is interesting to note that Boas is one of the major targets of anti-Negro writers today. See Carleton Putnam, *Race and Reason: A Yankee View* (Washington, 1961), 18, 23–27, 47–50; and George, *The Biology of the Race Problem,* 78–87.

2

THE RATIONALE
OF HISTORY AND HISTORIANS

I love the old South of the days of my youth, the land of peace and plenty, of blue blood, aristocracy, and happy niggers.

JOHN AMBROSE PRICE (1907)

The racism to which scientists capitulated also ensnared historians. Science alone was unable to fill the needs of racists, and for this reason they turned to other disciplines for added support. More often than not, the tenets of scientific racism had originated with Europeans or with American intellectuals and were incompletely understood by the layman. What was needed, therefore, was a supplement to science—a simple, straightforward explanation of the obvious inferiority of Southern Negroes and a rationalization of historical developments which produced that inferiority. This was the task of historical racism, and the task had special appeal to

Southerners and popularizers of anti-Negro ideas. That history was used and abused by racists was the fault of disinterested scholars as well as designing racists. The one was careless in research and uncritical in reasoning; the other sought respectable authority for racial prejudice.

Historians of the late nineteenth century, though little interested in the Negro, were often attracted by the idea of Teutonic superiority. Utilizing the ideas of Darwin and Spencer and the methodology of natural science, such scholars as Herbert Baxter Adams, Andrew D. White, John W. Burgess, Henry Cabot Lodge, and Moses Coit Tyler contributed significantly to the authority and appeal of Teutonism. Applying the evolution hypothesis to social development, they concluded that societies like individuals have a beginning, youth, maturity, and old age. The United States was to them a youthful society at the threshold of maturity and destined to be the apex of Western civilization. Americans, at least Anglo-Saxon Americans, were a chosen people, the instrumentality by which God and nature would achieve the grandest civilization in human history. Being a chosen people, however, was a supreme challenge, a precious trust, and not to be abused. Americans must remember that they are Aryans or Anglo-Saxons or Teutons and act accordingly. They must continue the historical process of Anglo-Saxon expansion and spread their civilization to backward and benighted peoples. They must also preserve the purity and excellence of their racial stock. Non-Teutonic peoples must in the future be excluded from the country. Those already here must not intrude themselves in Anglo-Saxon life and development.[1]

These aspects of American thought have received detailed attention from historians. Facets of historical racism relating to the Negro, however, have been virtually neglected.[2] Yet, the relationship be-

---

1 See Barbara Miller Solomon, *Ancestors and Immigrants* (Cambridge, 1956); Edward Norman Saveth, "Race and Nationalism in American Historiography: the Late Nineteenth Century," *Political Science Quarterly*, LIV (September, 1939), 421–41; and Saveth, *American Historians and European Immigrants* (New York, 1948). See also, John Higham, *Strangers in the Land, Patterns of American Nativism 1860–1925* (New Brunswick, N. J., 1955), 131–57, 270–77; Harvey Wish, *The American Historian* (New York, 1960), 236–64; and Stow Persons, *American Minds* (New York, 1958), 276–97.

2 See however Jacob E. Cook, "The New South," in Donald Sheehan and Harold C. Syrett (eds.), *Essays in American Historiography, Papers Presented in Honor of Allan Nevins* (New York, 1960), 67–73.

tween racial discrimination and historical scholarship on the "Negro question" was more than coincidental. Politicians, of course, did not consult historians before formulating race policies, but historians and pseudo historians so accurately reflected popular opinion that they could be and were often cited as authority for racial policies. Both academic historians and the popularizers of history endorsed a rationale which assigned to Negroes a permanently inferior status in American life.

Among anti-Negro historians between 1900 and 1930, three groups are distinguishable. There was first a substantial number of race theorists after the fashion of Gobineau and Chamberlain; second, a significant group of academic historians primarily interested in nineteenth-century America; and third, a large group of novelists, popularizers, and pseudo historians also interested in American history and the Negro. Whereas the first two groups had nothing in common, the third drew heavily upon both the others and interpreted their ideas for the American public. The anti-Negro literature of the three groups was in many respects as significant as that of scientific racism.

The first of these groups emphasized the relationship between history and race, a relationship which they felt to be primal. "Would you understand what is happening in the world, why nations act as they do, what their relations are to America, and what our policy should be toward them?" Lothrop Stoddard, most prolific of this group, asked readers of the *Saturday Evening Post* in 1924. If so, racial factors involved must be comprehended, for "the relative strength and importance of the different racial elements in a nation will largely determine every phase of that nation's life, from its manners, customs, and ideals to its government and its relations with other nations." To understand a nation, in other words, one must understand its racial composition and the racial changes it is currently undergoing. "How the racial interpretation of history clarifies and vitalizes the record of human events!" Stoddard exclaimed. "So many mysteries explained; so many riddles solved; such seemingly tangled situations become simple and understandable! And all this because we are at last looking at things in terms of basic reality." [3]

Stoddard and Madison Grant, the nation's most influential race

---

3 Lothrop Stoddard, "Racial Realities in Europe," *Saturday Evening Post,* CXCVI (March 22, 1924), 14–15; and Stoddard, "The New Realism of Science," *Saturday Evening Post,* CXCVII (September 6, 1924), 38.

theorists, detailed this racial interpretation of history, and their efforts were supplemented by throngs of less able and less important writers. Grant's importance lies in the fact that he synthesized for Americans the salient ideas of scientific and historical race theory. His most important work *The Passing of the Great Race, or the Racial Basis of European History* (1916) was revised and reissued three times within five years; it was easily the most significant single piece of racist literature produced in this period by an American. A wealthy New York bachelor, Grant was a forceful and persuasive writer and contributed significantly to the crystallization of American sentiment against European immigration. The most important role in popularizing historical racism, however, was Stoddard's. Born and reared in New England of old American stock, Stoddard was a curious combination of the best and worst elements of that section's social-intellectual heritage. He was educated at Harvard (B.A., 1905, Ph.D., 1914), where he was exposed to the theory that national institutions reflect racial capacity and racial psychology. Imbued with this idea, he spent his lifetime developing and popularizing the racism then favored by New England's social and intellectual elite. Well read in the social and natural sciences, he viewed history as a perpetual struggle between races. His task, he felt, was to make that struggle known to Americans, and toward that end he detailed its implications for this country in particular and the Western world in general. In more than one respect he was the climax of the nativist-racist movement among New England intellectuals.

More perhaps than any other individual, he popularized the racism of his generation. In such works as *The Rising Tide of Color Against White World Supremacy* (1920); *The Revolt Against Civilization, The Menace of the Under Man* (1923); *Racial Realities in Europe* (1924), which was serialized in *Saturday Evening Post; Re-Forging America, The Study of Our Nationhood* (1927); and *Clashing Tides of Color* (1935); and in numerous articles, interviews, and speeches he repeated the ideas of Gobineau, Chamberlain, and Grant. Civilization, he declared, was a product of the creative intelligence of white men, especially Nordics, but only aggressive and racially pure Nordics retained the potential for civilization. Yet civilization itself created conditions which encouraged degeneracy. Small families, civil wars, racial tolerance, democracy, humanitarianism, and religion each tended to undermine racial exclusiveness and promote racial intermixture. Past civilizations had failed to overcome these evils, and as a result history was a "series of racial tragedies." Race after race of whites had entered the threshold of civilization "in the pink of condition, full of superior strains slowly selected and accumulated by the drastic methods of primitive life." One by one, however, they had "been insidiously drained of their best until, unable to carry on, they [sank] back into impotent mediocrity." Civilization itself had been saved only by the continued appearance of superior barbarian races who replaced older, degenerating civilizations.[4]

In this view of history Stoddard repeated one of the basic tenets of historical and intellectual racism. Like other general ideas of racism, it applied equally to all races and it also assumed that the Negro race was inferior to all others. All civilizations, so the idea ran, even those of India, the Far East, the Aztecs, and the Incas,[5] had been created by white men. Eventually, however, migrations, wars, and assorted other racial misfortunes caused some of these civilizations to fall into the hands of other races. Those in the Far East had been perpetuated, though in stagnant form, by Mongolians. The Negro, however, had destroyed all civilizations in which he had been given a voice—ancient Egypt, for example, and modern Haiti.

The history of Greece and modern Europe was illustrative. Ancient Greeks had been "typical Germans"—tall, blond, blue-eyed, and fair-haired Nordics. "The age of Pericles and Alexander, with its grand achievements in molding the destinies of the civilized world" had been "a striking illustration of the supreme mission of the white race." But unable to unite politically, the Greeks had expended their racial stocks in fratricidal wars, at the same time inundating the Greek homeland with hordes of racially inferior slaves. Immediately miscegenation commenced, and a "rapid, almost sudden decline in the intellectual productivity of the Greek people" occurred. Centuries later the process was repeated in Rome, which also succumbed to racial miscegenation and degeneration. Invading hordes of Teutonic barbarians had not destroyed Roman civilization. On the contrary, they had rescued it from racial degenerates and preserved it for posterity. During the Middle Ages these "blond barbarians" settled in northern Europe, protected their racial purity, and then during the Renaissance burst forth with modern Western civiliza-

---

4   Stoddard, *The Revolt Against Civilization*, 83.
5   On the Aztecs and Incas see George Mallison, *Color at Home and Abroad* (Boston, 1929), 99–106; and Ernest Sevier Cox, *White America* (Richmond, 1923), 160–67.

tion. In the Reformation their Nordic individualism rebelled against the tyranny of un-Nordic Catholicism, and soon their political genius produced the modern nation-state. From their north European homeland they expanded over America, Africa, Asia, and Australia, illustrating in the process the Nordic's unique ability as adventurers, explorers, and colonizers. Columbus, for example, had been an Italian Nordic sent to America by those "red haired Goths," Ferdinand and Isabella. Sometimes, as in the case of Spain and Portugal, the Nordics had overexpanded themselves or intermarried with "native" populations, consequently decimating their racial stocks. In the Anglo-Saxon colonies of North America, Australia, New Zealand, and South Africa, however, they remained pure and vigorous and established flourishing civilizations.[6]

National policy, said Stoddard, should be based upon this view of history. The white race, he believed, had reached its zenith in the nineteenth century when it ruled mankind in its own self-interest. Falling prey to overcivilization, industrialization, urbanization, and civil war, however, the race had deteriorated, and its misfortune had made the colored man restive. By 1918 the Negro was threatening white supremacy, and a union of whites, or at least of Nordics, was imperative. Nordic nations must initiate "deep-going eugenic reforms," forget "delusions" like environmentalism and natural equality, drop humanitarian and religious interest in "natives," and rigidly enforce laws against racial mixture. They must also ignore any injustices which result from these policies. At stake was the future of civilization, before which everything else must give way.

In the world order envisaged by Stoddard, Negroes had a lowly place indeed. A congenital barbarian, the Negro had ravaged and ruined many civilizations, but had never created one of his own. An impartial observer might remark that the incapacities here assigned to the Negro were sufficient to neutralize any threat which the race offered to white civilization. But such, Stoddard emphasized, was not the case at all. It was true that the race represented no military threat, but this only intensified the danger from subtler means of

6 Woodruff, *The Effects of Tropical Light on White Men*, 234; Walter Guild, "A Plea from the South," *Arena*, XXIV (November, 1900), 487; McDougall, *The Group Mind*, 340; Lothrop Stoddard, *The Rising Tide of Color Against White World Supremacy* (New York, 1920), 174; David Starr Jordan, "War and Race Decadence," *Independent*, LIX (December 21, 1905), 1476; and Alfred P. Schultz, *Race or Mongrel* (Boston, 1908), 92–94.

"pacific penetration." Negroes were "highly prolific, often endowed with extraordinary physical vigor, and able to migrate easily." They flocked naturally to cities where their low wages upset the white man's living standards and encouraged him to have small families. There also the masses of both races were thrown together and traditional safeguards against intermixture were weakened.[7]

For these reasons Negroes in the United States should be segregated and interracial competition eliminated. Too numerous and too valuable as a labor force to be deported, the race might instead be herded onto reservations as were Indians in America or Negroes in South Africa. Unless they cooperated with responsible whites and accepted their proper place in American society, however, they might be removed to an environment more suited to their racial aptitudes.[8] Above all, they must shun agitators who peddle discontentment and doctrines of racial equality.

As an intellectual movement American racism thus paralleled national and Southern policies of racial discrimination and segregation. Madison Grant, for example, in language strikingly similar to that of Southern politicians and extremists declared that Negroes were so backward and unassimilable that they constituted a racial problem by their mere presence. The South, he believed, was the best place in America for Negroes; only there did whites understand the race and treat it properly—with firmness and kindness. Southerners, moreover, liked Negroes, at least as long as they kept in their proper relation to the whites, and race tensions in the South were rare. The migration of Negroes to the North, however, was certain to produce trouble in the future.[9]

Of course, intellectual racists rejected the crude extremism of the lyncher and the mob's disregard for law and order, but they endorsed the racism which ultimately justified those excesses. Therefore, they were popular in the South for their attitudes toward the Negro, just as they were popular in the North and East for their attitudes toward the immigrant. The Northerner, however, was prone to forget that he appealed to the same authority as did Southern segregationists, whom he sometimes disparaged as bigots. Thus, he could applaud the application of Grant and Stoddard's

7   Stoddard, *The Revolt Against Civilization*, 5–6.
8   Lothrop Stoddard, *Re-Forging America, The Story of Our Nationhood,* (New York, 1927), 255–325.
9   Grant, *The Conquest of a Continent,* 282–85.

theories to European immigration and at the same time be distressed by their application to the Southern Negro.

As this indicates, anti-Negro attitudes were prominent in nativist literature, despite the fact that most nativists had little immediate interest in the "Negro problem." Before World War I the average nativist probably felt that no such problem existed. Until that time few Negroes lived outside the South and those who did were frequently students, skilled artisans, or neat and trim domestics—hardly the source of major racial problems. Nativists were also deceived by the facade of interracial harmony which the South presented, and, despite periodic outbursts of violence in the region, it was generally felt that Southern Negroes were contented. Most nativists, moreover, considered racial problems from the viewpoint of eugenics and genetics, that is, they were chiefly concerned about amalgamation and intermarriage between whites and Negroes. Like Southerners, they usually ignored amalgamation which resulted from illicit and unsanctioned relations between the races, because such relations never resulted in marriage and the offspring was always relegated to the Negro race. In this way, they felt, the white man remained "pure" and the "danger" of amalgamation was neutralized. But this does not mean, to repeat, that they ignored the Negro. It means instead that they considered him a minor problem. It also means that they wrote of him with more contempt and greater self-assurance than they did of immigrants.

The views of Alfred P. Schultz, Clinton Stoddard Burr, and Charles Conant Josey were typical. Schultz, a perfervid disciple of Houston Stewart Chamberlain, expressed the ideology of nativism in its most repugnant and impassioned form. Obsessed with the idea that "mongrelization" was pernicious and that it represented a real danger to American civilization, he anticipated the writings of Grant and Stoddard. Like other nativists he was chiefly interested in immigration restriction, but his contempt for the Negro was more outspoken than that of most nativists. Since emancipation, he declared in *Race or Mongrel,* the nation's Negro policies had been completely misguided. As a slave the Negro had been "at least a good working-tool," but as a free man he was arrogant, indolent, and unreliable. The race had attempted to take an impossible short cut from savagery to civilization, and his efforts had been foolishly abetted by whites who gave him the ballot and political equality. Here as elsewhere, however, his political endeavors had failed signally. In Haiti and Santo Domingo, where the Negro had had a unique opportunity for self-development, he had been content "to pour alcohol into himself, chew tobacco, rip bellies open from time to time, and keep on the good side of the medicine man." American Negroes, warned Schultz, would similarly degenerate unless reduced to a serflike status and ruled by the iron hand of white men.[10]

Burr and Josey were calmer and more moderate in discussing the Negro. One of the country's leading nativists, Clinton Stoddard Burr eulogized Nordics and their role in the nation's "racial history." His *America's Race Heritage* was an effort to demonstrate that Americanism was "actually the racial thought of the Nordic race" and that Nordics alone possessed the "moral fiber, intellectual character and hereditary traits" to perpetuate it. Therefore, amalgamation with alien races was dangerous, and to guard against it European immigration must be halted and the Negro relegated to special reservations. Or, "if our idealism is great enough," the race might be deported to Africa or South America.[11]

Burr couched his discussion in an ostensibly sincere concern for the Negro, and in this respect he resembled Dartmouth psychologist Charles Conant Josey. Josey, however, was concerned with the other facets of the "Negro problem." Democracy, internationalism, and Christianity, he declared in *Race and National Solidarity*, and not amalgamation, were the real threats to white supremacy and Western civilization. By undermining race consciousness and weakening the white man's resolve to remain supreme, these products of over-civilization were destroying, however surreptitiously, the basis of world civilization, and the process was encouraged by unsuspecting and misguided whites. The fate of civilization, said Josey, rested upon the willingness of whites to retain political and military suzerainty over the colored man.[12]

The ideas of nativism and intellectual racism were derived from Grant and Stoddard, who in turn had received their inspiration from the chief spokesmen of European and American racism. Unlike Southerners, these spokesmen were primarily concerned with Euro-

10 Schultz, *Race or Mongrel*, 340–47.
11 Clinton Stoddard Burr, *America's Race Heritage* (New York, 1922), 136, 208–209, 153–57.
12 Charles Conant Josey, *Race and National Solidarity* (New York, 1923), v, 51.

pean "races"; consequently the task of detailing the implications of intellectual racism for the Negro remained. This task was assumed by a group of theorists, largely Southerners, who reflected the South's obsession with Negroes and the Southerner's self-assurance in discussing them. Combining two dissimilar traditions, they condemned the race with both. To the nativist's denunciation of Negroes upon intellectual, scientific, and historical grounds, they added the Southerner's assurance that inferiority was manifest by the immorality, ignorance, and depravity of Negroes in the South. Only Southerners, they felt, could competently and impartially judge the race.

Representative of these writers were Ernest Sevier Cox and James Denson Sayers. Cox, a Virginian, was perhaps the most important race theorist residing in the South in the period between World Wars I and II. His chief work *White America* was the most authoritative statement of intellectual-historical racism written by a Southerner. In 1937 an anonymous "prominent citizen" who desired "to promote the cause of 'Repatriation,'" privately reprinted *White America* and distributed free copies to members of Congress and to legislators of certain states. Unlike most Southern theorists, Cox actively sought to influence the nation's race policies. Besides authoring such polemics as *White America* and *The South's Part in Mongrelizing the Nation* (1926), he organized Anglo-Saxon clubs which were dedicated to the superiority of old American stocks, lobbied for enactment of the state antimiscegenation and race registration law in Virginia in 1924, led a movement after World War I to deport American Negroes to Africa, supported the black nationalism of Marcus Garvey, wielded a direct influence upon demagogues such as Theodore Bilbo, and lectured widely throughout the South. Eventually, he came to be rather well known among Southerners, although his influence never approached that of Stoddard or Grant.

Described by H. J. Eckenrode as a brilliant classic on the race question,[13] *White America* was the result of extensive study and travel by Cox. For fifteen years he visited areas of the world where substantial numbers of Negroes and whites lived together and studied various aspects of racial friction and adjustment. He was convinced that continued close contact between the races invariably

---

13   Quoted in Cox, *White America,* 400.

produced one of two results—amalgamation or extinction of the inferior race, perhaps by deportation. The fact that Southern whites were racially pure after three centuries among Negroes did not weaken his conviction. Instead, it constituted "the greatest miracle in the record of the contact of races," explainable only by the Anglo-Saxon's faithfulness to his race and its institutions. Amalgamation, however, was proceeding apace in the South and unless the Negro were deported would presently solve the race problem in its own sinister way. *White America* was thus a plea for racial purity, an end to be achieved by repatriating American Negroes in Africa.[14]

Cox's basic ideas, and those of Grant and Stoddard, were repeated by the vituperative Louisianian, James Denson Sayers. The details of Sayers' life are obscure, but he claimed, like Cox, to have traveled extensively and studied racial problems in all areas of the world. Although he denied seeing *White America* before completing his own manuscript, his forebodingly entitled *Can the White Race Survive?* was simply a rehashing of Cox's ideas. His purpose was to inspire the whites to greater appreciation of their racial heritage and thereby block the impending amalgamation of the races. Negro blood, he wrote in a passage of typical awkwardness, was "a voracious, insidious quagmire into which the blood of the conquering Man sinks, is today sinking, [and] against whose merciless pulling down power the sword and cannon are as useless as a baby's toy." To vivify his warning, he added to his work a frontispiece which pictured the Capitol crumbling in the midst of a dense jungle-like growth while two Negroid figures with a spear in hand stare in wonderment at the awesome ruin. This was Sayers' idea of the ultimate consequence of the racial amalgamation of Americans.[15]

Academic historians were unimpressed by the theories of intellectual racism, whether expressed by Stoddard and Grant or by Cox and Sayers. H. J. Eckenrode, an exception to this generalization, appears in this respect to be unique. A Virginian who earned a Ph.D. at Johns Hopkins in 1905, Eckenrode was successively Virginia state archivist, professor of economics at the University of Richmond, and after 1927 state historian of Virginia. A facile and prolific writer, he

---

14   *Ibid.*, 247. Cox reiterated these ideas in *The South's Part in Mongrelizing the Nation* (Richmond, 1926), and in *Teutonic Unity* (Richmond, 1951). Cox was one of the few race theorists of the 1920's still expounding his views after World War II.

15   James Denson Sayers, *Can the White Race Survive?* (Washington, 1929), 6.

produced a number of works on the Revolutionary, antebellum, and Reconstruction periods of American history, including biographies of Nathan Bedford Forrest, Rutherford B. Hayes, and Jefferson Davis.[16] His biography of the Confederate president, "an effort to apply anthropological science to American history," appears to be the only instance in which an academic historian applied the racial theories of Stoddard and Grant to American history.

Southern whites, he wrote, were Anglo-Saxons, a predominantly and characteristically Northern race, who had been "tropicized" by long exposure in the hot, sunny climate of the Southland. As "tropicals" rather than "temperates," as "Nordics baked in the sun," they had lost certain of their Nordic characteristics but retained others in an exaggerated, un-Nordic degree. They had lost the Anglo-Saxon's respectability and idealism and the Northerner's moroseness, irritability, and avarice. They had retained the Anglo-Saxon's pluck, resourcefulness, and initiative. Surrounded by hordes of Negro slaves, they had developed "a towering race pride and an inclination to ride over racial groups considered inferior." In the process they had also discarded the Anglo-Saxon doctrine of the brotherhood of man, which caused the Yankee's incessant prating about racial equality, and replaced it with political cajolery and naked force in dealing with Negroes. The result was the "hot-blooded, genial [Southerner] who would lend [his] last dollar to a friend and kill him for an ill-judged word." [17]

In spite of this Eckenrode ironically concluded that antebellum Southerners were better Nordics than their racial compatriots of the North. Such Nordic virtues as personal courage, masterfulness, and reckless generosity, he pointed out, were imperative in the antebellum South, where Nordicism, despite the hot climate, found plantation life congenial. Above the Mason-Dixon line, however, the reverse was the case, for the North in 1860 was being "un-Nordicized" by industry, democracy, and non-Nordic immigration. Two separate peoples were developing, and the non-Nordic world of the North was unable to understand the impulsive, reckless, and affectionate Nordics of the South. This to Eckenrode was the real cause of the

---

16 Eckenrode's ideas are best expressed in his *Jefferson Davis, President of the South* (New York, 1923); *Rutherford B. Hayes, Statesman of Reunion* (New York, 1930); and *Bottom Rail on Top, A Novel of the Old South* (New York, 1935).

17 Eckenrode, *Jefferson Davis*, 13–15.

Civil War. Viewed correctly, he insisted, the war was "between that part of the Nordic race which was prepared to renounce its tradition of mastery for equality, modernism and materialism, and that part of the race which was resolved, despite modernity, to remain true to its ruling instinct." Secession, thus, resulted from "the antagonism of the tropic Nordicism of the lower South for the meddling, non-Nordic industrial civilization of the North." The Nordic instinct of self-government left the South no other alternative. Slavery was but an incident in the conflict; the determining factors were Nordic blood and hot climate. The Confederacy had been an "effort of the Nordic race to save itself. Had it succeeded, a great Nordic empire might have stretched from the Potomac to Cape Horn." But it failed, and its failure ended the dream of a Nordic empire of the tropics. At Appomattox the last hope of the Nordic race expired.[18]

Whereas one facet of historical racism sprang from overimaginative theorizing, another more important facet was the achievement of "disinterested" research by academic historians. Uninfluenced by Stoddard's racial interpretation of history, these historians were seldom aware of racial bias and were not in their own minds prejudiced against the Negro. Like most Americans of their day they felt that Negroes were inferior, but they accepted this as a fact of life rather than an expression of bigotry. If they had been troubled to defend themselves upon this point (which they were not), they would have pointed to the black man's history in America as conclusive proof of their assertion. In slavery as in freedom, they felt, the Negro had demonstrated his racial incapacity, and for this reason they endorsed segregation and disfranchisement. Their approach to race problems was paternalistic and sympathetic, and like scientists who endorsed this approach they were unaware of the inner contradiction of their position.

The similarity between anti-Negro elements in science and history, however, does not end here. Anti-Negro historians, too, were among the first generation of their profession trained in scientific methodology. Products of the new graduate seminars at Johns Hopkins, Columbia, Chicago, and Harvard universities, they were professional historians in every sense of the term, and their researches carried the authority of professional competence. But as the first historians to give systematic attention to the Negro, Reconstruction,

---

18   *Ibid.*, 17, 20–21, 359, 366.

and the New South, they were responsible for the anti-Negro prejudices which pervaded the study of these subjects after 1900. Writing at the time the South legalized and systematized its racial policies, they did to Negroes what Stoddard and Grant did to immigrants—created an intellectual rationale to justify policies of discrimination and exclusiveness. Although perhaps unintentional, this achievement made them widely influential among racist elements in the South.

The ranks of anti-Negro historians included such eminent scholars as James Ford Rhodes, John W. Burgess, William Archibald Dunning, and Dunning's most influential student Walter L. Fleming. Rhodes's weighty and respected *History of the United States from the Compromise of 1850* was liberally sprinkled with his anti-Negro views, as was Burgess' influential *The Civil War and the Constitution* (1901) and *Reconstruction and the Constitution* (1902)[19] Though Northerners, both Rhodes and Burgess believed explicitly that Negroes were inferior to whites, that the colored man's interests were secondary to those of white men, and that the basic error of Radical Reconstruction was its attempt to make an innately inferior race equal or superior to Southern whites. This, of course, had always been the Southern point of view and its espousal by Rhodes and Burgess as well as lesser historians occasioned little criticism in academic circles. That it was accepted as the correct view was in no small degree the achievement of William Archibald Dunning.

At Columbia University between 1886 and 1922 Dunning trained a generation of historians to write Reconstruction history from the anti-Negro premises of Rhodes and Burgess. Committed to the principles of scientific history, he was not inclined, as Rhodes was, toward dogmatism and moral judgments. Thus, despite the fact that his anti-Negro preconceptions were obvious, he gave the impression of detachment, and his prestige as a scholar was accordingly enhanced. Through students such as Walter L. Fleming,[20] Ulrich Bon-

19 James Ford Rhodes, *History of the United States from the Compromise of 1850* . . . (7 vols.; New York, 1904–1920). For a brief account of the anti-Negro attitudes of these historians see Wish, *The American Historian,* 209–64. On Rhodes and the Negro see Robert Cruden, *James Ford Rhodes, the Man, the Historian and His Work* (Cleveland, 1961).
20 See for example Fleming's *The Sequel to Appomattox* (New Haven, 1919), 115–16. For a grossly unfavorable picture of the Negro see his "The Servant Problem in a Black Belt Village," *Sewanee Review,* XIII (January, 1905), 1–17.

nell Phillips,[21] J. G. de Roulhac Hamilton, and Charles W. Ramsdell, he inspired a new school of historians devoted to the study of Reconstruction and the postwar South.[22] Dunning's own *Essays on the Civil War and Reconstruction* (1897) and *Reconstruction, Political and Economic, 1865–1877* (1907), the latter a volume in the American Nation Series, summarized the views of this school. Like the historians whom he inspired, Dunning was chiefly concerned with vindicating the South and its racial policies since the Civil War. "The freedmen were not," he declared, "and in the nature of the case could not for generations be, on the same social, moral, and intellectual plane with the whites," and any program which ignored this fact was doomed to failure. Slavery had succeeded as a social system precisely because it acknowledged this "fact of racial inequality," and as Southerners recognized in 1865, freedom in no way altered racial capacity. The prostrate South had sought a new *modus vivendi* in race relations and toward this end enacted the Black Code, which legalized the Negro's inferior status and protected his race against exploitation without at the same time sacrificing the paramount rights of white men. Although "faithful on the whole to the actual conditions with which they had to deal," these policies had been misunderstood by Radicals and Negroes, who based their program upon false premises of racial equality. Especially harmful had been the enfranchisement of Negroes, "as reckless a species of statecraft, as that which marked 'the blind hysterics of the Celt' in 1789–95." Unable to vote intelligently, the enfranchised Negro, nevertheless, "came gradually to understand and crave those more elusive privileges that constitute social equality, . . . the end towards which the ambition of the blacks tended consciously or unconsciously to direct itself." Soon they were demanding "mixed schools" and complaining of social discriminations. As a result came

---

21   See for example Phillips' *American Negro Slavery* (New York, 1918); "The Plantation as a Civilizing Influence," *Sewanee Review*, XII (July, 1904), 257–67; and *Life and Labor in the Old South* (Boston, 1937).

22   See such works as Walter L. Fleming, *Civil War and Reconstruction in Alabama* (New York, 1905); James W. Garner, *Reconstruction in Mississippi* (New York, 1901); J. G. de Roulhac Hamilton, *Reconstruction in North Carolina* (New York, 1914); Charles W. Ramsdell, *Reconstruction in Texas* (New York, 1910); C. Mildred Thompson, *Reconstruction in Georgia* (New York, 1915); Ella Lonn, *Reconstruction in Louisiana after 1868* (New York, 1918); and William Watson Davis, *The Civil War and Reconstruction in Florida*, (New York, 1913).

an upsurge in "the hideous crime against white womanhood which now assumed new meaning in the annals of outrage." [23]

Endorsed by Dunning, Rhodes, and Burgess, anti-Negro ideas came to pervade the study of nineteenth-century American history. The works of Philip Alexander Bruce, Frank L. Owsley, Dunbar Rowland, Albert Bushnell Hart, Francis Pendleton Gaines, Hubert Howe Bancroft, Holland Thompson, the state historians of Reconstruction cited previously, and, less overtly, Woodrow Wilson reflected the extent to which historians accepted anti-Negro attitudes,[24] as did the massive, cooperative work *The South in the Building of the Nation.* A monument to the development of historical scholarship in the South, this last work was also a memorial to the racism of Southern historians.[25] Its references to the Negro indicate that Southern historians did not materially disagree with popular Southern views concerning the Negro and racial policies, and the fact that they gave relatively little attention to Negroes enhanced the impression that the race's contribution to Southern history had been entirely negative.

Historians, as previously indicated, gave no attention to theories of intellectual and historical racism, but such theories were utilized, in altered form and emphasis, by certain novelists, popularizers, and

---

23   William Archibald Dunning, *Reconstruction, Political and Economic 1865–1877* (New York, 1907), 57–58, 213.

24   See Philip Alexander Bruce, "Evolution of the Negro Problem," *Sewanee Review,* XIX (October, 1911), 385–99; Bruce, "Race Segregation in the United States," *The Hibbert Journal,* XIII (July, 1915), 867–86; Frank L. Owsley, "The Irrepressible Conflict," Twelve Southerners, *I'll Take My Stand, The South and the Agrarian Tradition* (New York, 1930), 61–91; Owsley, "Scottsboro, The Third Crusade: The Sequel to Abolition and Reconstruction," *American Review,* I (June, 1933), 257–85; Dunbar Rowland, *A Mississippi View of Race Relations in the South* (Jackson, 1902); Hart, *The Southern South;* Francis Pendleton Gaines, *The Southern Plantation, A Study in the Development and Accuracy of A Tradition* (New York, 1925), 158, 224, 227; Hubert Howe Bancroft, *Retrospection Political and Personal* (New York, 1912), 369–74; J. G. de Roulhac Hamilton, "Southern Legislation in Respect to Freedmen 1865–1866," in *Studies in Southern History and Politics Inscribed to William Archibald Dunning* (New York, 1914), 137–58; and Woodrow Wilson, *Division and Reunion 1829–1909* (New York, 1910), 125–27, 166.

25   See for example Alfred Holt Stone, "The Negro in the South," in *The South in the Building of the Nation* (13 vols.; Richmond, 1909), X, 166–83; John Preston McConnell, "Virginia in the New Nation," in *ibid.,* I, 131, 136, 139, 147–48; and William Shannon Morrison, "South Carolina, 1865–1909," in *ibid.,* II, 95, 102–103.

pseudo historians and, thus, constituted a link between historians and race theorists. The connection, however, is tenuous and consists largely of the fact that each of the groups believed in racial inequality and Negro inferiority. As such, it indicates the extent to which anti-Negro ideas permeated all levels of American thought rather than any direct relationship between historians and race theorists.

The significance of the popularizers, however, is not to be gainsaid. The theories of Grant and Stoddard concerned Negroes only incidentally and seem never to have appealed directly to Southern opinion. Apparently, indeed, Southerners were unaware of these theories or, more likely, they failed to comprehend their implications for Southern race policies. At any rate popular Southern literature seldom mentioned them. And since the monographs of historians were read only by other historians, the responsibility for interpreting and reporting historical racism fell to novelists and popularizers.

Among them several groups are distinguishable. Most important is a large and varied assortment of reputable literary figures from Thomas Nelson Page around 1900 to Allen Tate and the Southern Agrarians around 1930. Consciously and conscientiously Page sought to understand the Negro and the "Negro problem," and on those subjects he sought to win Northern sympathy for the Southerner's point of view. As much as any individual he contributed to the crystallization of Southern mythology concerning the Old South and the Negro. In such works as *The Negro: The Southerner's Problem* (1904), *In Ole Virginia; or, Marse Chan, and Other Stories* (1910), and in numerous articles and speeches, he pictured the Negro as a docile, stupid, and faithful simpleton, blissfully happy whether slave or menial, and totally incapable of desiring or enjoying equality with the white man. Tate, however, was only incidentally concerned with the Negro, whom he saw as part of a larger problem. In less nostalgic tones, but with the same sense of assurance, he and his fellow Agrarians, notably Robert Penn Warren, Andrew Nelson Lytle, and Frank L. Owsley, repeated the ideas of Page. In the agricultural utopia envisioned by the authors of *I'll Take My Stand* (1930), the Negro would be a perpetual menial in a static society.[26] Like Page, the Agrarians considered themselves seri-

---

26   See Allen Tate, *Stonewall Jackson, The Good Soldier* (New York, 1928); Tate, *Jefferson Davis: His Rise and Fall* (New York, 1929); Tate, "A View of the Whole South," *American Review*, II (February, 1934), 411–32; Robert Penn Warren, "The Briar Patch," in Twelve Southerners, *I'll Take*

ous students of social and economic problems, and as such they were among the soberer elements of Southern paternalism. As Southerners, however, they insisted upon white supremacy and racial inequality.

A second group who popularized historical racism had less literary merit and influence than Page or Tate and was much harsher in its attitude toward the Negro. Consisting of such writers as the pseudo historians James Elbert Cutler and Winfield H. Collins, this group was blatantly contemptuous of the Negro. Cutler's *Lynch Law* (1905), for example, published while he was an economics instructor at Wellesley, showed more concern for lynchers than lynched. Collins, also a student of lynching, reflected the same viewpoint in *The Truth about Lynching and the Negro in the South* (1918), which he subtitled "In which the Author Pleads That the South Be Made Safe for The White Man." [27]

A final group of popularizers, who made similar use of history, was typified by the Methodist minister-turned novelist Thomas Dixon. In *The Clansman, An Historical Romance of the Ku Klux Klan* (1905), *The Leopard's Spots, A Romance of the White Man's Burden* (1902), and several less important novels, Dixon acquainted the American public with the extreme ideas of historical and intellectual racism. *The Clansman*, for example, was the basis for D. W. Griffith's epic motion picture *The Birth of A Nation*. Built around the theme that Negroes are vicious and depraved animals, Dixon's novels carried historical racism to its ultimate and logical conclusion. Scholars who had originated or systematized those ideas were repelled by the form which Dixon gave them. Yet their endorsement of orderly and paternalistic segregation made the American public more receptive to the extremism of Dixon.

That various groups of historical racists differed only in degree and not in substance is illustrated by their account of the Negro's role in American history. That role, they all agreed, was negative

---

My Stand, 252–55; Warren, *John Brown, The Making of a Martyr* (New York, 1929); Andrew Nelson Lytle, "John Taylor and the Political Economy of Agriculture," *American Review*, III (September, 1934), 432–47; and Frank L. Owsley, "The Pillars of Agrarianism," *American Review*, IV (March, 1935), 529–47.

27 Also representative of this group were Charles Morris, *The Old South and New* (Washington, 1907); Theodore D. Jervey, *The Slave Trade, Slavery and Color* (Columbia, 1925); and John C. Reed, *The Brothers War* (Boston, 1905).

and passive. Whether slave, freedman, or the "New Negro" of the twentieth century, the race was significant only as an object of controversy among whites. Before the Missouri Compromise, therefore, Negroes were of little interest to racists. By that time Northerners had already abolished slavery, but this, racists hastened to point out, was due to climate and economic selfishness and not to moral or religious scruples. Southerners, however, were forced to retain slavery for several reasons. In the region's subtropical climate the Negro had thrived, but more importantly, New England traders had brought so many Negroes to the South that slavery was an essential means of race control. That slavery had ever existed was the fault of Yankees. That it continued was due to the Southerner's sense of obligation to his slaves and to his fellow Caucasians.[28]

More important than the origin of slavery, however, was the commonly held belief that Negroes were peculiarly adapted to servitude. More than any other human type, it was alleged, the Negro was "marked out by his mental and physical characteristics as the servant of other races." Possessing the servile virtues of "great physical strength, docility, cheerfulness of disposition, a short memory for sorrows and cruelties, and an easily aroused gratitude from kindness and just dealing," he was a born slave.[29] Thus, slavery had been an idyllic life for him, the greatest benefit that any large part of the Negro race had ever received, and "so far from being wrong morally, was righteousness, justice and mercy to the slave." It transformed savage animals and wanton idlers into rational men and industrious serfs. "It found the Negro rioting in benighted ignorance, and led him to the threshold of light and knowledge. It clothed nakedness in civilized habiliments, and taught a jungle idolator of Christ and immortality." It supplied the Negro's food and clothing, nursed his illnesses, and otherwise removed care and responsibility from him. Consequently, slaves had been contented, happy, and harmless.[30] When viewed in this light, slavery was nei-

---

28   See for example Morris, *The Old South and New*, 280.
29   Stone, "The Negro in the South," in *The South in the Building of the Nation*, I, 166–69; and Phillips, *American Negro Slavery*, 8. Phillips described Negroes as the world's premium slaves.
30   Reed, *The Brothers War*, viii, 182; Thomas, *The American Negro*, 21; and John Ambrose Price, *The Negro Past, Present, and Future* (New York, 1907), 45–46. The New York *Herald-Tribune*, Nov. 14, 1931, quoted novelist William Faulkner as saying that "Negroes would be better off under the conditions of slavery than they are today." "The Negroes would be better off," he said, "because they'd have some one to look after them. I

ther a convenience for whites, an exploitation of Negroes, nor even a tyranny born of necessity. It was, instead, "a positive good"—the phrase is Allen Tate's as well as John C. Calhoun's—a social adaptation to the Negro's incapacity. It was a "cruel kindness," wrote Hubert Howe Bancroft, which snatched the Negro from the kettle of the cannibal.[31]

Since slavery was a benevolence, abolition was an evil. "With their bitter contempt for the compromises of the Constitution, their ruthless program of abolition whether with or without constitutional warrant, and their readiness for separation from the southern States should abolition prove impossible,"[32] abolitionists were frequent objects of racist invective. "There were people in New England who wanted to destroy democracy and civil liberties in America by freeing the slaves," wrote Allen Tate. "They were not very intelligent people; so they didn't know precisely what they wanted to destroy. They thought God had told them what to do. A Southern man knew better than this. He knew that God only told people to do right; He never told them *what* was right." To the extremist John Ambrose Price, "abolitionism was a propaganda composed of the fanatics of the North and South, headed by the dogma of Thomas Jefferson, 'All men are born free and equal.'" He traced its success to *Uncle Tom's Cabin,* "a book of rot" written by "a shrewd Yankee woman who many years before the Civil War was in *need* of *money* and conceived that novel which led to this war." Such was the irresponsibility against which the South fought! Recognizing the shortsightedness and injustice of abolition and the unreadiness of Negroes for freedom, its position was statesman-like and disinterested. Eventually, however, it was overwhelmed by superior numbers.[33]

The Civil War was, thus, the fruit of abolitionist irresponsibility, and for that catastrophe the North was largely to blame. Slavery had been a means of race control, and attacks upon it had been attacks upon the white man's security. The real problem had not been slavery itself, but the presence of Negroes in substantial numbers. Throughout the sectional controversy, the South's concern had been

---

don't think it would be as good for the white people as for the Negroes to have slavery come back."
31 Bancroft, *Retrospection, Political and Personal,* 368; Tate, *Stonewall Jackson,* 39.
32 Wilson, *Division and Reunion,* 166.
33 Tate, *Stonewall Jackson,* 25; and Price, *The Negro Past, Present, and Future,* 83.

to avert the kind of racial violence which Yankee interference eventually produced. Its position, moreover, had been legally and constitutionally correct. Secession was an inherent right of sovereignty as Calhoun had often demonstrated and as Theodore Roosevelt had accepted in the "secession" of Panama from Colombia. Southerners had fought not to perpetuate human bondage but to protect their "rights according to the laws of God and man," rights which they "held under the old constitution, made by a slave-holding aristocracy." [34]

One catastrophe, however, produced another. Civil War was followed by emancipation. For all its beneficence, the Negro's apprenticeship in slavery had been too brief, and emancipation was another in the list of Northern blunders in racial policy. Not only was it an additional rape of the Constitution, but it was also unjust to the Negro, who was unready for freedom. "It was something like throwing our domestic animals into the forest and desert where they, without knowledge of the new environment must live, if they can live, only in competition with their wild brothers," and the freedmen had been unequal to the task. "Broken loose from their moorings and set adrift on an unknown sea, these helpless beings were in a state of demoralization not easy to describe." The thin veneer of civilization, the result of a few generations of slavery, proved ineffectual against a more deeply implanted call of the wild. Religious, moral, and industrial retrogression commenced immediately, and ceasing largely from work, Negroes began to revert to savagery.[35]

None of this Northerners understood. Blindly they continued to believe that skin color was the only difference between races, and upon this fallacy they built a reconstruction program. Had Southern advice been followed, the Constitution would have been amended to acknowledge the inequality of races and give to Negroes minority representation in the government. But before Southerners could demonstrate the wisdom of this, a small clique of Radical Republicans commenced a campaign of misrepresentation to convince Northerners of the necessity of dealing drastically with the South. As the struggle between Congress and President developed, this con-

---

34   Price, *The Negro Past, Present, and Future,* 30–31; and Thomas Dixon, *The Leopard's Spots, A Romance of the White Man's Burden, 1865–1900* (New York, 1902), 335.

35   Tate, *Stonewall Jackson,* 263; Reed, *The Brothers War,* 180–81; Morris, *The Old South and New,* 349; and Eckenrode, *Rutherford B. Hayes,* 107.

spiracy became more and more systematic and unscrupulous. Southerners, however, chose to ignore this provocation and suggested instead a reconstruction program which conformed to social and racial reality. The black codes were a reasonable, temperate, and kindly first step in this program, and Southerners had adopted them with no ulterior motives. "Far from embodying any spirit of defiance towards the North or any purpose to evade the conditions which the victors had imposed," wrote Dunning, the codes were "in the main a conscientious and straightforward attempt to bring some sort of order out of the social and economic chaos which a full acceptance of the results of war and emancipation involved." [36]

But Southern efforts were wasted. Against conspiring Radicals, defeated Southerners were helpless and hopeless. They could overcome neither narrow partisanship nor "the popular misconception of the Negroes as beings who differ from ourselves only in the color of their skin and in the kink of their hair." The Radicals triumphed, and Southerners were subjected to a reign of terror more distressing than the war itself. Popularly known as Radical Reconstruction, this terror was the supreme folly, the transcendent disgrace of American history. It was at bottom a racial struggle between Southern whites and Negroes, although the latter were abetted by the race treason of Northern Radicals. At issue was the question, "Shall the future American be an Anglo-Saxon or a mulatto?" For the first time in history one group of Anglo-Saxons delivered another to be plundered and despoiled by semisavage Negroes. For the first time "proud sons of Anglo-Saxon sires" were subjugated to hordes of inferior and despicable Africans. The effort, however, was foredoomed, for like Caucasians the world over, white Southerners would suffer extermination rather than endure Negro rule.[37]

Therefore, Radical Reconstruction was a "riot of Africanism," an "attempt to reverse the order of Nature, turn society upside down, and make a thick-lipped, flat-nosed Negro, but yesterday taken from the jungle, the ruler of the proudest and strongest race of men evolved in two thousand years of history." [38] It was Charles Sumner's

---

36 Eckenrode, *Rutherford B. Hayes,* 109; Fleming, *Sequel to Appomattox,* 82; and Dunning, *Reconstruction, Political and Economic, 1865–1877,* p. 57.
37 Dixon, *The Leopard's Spots,* 161; Jerome Dowd, *The Negro in American Life* (London, 1927), 495.
38 Smith, *The Color Line,* 196–97; Rowland, *A Mississippi View of Race Relations,* 4; and Dixon, *The Leopard's Spots,* 98.

effort to deracialize Caucasian institutions and the Caucasian race. Sumner, said Frank L. Owsley, was vexed because his skin was not black, though Claude Bowers and Walter L. Fleming believed that the Massachusetts Senator loved the Negro only from a distance and "was the last man to share his bed with a black man." [39] Had Sumner succeeded, "the Southern States today would be simply a group of mongrel communities, their social character debased by universal miscegenation, and their political discredited by chronic tumult." [40]

In contrast to their treatment of Sumner, anti-Negro historians had nothing but praise for Andrew Johnson. Although a renegade Southerner, a foe of aristocracy and slavery, and technically even a "Black" Republican, Johnson was the great hero of Reconstruction. Enabled by his Southern background to understand the gravity of the situation, he "was appalled at the prospect of having great States come under the rule of ex-slaves, many of whom were still little less than savages and some of whom were but two or three generations removed from cannibalism." Such a policy, he realized, was sheer madness, but as he strove to save the South the Radicals in turn sought to destroy it.[41]

Lincoln received more varied treatment from anti-Negro writers. To most he was the great statesman of Civil War and Reconstruction, the martyred champion of intersectional goodwill. He was fully cognizant, they said, of the Negro's inferiority, and he premised his policies upon this fact. His "prophetic soul had pierced the future and seen with remorseless logic that two such races as the Negro and the Caucasian could not live side by side in a free democracy." [42] Freeing the slaves had been a first step only in solving the race question. To the Emancipation Proclamation he had attached a second step, a constitutional amendment authorizing the deportation of Negroes from the United States. If he had known that

---

39   Owsley, "The Irrepressible Conflict," in Twelve Southerners, *I'll Take My Stand*, 62; Claude Bowers, *The Tragic Era* (Cambridge, 1929), 335; and Fleming, *Sequel to Appomattox*, 123.

40   Chandler, "Introductory Outline to the History of the States," in *The South in the Building of the Nation*, I, xlviii; and Bruce, "Race Segregation in the United States," 868.

41   Eckenrode, *Rutherford B. Hayes*, 80–81; and Bowers, *The Tragic Era, passim*.

42   For the most extreme statement of this view see Thomas Dixon, *The Southerner, A Romance of the Real Lincoln* (New York, 1913); and his, *A Man of the People, A Drama of Abraham Lincoln* (New York, 1920).

the amendment would be ignored he would have opposed emancipation.

A second group of writers was not so sympathetic. Unable to forget that Lincoln waged war upon the South and freed the slaves, they lumped him with other Black Republicans. He received the presidential nomination in 1860, they declared, because he was "the only man who could disguise the sectional basis of the party and carry the border states north of the Ohio." A Black Republican from the outset, he thus shared heavily in his party's war guilt. Unable to understand the Southern point of view, he saw only "the black side of slavery, and refused to look upon the bright side." Had he conscientiously weighed and investigated the issue, he would have seen "a very bright side in favor of an institution which was for the uplifting and betterment of the Negro race." He chose instead to submit to abolitionist pressure and the result was Civil War and emancipation.[43]

Emancipation was almost innocuous, however, when compared to the cynical exploitation of the freedmen which followed. Union Leagues and Freedmen's Bureaus were established to destroy the friendly, confidential race relations in the South, to undermine the fundamental good nature of the blacks, and to encourage them in idleness and insolence. These efforts, however, were thwarted by the Negro's good nature and the heritage of interracial goodwill in the South, and the Radicals were forced to seek other means of fomenting racial unrest. They soon found an ideal solution to their problem—they enfranchised the ignorant and degraded freedmen. Described variously as "an act of unpardonable folly," "the crime of all the ages against civilization," and "the offspring of ignorance and passion," enfranchisement was looked upon as the most serious of all Radical blunders. Conceived in sin and brought forth in iniquity, it encouraged unrest and viciousness among Negroes and in turn produced race riots and conflicts. It had hopelessly dislocated the judicious evolutionary process of the Negro's political development.[44]

---

43 Andrew Nelson Lytle, *Bedford Forrest and His Critter Company* (New York, 1931), 32; and Price, *The Negro Past, Present, and Future*, 29.

44 Edgar Gardner Murphy, *The Problems of the Present South* (New York, 1904), 84; "Governor Vardaman on the Negro," *Current Literature*, XXXVI (March, 1904), 270; Thomas Nelson Page, *The Negro: The Southerner's Problem* (New York, 1904), 130; and Price, *The Negro Past, Present, and Future*, 247.

Against cupidity and peculation, against carpetbagger and scala-
wag, against bayonet and savage, the South fought for civilization.
In despair and dismay it witnessed the reversal of natural order and
saw black heels placed upon white necks. The sight was revolting.
As English-speaking white people, Southerners naturally found
black supremacy intolerable, and, though defeated and helpless,
they were forced to take action. Facing desperate problems, they
sought desperate solutions—they organized the Ku Klux Klan.
Necessitated by the Radical campaign of hate and social equality,
which was playing havoc with naturally kindly and trustful Negroes,
the Klan was, wrote Dunning, "the unorganized and sporadic expression of social demoralization." [45] According to Lawton B. Evans,
superintendent of public schools in Augusta, Georgia, and a contributor to *The South in the Building of the Nation,* the Klan was
"demanded by the rude times to preserve order, intimidate the Negroes and prevent the dissolution of the labor system upon which the
regeneration of the South depended. Much has been written of the
atrocities of this organization," Evans continued, "but one need only
consider the menace of several millions of Negroes no longer compelled to labor, long unused to self-control, inflamed by ruthless men
against their former masters, and muttering unheard of threats
against those they once held in reverence, to realize that some pre-
ventive measures were imperative to protect a defenseless society
against the incursions of that part of the Negro population that had
abandoned itself to its primitive barbarity." [46]

Although a product of the South's desperation, the Klan had been
spectacularly successful. It "regulated the conduct of bad Negroes,"
recounted Walter L. Fleming, "punished criminals who were not
punished by the States, looked after the activities and teachings of
Northern preachers and teachers, dispersed hostile gatherings of
Negroes, and ran out of the community the worst of the recon-
structionist officials." It "kept the Negroes quiet and freed them to
some extent from the influence of evil leaders." As a result, "the
burning of houses, gins, mills, and stores ceased; property became
more secure; people slept safely at night; women and children

45 John P. McConnell, "Virginia in the New Nation," in *The South in the
     Building of the Nation,* I, 136; and Dunning, *Reconstruction, Political and
     Economic, 1865–1877,* p. 187.
46 Evans, "Georgia in the New Nation," in *The South in the Building of the
     Nation,* II, 222.

walked abroad in security; the incendiary agents who had worked among the Negroes left the country; agitators, political, educational, and religious, became more moderate; 'bad niggers' ceased to be bad; labor became less disorganized; the carpetbaggers and scalawags ceased to batten on the Southern communities." [47]

The South was, thus, redeemed and the horror of Reconstruction ended. But not quite. The Radicals had done their work too well. Reconstruction had been too thorough and too disruptive to be so easily concluded. Its legacies remained to haunt the South, exerting a baleful influence upon race relations and politics. Southern whites were again ascendant, but their ascendancy was circumscribed by the malignant inheritance of Radicalism.

To anti-Negro historians, the most significant fact about Reconstruction was the proof it offered that the Negro had not yet developed "a sense of political or social order beyond what he brought with him from his native country." He always voted as a Negro, they said, and never as a man. During Reconstruction he allowed himself to become a tool of Radicalism, cynically exploited by "savage political leaders like Thaddeus Stevens." His efforts at lawmaking, wrote Claude Bowers, turned state legislatures into "monkeyhouse[s]—with guffaws, disgusting interpolations, [and] amendments offered that are too obscene to print." As a political integer he was not only grotesque but dangerous as well, and for this reason whites were justified in using intimidation, fraud, and violence against him. The remedy for this travesty of democracy was complete disfranchisement, but this obvious solution was blocked by Northern demagogues and the Fifteenth Amendment.[48]

Reconstruction was similarly unsettling in its impact upon social relations. Radical doctrines of social equality, sustained by political power and intensified by the Negro's natural affinity for white women, had destroyed the Negro's satisfaction with social separateness and inferiority. Freedmen were told repeatedly that "they were as good as white men, entitled to sit in the white man's parlor, [and] to take to wife the white man's daughter." As a result they became "commonly arrogant, frequently impertinent, sometimes insulting," and generally dissatisfied with their place. Thus, it became necessary to use force, intimidation, and violence to keep them

---

47   Fleming, *The Sequel to Appomattox*, 258.
48   Shaler, *The Neighbor*, 138; Owsley, "The Irrepressible Conflict," in Twelve Southerners, *I'll Take My Stand*, 62; and Bowers, *The Tragic Era*, 364.

circumspect and respectful. Intimidation was the necessary response to "uppity-ness," coercion an answer to insolence, lynching a defense against rape. And the one must continue until the other ceased.[49]

The Negro's desire for political and social equality was the source of another result of Reconstruction, a notable increase in racial antipathy. Race relations in the South had always been harmonious, even idyllic, insisted racists, but Radical agitation had destroyed this interracial goodwill, and the races were now growing further apart. Whites were dropping their historic concern for Negroes and without the white man's guidance and sympathy Negroes were experiencing a moral, physical, and economic deterioration. Emancipation had halted their training in technical and industrial skills, and antipathy toward the white man deprived them of civilized discipline and encouragement. As a result the free Negro was unable to advance in American society. Released from the firm but understanding control of the planter, he was slowly but surely tending to revert to savagery.[50]

Consequently, racists were convinced that Southern race problems stemmed directly from political and social policies initiated by vindictive Radicals and maintained by misguided visionaries. The most obvious lesson of Reconstruction was the inability of "outsiders" to comprehend the nature of Southern problems. However well intentioned, reformers could best help by surrendering to the South complete control of its peculiar institutions. Unanimously accepted by Southerners, this view also filtered into the North. Charles Francis Adams, for example, whose African travels reinforced his belief in racial inequality and Negro inferiority, expressed it well:

One thing is clear, [he wrote] the work done by those who were in political control at the close of our Civil War was done in utter ignorance of ethnologic law and total disregard of unalterable fact. Starting the movement wrong, it will be yet productive of incalculable injury to us. The Negro, after emancipation, should have been dealt with, not as a political equal, much less forced into a position of superiority; he should have been treated as a ward and dependent—firmly, but in a spirit of kindness and absolute justice. We will in America make small progress towards a solution of our race problem until we approach it in less of a theoretic and

---

49   William S. Morrison, "South Carolina, 1865–1909," in *The South in the Building of the Nation*, II, 95–102.

50   Schultz, *Race or Mongrel*, 240; Tillinghast, "The Negro in Africa and America," 201, 226; and Randle, *Characteristics of the Southern Negro*, 72–73.

humanitarian, and more of a scientific spirit. Equality results not from law, but exists because things are in essentials like; and a political system which works admirably when applied to homogeneous equals results only in chaos when generalized into a nostrum to be administered universally.[51]

The ideas of historical racism were bearing their fruit. Even New England was deserting the Negro.

The decline of anti-Negro ideas among historians was a gradual process which made its greatest progress after 1930. For this reason, it is largely outside the scope of this study. A few observations on the subject, however, seem pertinent. As a discipline, history never capitulated to anti-Negro ideas as completely as did eugenics, psychology, and sociology. Historians of slavery, Reconstruction, and the New South were only a small segment of academic historians, and their expression of racist views should not distort the general picture. Concerning the Negro, the sin of most historians was one of omission rather than commission. More often than not, they expressed their disregard for the race by exactly that—disregarding it altogether. Contributors to *The South in the Building of the Nation,* for example, were so preoccupied with the South's virtues and the Negro's aspirations for equality, that they overlooked his positive contributions to Southern life. In this manner they strengthened the impression that he had contributed nothing and enhanced the idea that he was by nature a hewer of wood and drawer of water. Historians of the colonial period, the Revolution, and the settlement of the West similarly underemphasized his role in national development. These historians, however, were generally unconcerned with questions of race and made no effort to demonstrate the Negro's alleged inferiority. Thus, as the nation reassessed its racial attitudes and policies and as science reexamined its treatment of the Negro, most academic historians readily followed suit. Never having indulged in the excesses of extremism, they had no deeply ingrained or publicly expressed views to renounce.

For historians of slavery, Reconstruction, and the New South, especially of Reconstruction, the change was not so simple or so readily made. Reconstruction historians invariably supported the white South in its struggles against Radicals and Negroes. To them,

---

51 Adams, "Reflex Light from Africa," *Century Magazine,* LXXII (May, 1906), 107.

the South's stand on legal, constitutional, and social questions was not only correct, but desirable and realistic as well. They assumed as an axiom that the white man's interests were paramount to those of the Negro, and they believed that white supremacy was both justified and desirable. They also assumed that a moderate Reconstruction policy was wisest, for only in this way could the Southern white be safeguarded against the Negro. These assumptions, they felt, were pragmatic and responsible, in pointed contrast to the doctrinaire and visionary policies of the Radicals.

This interpretation of Reconstruction continued long after 1930. Indeed, in a somewhat diluted form, it is still the most widely accepted view of the troubled postwar era. Professor E. Merton Coulter, whose *The South During Reconstruction, 1865–1877* is the only detailed study of the period by an academic historian since World War II, accepts all major tenets of this interpretation. The Negro's participation in Reconstruction politics, declares Coulter, was "the most spectacular and exotic development in government in the history of white civilization," an event to be "shuddered at, and execrated." Coulter is, however, a Southerner and an admitted partisan of the South. It is necessary, therefore, to look elsewhere to appreciate the extent to which anti-Negro preconceptions still color the interpretation of Reconstruction. To do this one need look no further than college textbooks, the more widely used of which reflect rather accurately the trends of historical interpretation. The immensely popular texts of John D. Hicks, *The American Nation* (1955 edition), and James G. Randall, *The Civil War and Reconstruction* (1953 edition), to cite only two conspicuous examples, approach Reconstruction with premises strikingly similar to those of Dunning. "For a time," wrote Professor Hicks, Andrew Johnson "may have toyed with the idea of Negro suffrage, but, if so, his common sense and his southern background soon led him to give it up." Hicks was, of course, in no sense a racist historian, but with this statement racists of all opinions would agree—no man with "common sense" could favor Negro suffrage. Professor Randall wrote with similar preconceptions. One of the leading Civil War and Reconstruction scholars since Dunning, Randall still referred to Thaddeus Stevens and the Radical "conspiracy" against the South. "One of the controlling elements in the whole reconstruction story," he wrote, "was the fact that in party counsel and in congressional action the votes of hundreds of men affecting the happiness of millions of people were

swayed by the domineering force of this hater of the South." [52]
Thomas Dixon's descriptions of Stevens were hardly more outspoken.

All this, to keep a proper perspective, does not mean that Randall
and Hicks or other historians of Reconstruction are especially committed to the idea that Negroes are racially inferior to whites. It
means instead that the history of Reconstruction has never overcome
the influences of an earlier generation of racists. It also raises a
problem of interpretation which has always plagued historians of the
American Negro. Like others of their profession, historians of the
Negro reflect the society in which they write, and in American
society the Negro has always been in many respects "inferior." As a
race he has had the lowest standard of living, the poorest education,
the least opportunity, and as a result the highest crime rate, the most
conspicuous immorality, and the least respect for middle-class values. Historians and racists of an earlier generation took these factors
as proof that the race was innately inferior and sprinkled their
writings on the Negro with moralizings about racial inequality. Since
1925 historians of the Negro have gradually dropped this overt
moralizing about racial inequality, but they have generally retained
the anti-Negro viewpoints by which racists originally justified that
moralizing. They have refused, in other words, to examine objectively the history of the Negro. In discussing the white man, they
never mention the subject of race, but once the Negro enters their
account the subject of race immediately appears. Reconstruction,
therefore, has rarely been discussed apart from race, and the Negro's
record therein is never that of a group of individuals varying widely
in intelligence, ability, experience, education, and morality. Instead,
it is the record of an inferior race whose actions are instinctively
determined by certain well-recognized and generally undesirable
racial drives. Consequently, the corruption of Negro legislators is an
expression of racial incapacity, although the corruption of white
lawmakers is a random example of individual scoundrelism. At one
time or another, every facet of Reconstruction has been subjected to
this racial test.

Beginning in the 1930's, however, some historians began to recog-

---

52   E. Merton Coulter, *The South During Reconstruction 1865–1877* (Baton
Rouge, 1947), 141; John D. Hicks, *The American Nation* (Cambridge,
1955), 15; and James G. Randall, *The Civil War and Reconstruction* (Boston, 1953), 725.

nize the deficiencies of writing Reconstruction history from a narrowly anti-Negro point of view.[53] Gradually, they have come to understand that the alternative to pro-white is not necessarily pro-Negro but a broader view which encompasses the interests of both races. Historians are, thus, reassessing the entire period of Reconstruction and are discovering a hitherto unsuspected merit in the program espoused by Radical Republicans. As a result, Reconstruction appears in an altered historical perspective. Like the earlier views, this reinterpretation, which is only recently under way,[54] is a reflection of the society in which historians live. The Negro is today receiving increased attention as a result of civil rights controversies, and he appears before Americans in an entirely new light. He is now an articulate lawyer filing a legal brief with the federal courts, or a well-dressed college student demonstrating against legal and social discriminations. As such, he no longer fits the stereotype upon which historical racism was based. Perhaps an important result of current racial controversies will be a more objective evaluation of the Negro's role in American history. With that, it is to be hoped, the remnants of historical racism will disappear.

---

53   See for example, Francis Butler Simkins, "New Viewpoints of Southern Reconstruction," *Journal of Southern History*, V (February, 1939), 49–61; and Howard K. Beale, "On Rewriting Reconstruction History," *American Historical Review*, XLV (July, 1940), 807–27.

54   Eric McKitrick, *Andrew Johnson and Reconstruction* (Chicago, 1960); David Donald, "Why They Impeached Andrew Johnson," *American Heritage*, VIII (December, 1956), 20–25; Fawn Brodie, *Thaddeus Stevens, Scourge of the South* (New York, 1959); David Donald, *Lincoln Reconsidered* (New York, 1961), 103–27; and John Hope Franklin, *Reconstruction After The Civil War* (Chicago, 1961). For discussions of these recent developments in Reconstruction historiography see Mark M. Krug, "On Rewriting of the Story of Reconstruction in the U.S. History Textbooks," *Journal of Negro History*, XLVI (July, 1961), 133–53; and Bernard A. Weisberger, "The Dark and Bloody Ground of Reconstruction Historiography," *Journal of Southern History*, XXV (November, 1959), 427–47.

3

THE USES OF RELIGION

He who doubts that the Negro was created a servant to his brethren, doubts the Word of God.

JOHN AMBROSE PRICE (1907)

As an element of anti-Negro thought, religion was hardly less important than science or history. The concern of racists with the origin of man and his division into races was sufficient in itself to lead them to the Bible and fundamental Christianity, but other important considerations pushed them in the same direction. To be complete, anti-Negro thought must appeal to all levels of American society, and to most Americans religion was a vital force, an intimate part of life. An exclusively "profane" racism was, therefore, unsatisfactory, or rather incomplete. It must be supplemented by religious authority, by scriptural proof of racial inequality. Religious racism was by its very nature most appealing to the ignorant and uneducated, to those, that is, whose racial views were prejudiced and emotional rather than rational or scientific. It was, thus, a valuable component of anti-Negro thought.

Throughout American history popular notions toward the Negro have had biblical and religious justifications. Seventeenth-century slaveholders had feared that the Christianizing of Negroes was incompatible with slavery, but self-interest and a firm assurance that Negroes were by nature servile and inferior helped overcome their misgivings. Even though the nation's treatment of Negroes was always discriminatory, it was never completely devoid of religious overtones. Generally speaking, however, these overtones have manifested themselves in disparate and sometimes antagonistic influences. Most importantly, religious authority has been used to buttress discriminatory and repressive policies—slavery at first, and later segregation. Yet weaker, more sporadic efforts have also been made to condemn those policies as irreligious or outrightly sinful. Another influence, more difficult to assess than the others, is the historic tendency of religious bodies in this country to neglect the Negro and racial problems altogether. Like most Americans, church groups find these problems embarrassing or distasteful, but their lack of concern has profoundly influenced racial policies. It has had the effect of a passive endorsement of the *status quo.*

The religious phases of anti-Negro thought in the twentieth century derive from proslavery arguments of antebellum Southerners and from modifications of those arguments by racists of the postbellum period. As they appear today on the printed page, proslavery and prosegregation arguments are strikingly similar, but this similarity does not conceal important shades of difference. Proslavery literature more frequently reflected the paternal aspects of plantation life and as a result lacked much of the hatred and bitterness of post-Reconstruction writings. The literature of both periods, however, placed substantial reliance upon religious authority. Professor Thomas R. Dew, Chancellor William Harper, Josiah Priest, and George Fitzhugh, for example, each found biblical and moral justifications for slavery,[1] whereas such varied postbellum spokes-

---

1 See *The Pro-Slavery Argument; as Maintained by the most Distinguished Writers of the Southern States* . . . (Philadelphia, 1853); Josiah Priest, *Bible Defense of Slavery* . . . (Glasgow, Ky., 1851); and George Fitzhugh, *Sociology for the South, or the Failure of a Free Society* (Richmond, 1854).

men as Hinton Rowan Helper, Atticus G. Haygood, and Josiah Strong used similar justifications for policies of repression and discrimination.[2] Between 1900 and 1930 this tradition of religious racism persisted. Anti-Negro theorists and writers continued to exploit Christianity and the Bible, and organized religious bodies still endorsed or failed to condemn racist policies. Long after scientists and scholars had dropped their belief in racial inequality, anti-Negro ideas endured among many American church groups. Especially true of fundamental churches in the South, this fact indicated the peculiar way in which American churches reflect popular opinion.

This facet of American church history has been treated in detail by historians.[3] Church records and church literature have been examined and conclusive evidence submitted that American Protestantism has always discriminated against Negroes—a fact which, though obvious, needed documentation. A second aspect of religious racism and an integral part of the first, however, has been ignored. There has been no systematic exposition of that phase of anti-Negro racism which rested upon religious and biblical authority. Although rarely accepted as such, this cluster of anti-Negro ideas rationalized and justified the racial practices of American Christians. The purpose of this chapter is to detail these ideas of religious racism and to explain their usefulness to segregationists. It is not my purpose to explain the racial practices of individual religious denominations, for this would duplicate the researches of Professor Robert M. Miller and others. I hope, instead, to illustrate the uses of biblical interpretations and popular religious ideas as a defense for discrimination and segregation.

As indicated above, American churches in the early twentieth century ignored both the Negro and the "Negro problem." Before 1930 churches rarely took official cognizance of either, and, when they did, they limited their actions to the adoption of platitudinous resolutions of no effect upon individual members or congregations. A characteristic of all Protestant churches of national significance, this practice was especially significant for large fundamentalist denomi-

---

2   Helper, *Nojoque; A Question for a Continent* (New York, 1867), 238–51; Haygood, *Our Brother in Black, His Freedom and His Future* (Nashville, 1881); and Strong, *Our Country: Its Possible Future and Its Present Crisis* (New York, 1885), 208–27.

3   The best account is Robert Moats Miller, *American Protestantism and Social Issues 1919–1939* (Chapel Hill, 1958), 291–313, 131–36. See also Frank S. Loescher, *The Protestant Church and the Negro* (New York, 1948).

nations in the South. As important social institutions in a conservative society, Southern churches were not inclined to embroil themselves in sociopolitical controversies. Southern congregations were exactly that—Southern—and products of the South's social-intellectual heritage. Their attitude toward the Negro was that of Southerners in general and, as such, was beyond the immediate influence of outside pressures. Throughout the period, however, religious leaders and church officials often discussed the Negro and racial problems. Generally sympathetic to the Negro, they couched their views in temperate language and, thus, had considerable influence among moderates and reformers. Like other moderates and reformers, they had no basic quarrel with segregation and white supremacy, and for this reason they were especially useful to racists.

Bishops Charles B. Galloway, Theodore DuBose Bratton, and William Montgomery Brown were representative of Southern church leaders who interested themselves in the Negro. A moderate, a reformer, and an extremist, respectively, they indicated the variety of attitudes among Southern churchmen—and also the historian's difficulty in defining those attitudes. Concerning the Negro, it seems that Southern church leaders, like Southerners in general, were drawn between antagonistic impulses. They knew and liked and, in their own way, respected individual Negroes, but they were also convinced of the race's inferiority and the necessity of maintaining white supremacy. Inclined on the one hand toward kindliness and paternalism, but faced on the other with the actualities of segregation and discrimination, they equivocated. Segregation, they decided, was neither repressive nor harmful, and Southerners were genuinely concerned with the Negro's welfare. When white supremacy was threatened, they turned instinctively to extremism, but in the normal course of events they preferred a softer, more moderate approach. For this reason the implications of their writings are not always apparent. It seems probable, indeed, that they often had a double meaning—one for periods of racial tranquility and another for periods of unrest—and this without conscious hypocrisy. Their seeming harshness was not always intended as such, nor their ostensible reformism an appeal for change. They wrote under the stress of internal difficulties and tensions, and to understand their literature these difficulties and tensions must be recognized and understood.

Charles B. Galloway, a Mississippian, was in the early years of this century a bishop of the Methodist Episcopal Church, South. In 1904 he was invited to address the Conference for Education in the South, at Birmingham, Alabama, upon the subject "The Negro and the South." [4] Neither the Bishop nor the educators in his audience were extremists or race baiters, and his address reflected the moderation of the occasion. "All our dealings with [Negroes] should be in the spirit, and according to the ethics of the Man of Galilee," he declared. "What is best for them now should be the measure of present duty, leaving the future to His hands who knows the end from the beginning. We must insist that the negro have equal opportunity with every American citizen to fulfill in himself the highest purposes of an all-wise and beneficent Providence." The crux of the matter, of course, was the "highest purposes" of Providence, and the Bishop felt compelled to elaborate upon this later. "In the study of this momentous question," he continued, "some things may be considered as definitely and finally settled." First of all, "whether it be prejudice or pride of race," the South will never permit "social mingling of the races." Secondly, the two races will continue to "worship in separate churches and be educated in separate schools." Finally, whites will retain political supremacy, for "intelligence and wealth will and should control the administration of governmental affairs." This, in rather blunt language, was the spirit and ethics of the Man of Galilee.

The distinction between moderation and extremism was a matter of emphasis and attitude rather than a fundamental difference of opinion. This fact is pointedly illustrated by a comparison of Galloway's views with those of the Right Reverend William Montgomery Brown, D.D. A native of Ohio, Brown spent his adult life as an Episcopal clergyman in Arkansas where he was eventually elevated to a bishopric. In Arkansas he first encountered the "Negro problem," which to him was a strangely interesting social phenomenon. The more he studied the problem, the more he became obsessed with defining its nature and solving it, and toward these ends he prepared a vitriolic, rambling, and repetitive work, *The Crucial Race Question, or Where and How Shall the Color Line Be Drawn.*[5]

---

4 Galloway, *The South and the Negro* (New York, 1904), 8.
5 William Montgomery Brown, *The Crucial Race Question, or Where and How Shall the Color Line Be Drawn* (Little Rock, 1907), 12, 118, 125, 135.

Although he was a "Southernized Northerner" and a respected Episcopal clergyman, his attitude toward the Negro was that of the
Southern extremist. In *The Crucial Race Question* he attempted to
prove that Negroes were bestial and degenerate in order to show the
necessity for extending the color line to all phases of race relations.
The object of racial policy, he said, is the maintenance of racial
purity among whites. Amalgamation must be avoided at all costs
because it thwarts God's plan. The vehicle for achieving amalgamation was social equality, for "if a representative of one race admits
one of another to his table, he opens a wide door to . . . the
thwarting by intermarriage, of God's plan in the creation of different
races." Happily, however, the white man was protected by a law of
nature, "a deep-rooted, God-implanted instinct" of racial prejudice
which made Negroes repulsive to him. "From every point of view,"
Brown reasoned, "the conclusion is unavoidable that it is not only
right for Anglo-Americans to recognize the Color Line in the social,
political, and religious realms, but more than that it would be a great
sin not to do so."

The complexity of attitudes among Southern churchmen is further
illustrated by Bishop Theodore D. Bratton. Like Galloway, Bratton
was a Mississippian, and like Brown he was an Episcopalian. To a
greater extent than either, however, he sought to effect meaningful
reforms in Southern race policies. Active in religious, civic, and
reform organizations, he was concerned with the full range of Southern social and economic problems. Through writings, lectures, and
religious activities and through such organizations as the Southern
Sociological Congress of which he was president in 1918, he promoted interest in the Negro and understanding of racial problems.
His chief work *Wanted—Leaders! A Study of Negro Development*
differed radically in tone from the writings of Brown and Galloway,
for Bratton blamed environment and lack of opportunity for much of
the Negro's backwardness, and he recognized different abilities and
stages of development among Africans.[6] He also blamed unscrupulous and selfish whites rather than ignorant and savage Negroes for

---

6 Theodore DuBose Bratton, "The Christian South and Negro Education,"
   Sewanee Review, XVI (July, 1908), 290–97; Bratton, *Wanted—Leaders!
   A Study of Negro Development* (New York, 1922), 215, 220, 223, 229;
   and Bratton, "Race Co-operation in Church Work," in James E. McCulloch
   (ed.), *Battling for Social Betterment, Southern Sociological Congress . . .
   1914* (Nashville, 1914), 146.

the excesses of Reconstruction and the racial bitterness which followed that unhappy era. The South's race problem, in his view, was a result of political demagoguery, and its solution lay in "the Christian thought and sentiment and the labor of Christian men of science." The Christian's obligation, he believed, was obvious—to give "righteous obedience to God's law of justice, and conformity to God's law of love." To Bratton this meant setting a moral and spiritual example for Negroes and offering them increased educational, economic, and political opportunities, including the right to vote. But it did not include—and emphatically not—an iota of social equality. In Bratton's view the heart of the race problem was "not how to escape doing justice, but how to be just without destroying racial integrity." The vast majority of Negroes, he declared, were "still children intellectually" and "little short of [the] savage morally," and to give them equality was not in the best interest of anyone. Like Galloway and Brown, then, Bratton wanted no basic alteration in Southern racial policies. Yet he did propose to ameliorate the Negro's condition by making segregation less oppressive and subordination less desperate.

As Bratton, Brown, and Galloway indicated, church leaders viewed religion as a source of inspiration and guidance in race relations. Other racists, however, had different uses for it. Because it offered an explanation for the origin of man, the appearance of races, and the source and nature of racial inequality, it was for many theorists and popularizers a substitute for science. To fundamentalists evolution and science were atheistic explanations of human development, much less satisfactory than religious faith, biblical history, and the Mosaic account of creation. But despite their rejection of evolution, they never found a generally acceptable alternative. Many of them were overly concerned with faith and literalism and sought no alternative, whereas those who did were unconcerned with systematic thoroughness and logical consistency. As a system of ideas, therefore, religious racism was more disorganized and incomplete than scientific or historical racism.

The central theme of religious racism was the idea that racial inequality is the work and the will of God. For reasons unknowable to man, the idea ran, an infinitely wise but inscrutable Creator had ordained and created separate and easily distinguishable races. Each He endowed with qualities and capacities befitting its role in the providential design, and each had developed in conformity with

His plan. As Senator John W. Daniel of Virginia declared in 1899, each had different qualities which "God has created in order that they may fulfill separate and distinct missions in the cultivation and civilization of the world." [7] Such generalities of course are vague and meaningless, but they were widely accepted as sufficient evidence of the Negro's inferiority. In their own minds at least, those who accepted them simply recognized God's work, saw it was good, and accepted its implications. Should anyone press them further, they replied that racial inequality was obvious. Had not the different races achieved unequal levels of civilization? Did not Caucasians enjoy a special relationship with God? For those who asked such questions only one answer, an emphatic affirmative, was possible. The white man, they felt, could ill afford to violate God's law by sharing his institutions or his blood with others. "We believe," said one of Thomas Dixon's characters, "that God has raised up our race, as he ordained Israel of old, in this world crisis to establish and maintain for weaker races, as a trust for civilization, the principles of civil and religious liberty and the forms of constitutional government." [8]

Literal-minded religionists, however, were not always satisfied with such generalities. They wanted additional evidence, special biblical authority for racial inequality. They turned, therefore, to the oft-repeated story that the Negro's inferiority was a perpetual curse which God through Noah had placed upon the descendants of Ham. The marks of this curse—black skin, physical inferiority, and mental incapacity—were signs of God's displeasure and from them there was no escape. As the cursed of God, the Negro could never expect equality for he was unworthy of the white man's civilization. [9] This view, of course, made the Negro's inferiority an afterthought of God rather than the design of Providence, but the inconsistency was never discussed by racists.

Concerned chiefly with practical implications rather than philosophical thoroughness, religious racists did not generally elaborate upon God's role in creating inequality. (This they left for a small group of extremists who are discussed below.) More often than not they merely stated a truism which, like other truisms of fundamental

---

7   Quoted in Richard Hofstadter, *Social Darwinism in American Thought, 1860–1915* (Philadelphia, 1945), 166.
8   Dixon, *The Leopard's Spots*, 439.
9   See for example, Hill, *Negro, National Asset or Liability?* 54–60.

religion, was its own proof. They ignored unanswered and bother-
some questions on the Adamic creation, neglected Orientals and
other racial stocks, and even disregarded the Christian concept of
the brotherhood of man. Yet their ideas were enormously influential
in popular opinion and were widely accepted as consonant with
biblical authority and natural order. They told the faithful, the
irrational, and the uneducated what they already felt but wanted
confirmed—that blacks are inferior and whites superior, that segregation is righteous and discrimination just, and that Negroes by
nature are hewers of wood and drawers of water.

A sampling of their views will indicate their disregard for reason
and veracity and show also the difference between popular religious
racism and the views of Bishops Bratton, Galloway, and Brown. God
made Negroes a most inferior race, declared John Ambrose Price, a
race of servants whom He "cursed . . . with servitude for our
benefit and theirs." He constructed them on a very different plan
from the whites and gave them distinguishing characteristics peculiarly adapted for the position they occupy among us. Specifically,
their "inferior physical structure and [depraved] moral organization" were adaptations for perpetual servility and servitude. In
placing "the curse upon the posterity of Ham," said Price, "God
never promised to remove it, and He never will." [10]

The implications of Price's views were more important than their
authenticity, and they were developed in detail by such extremists as
Representative Frank Clark of Florida and Senator J. Thomas Heflin
of Alabama. "If God Almighty had intended these two races to be
equal," Clark told his colleagues in the House of Representatives,
"He would have so created them." Instead, He created "the Caucasian of handsome figure, straight hair, regular features, high brow,
and superior intellect," while He gave the Negro "a black skin, kinky
hair, thick lips, flat nose, low brow, low order of intelligence, and
repulsive features." Such differences, of course, were not the result of
either accident or mistake on the part of the Creator, who knew what
He was doing and did just what He intended to do. Echoing and
expanding Clark's views, Senator Heflin assured the Congress that
God had a purpose in making separate and distinct races. He intended white men to rule the world and for this reason made them
superior to other races, the climax and crowning glory of creation.

---

10   Price, *The Negro Past, Present, and Future,* 42, 69, 128–29, 134.

"In His infinite wisdom," said Heflin, as the history of the human race demonstrated, the Creator "clothed the white man with the elements and the fitness of dominion and rulership," and, wherever the white man "planted his foot and unfurled the flag of his authority," he immediately became dominant. Wherever he encountered colored races he immediately subjugated them and perpetuated his supremacy by any means necessary. It should thus be "apparent to all intelligent students of history" that whites in the United States will continue to control the Negro. It is the Creator's will that they do so, and no amount of legislation or quibbling can improve on the Almighty's handiwork.[11]

Religious racists mentioned thus far were monogenists. They accepted the Mosaic account of creation, as they understood it, and they felt, though only vaguely, that all mankind was descended from Adam. This point, however, they seldom stressed, although not for fear that it contradicted their other ideas on racial origins or inequality. They simply felt that further speculations were superfluous. In this respect they differed from a second group of religious racists whose conjecturings and conclusions were much less limited. Members of this group suggested, vaguely, that God had created only one race, Caucasians, or at least only one race in His own image and that He was largely uninterested in the others. God Almighty, insisted the loquacious Georgia Congressman William C. Lankford in 1922, "took the dust of the earth and molded it into His own image, into the form of a man and breathed into its nostrils His own creative everlasting, immortal breath, and the image came forth a human being, a living soul, all dominating, all conquering, everlasting, eternal, immortal; a part of God Himself; a Caucasian, a white man, and God gave that first white man dominion over all things, and told him to reach to the bottom of the sea and up to the highest skies and understand and know the mysteries of all time and space, and that first man, a white man, went forth to solve, understand, conquer, and know the universe in which he had been placed."[12]

In this long and rambling sentence Lankford illustrated the major characteristics of this group. By indirection he was a polygenist, but he gave no thought to the possibility that his views were inconsistent

---

11 *Congressional Record,* 60th Congress, 1st Session (February 22, 1908), Appendix, 40; *ibid.,* 71st Congress, 2nd Session (February 7, 1930), 3234; *ibid.,* 71st Congress, 1st Session (May 22, 1929), 1722.
12 *Ibid.,* 67th Congress, 2nd Session (January 18, 1922), 1371.

with popular understanding of the story of creation. Like others of this group he was chiefly concerned with the white man, whose origins he explained in detail. His—and their—interest in the Negro was of a different nature. They accepted the idea that black skin was a curse from God, but they disliked the suggestion that Ham, and thus Noah and Adam, was the ancestor of all races. Adam was of course a white man—some even said an Aryan—and all white men were descended from him. But nothing in the Bible justified the contention that the black man descended from Adam or Noah. "All Caucasian races can be traced to Noah by history, mythology, customs, language, and tradition," wrote E. H. Randle, but no other race can be so traced by any one of these methods.[13]

The ideas of popular religious racism ranged from Randle the extremist to Bishop Bratton the reformer. The two men differed fundamentally in their opinions of the Negro and their approach to race problems. Yet the racial policies which each endorsed differed in degree rather than kind. To Randle, segregation should be complete and repressive. To Bratton, it should be meliorative and paternal—but still segregation. Randle would base racial policies on the cynical self-interest of the white man. Bratton would sympathize with the Negro's aspirations for advancement within the framework of segregation. Even Randle, however, would not exclude Negroes from the human species: they were simply inferior human beings whose exploitation by the white man was justified. But a small group of religious racists were more extreme than Randle. To them the Negro was not a human being at all. He was instead the biblical beast of the field.

Chief spokesman of this most extreme of all anti-Negro groups was Charles Carroll, a Missourian who developed his ideas in *The Negro A Beast, or in the Image of God* (1900) and *The Tempter of Eve* (1902). Considering himself a man of science as well as a man of God, Carroll drew his ideas from several sources: popular religious racists, especially those writers who rejected evolution but who otherwise attempted to reconcile science and the Bible, and the most farfetched and discreditable prejudices which circulated in the late nineteenth century. Writing with the righteousness of a bigot and the zealousness of a crusader, he saw himself as an agent

---

13 Mallison, *Color at Home and Abroad*, 13; and Randle, *Characteristics of the Southern Negro*, 116.

of God for educating Americans to the true nature of creation. Specifically, he sought to prove that God had created the Negro not as a man, as Homo sapiens, but as an ape, the highest of apes to be sure, but an ape nevertheless. Adam (man), he declared, had been created in the white image of God as the final act, the crowning glory, of creation. Since man (the Caucasian) was the last act of creation, Negroes were *ipso facto* "pre-Adamic," that is, prehuman animals. Other so-called races—Mongolians, American Indians, Malayans—were also inhuman, being the bastard offspring of man's promiscuous and unholy mating with apes (Negroes).

The unorthodoxy of this view was not lost upon Carroll and he sought to explain it thoroughly. Over the centuries, he insisted, the story of creation had become garbled at crucial points by mistranslations of key biblical passages. A product of the translator's faulty understanding of Greek and Hebrew, these errors had been passed from generation to generation and had accumulated in the process the authority of long acceptance. Lately their authority had been enhanced by the Christian's revulsion against Darwinism and re-inforced by insidious fallacies such as charity, brotherhood, altruism, and the white man's burden. "When God's plan of creation, and the drift of Bible history are properly understood," wrote Carroll confidently, "it will be found that the teachings of scripture upon this, as upon every other subject, harmonize with those of science." But Carroll's of course was a peculiar science, and his interpretation of scripture was a grotesque product of his feverish imagination.

To summarize ideas as bizarre as his is difficult. Carroll is significant not for his influence upon popular opinion but because he illustrated the most extreme fringe of religious racism. His tone is thus more important than his ideas, and his tone is easily indicated. The Almighty, he declared, created man to civilize and dominate the earth, and to simplify man's task He provided work animals of various kinds. Those with four legs He called cattle, and those with two legs, beasts. As a part of the general scheme of salvation, then, He devised "a great labor plan for development of the resources of the earth," entrusting its execution to man, "who was designed to perform the mental labor," and to beasts (Negroes), "which [*sic*] in the capacity of servant[s], should perform the manual labor." The Negro was given characteristics which were essential to servitude—erect posture, a well-developed hand and foot, articulate speech, and a low order of mentality. But he was given no soul and no moral faculty, a fact which happily relieved the white man of religious or moral responsibilities toward him.[14]

To make his theory more plausible, Carroll reinterpreted the whole of biblical history from the Garden of Eden to the coming of Christ, emphasizing in the course thereof the disruptive role of the Negro. The tempter of Eve, for example, had been a Negro, not a serpent. Biblical scholars had simply mistranslated as "serpent" the Hebrew word which in reality meant "black." His discovery that the culprit in Eden was a Negro, said Carroll, solved many difficulties of interpretation. Not only did it explain the tempter's ability to speak, but it also accounted for Eve's lack of surprise at hearing it speak. Responsibility for the fall of man, however, was only the first of the Negro's sins. The wife whom Cain had taken in the land of Nod was a Negro, and the fact that Negroes were beasts explained her existence. Thus Cain and his wife had commenced the worst of all violations of God's law—man's amalgamation with the beast of the field—a violation which at once became the most prevalent of sins and the chief obstacle to God's plan of salvation. Disregarding God's injunction to the contrary, man promiscuously mongrelized himself with beasts, giving God no choice but to intervene. The results were first the destruction of Sodom and Gomorrah and second the destruction of the earth by water. At the time of the Flood, Noah and his family were the only pure whites left on earth, so God determined to eliminate the hordes of soulless mongrels and give man a new opportunity. Among the beasts on the Ark, however, were a pair of Negroes, and amalgamation commenced again soon after the Flood. Again God found it necessary to intervene, this time by sending His son Jesus Christ to "redeem man from atheism, amalgamation, and idolatry." Carroll wrote that "the drift of Bible history from the Creation to the birth of the Savior clearly indicates that he came to destroy man's social, political and religious equality with the Negro and mixed-bloods and the amalgamation to which these crimes inevitably lead, and to rebuild the barriers which God erected in the Creation between man and the ape."[15]

These views were by no means original with Carroll. In various forms they had circulated among extremists during the latter half of the nineteenth century, however always without much popular ap-

---

14   Charles Carroll, *The Negro A Beast, or In the Image of God* . . . (St. Louis, 1900), 87, 99, 221.
15   *Ibid.*, 246, 269.

peal. Carroll's ideas seem to have been expropriated, in wholesale fashion, from the Reverend Buchner H. Payne, who had developed them in 1872 in *The Negro: What Is His Ethnological Status?* Offering himself as a biblical scholar and logician, Payne was uninterested in rational or scientific proof of his assertions, although he did have a flair for manufacturing, in catechistic fashion, conclusions which "proved" his theories.

Now as Adam was white, [he wrote,] Abraham white, and our Savior white, did he enter heaven when he arose from the dead as a white man or as a negro? If as a white man then the negro is left out; if as a negro then the white man is left out. As Adam was the *Son of God* and as God is light (white) and in Him is no darkness (black) *at all*, how could God then be the Father of the negro, as like begets or produces like? And if God could not be the *Father* of the blacks because He was white, how could our Savior, "being the express image of God's person," as asserted by St. Paul, carry such a *damned color* into heaven where all are white, much less up to the throne? [16]

It is difficult to determine what, if any, influence Carroll's ideas enjoyed. In 1909 an observer suggested that *The Negro A Beast* had "become the Scripture of tens of thousands of poor whites," who maintained its doctrines "with an appalling stubbornness and persistence." Another reported four years earlier that the book was "said to be securing a very wide circulation among the poor whites of the cotton states." [17] These opinions, however, are mere surmises, and, since both observers found Carroll's views repulsive, they were inclined perhaps toward overstatement. The suggestion that Negroes are beasts of the field was so totally at variance with popular interpretations of the Bible that it probably had little influence among any group, even in the deep South. Carroll was never cited by popular writers, and few racists seem to have read his works. His views were simply the ultimate extension of religious racism. The average racist never felt it necessary to carry his thoughts so far.

---

16   "Ariel" [Buchner H. Payne], *The Negro: What is His Ethnological Status?* (Cincinnati, 1872), 87–88. For other expressions of these views see "Caucasian" [ps.], *Anthropology for the People, A Refutation of the Theory of the Adamic Origin of all Races* (Richmond, 1891); G. C. H. Haaskarl, *The Missing Link; or the Negro's Ethnological Status* (Chambersburg, Pa., 1898); Frank P. Ball, *Divine Creation versus the Theory of Evolution* (privately printed, 1925); and "The Negro and His Creator," *Outlook*, LXXVII (July 16, 1904), 635–36.

17   H. Paul Douglass, *Christian Reconstruction in the South* (Boston, 1909), 114; and Edward Atkinson, "The Negro A Beast," *North American Review*, CLXXXI (August, 1905), 202.

Whether he would have agreed with Carroll had he done so is problematical.

Although Carroll probably had little influence, his works brought a storm of protest from a few literal-minded religious racists whose sensibilities were wounded by his radicalism. Carroll had seized the initiative, however, and his opponents were in the uncomfortable position of racists defending the Negro. Rather than dismiss Carroll as a crackpot, which was the most common reaction to his views, a few writers insisted upon refuting him point by point. In the process they sometimes advanced theories of their own which were as novel and unorthodox as those they were so anxiously denouncing. Typical of Carroll's refuters was the Reverend W. S. Armistead, of Tifton, Georgia, who expressed his outrage in *The Negro is a Man* (1903). Adam's skin, like that of all pre-Noachians, declared Armistead, was red not white. Noah's sons, however, were red (Shem), white (Japheth), and black (Ham)—a truth not previously realized because, like Carroll, Bible scholars had erroneously assumed that like invariably begets like. When man began to spread over the earth, God saw that the dissimilar environments of Africa, Asia, and Europe demanded different types of men, and He accordingly differentiated mankind. Thus all races are human beings descended from Adam, and their differences in no way reflect inferiority or superiority. "The Negro is a *fac simile* [*sic*] of the white man," declared Armistead emphatically, "and, therefore, is of Adamic descent." [18]

Continuing his assault upon Carroll, the Georgian suggested that the tempter of Eve was neither a Negro nor a serpent, but a crocodile, the most cursed of all earthly creatures. Cain's wife, moreover, was not a Negro, and her existence was no dark mystery. When she and Cain married, there were already 400,000 males on earth and presumably an equal number of females. Mrs. Cain's maiden name was even revealed by Armistead—Miss Save Adam or Miss Azura Adam, or perhaps Miss Save Abel or Miss Azura Abel. She was also not a Negro, as the race did not yet exist, and Carroll's descriptions of Cain's amalgamation were nothing but fantasy. This did not mean, however, that Armistead, or God, endorsed racial intermixture. God made of one blood all the nations of men that dwell on

18   W. S. Armistead, *The Negro is a Man, A Reply to Professor Charles Carroll's Book "The Negro is a Beast or in the Image of God"* (Tifton, Ga., 1903), 161.

earth, Armistead admitted, but He scattered the races across the earth and separated them by continental barriers. In so doing, He "signified, aye, expressed in no uncertain terms, His *willingness,* aye, His *imperative desire,* that *race intermingling* or *intermarriage should* not *take place."* The nation should therefore dig *"deeper* the *foundations"* and build *"higher* the *walls* that *intervene Racial Social Equality.* God has drawn the line—a *continental one.* To ignore it would be to reflect on the wisdom of God; to remove it would be the ruin of the negro race; to abolish it would be to destroy the white race morally and religiously." [19] As a practical matter, then, Armistead arrived at the same conclusion as Carroll. The Negro had a "place" in American society and he should be kept in it. And when viewed from the Negro's standpoint, the racial policies which Carroll and Armistead endorsed differed principally in degree from those of Bishops Bratton and Galloway.

Religion was, thus, a popular and effective basis for theorizing on the origins of racial inequality and Negro inferiority. It was also a basis for interpreting the history of Negroes in the United States and explaining their proper role in contemporary society. Like other aspects of religious racism, this attention to history was a twentieth-century holdover of a nineteenth-century phenomenon. As such it enjoyed the authority of tradition and the respectability of age.

To many racists of the twentieth century, American Negro slavery was an instrumentality of God, and the Southern planter an agent of the Almighty. "God's mercifully overruling providence," Bishop Bratton wrote concerning slavery, "brought the negro race out of darkness into a light that has shone not only upon themselves here, but into the far darker recesses of their native Africa." Perhaps there had been a degree of unrighteousness in so selfish and material an institution, he conceded, for slavers and planters were sometimes influenced by the love of greed.[20] Yet generally speaking, they were helpless instruments in the hands of God. Southerners, of course, had not sought the responsibility and the onerous burden of civilizing and Christianizing the Negro, but God in his mysterious providence had demanded of them the sacrifice. It was not by chance, therefore, that Negroes were in this country, nor was it accidental that they imitated the white man and found in his example an

---

19   *Ibid.,* 537–39.
20   Bratton, "Race Co-operation in Church Work," in McCulloch (ed.), *Battling for Social Betterment,* 148.

inspiration for intellectual and moral advancement.[21] But God's ultimate purpose was not simply to expose a few Negroes to Caucasian civilization. This was His means to more important ends—He hoped eventually to civilize and Christianize all Africans.

Beyond this point, anti-Negro theorists differed in their accounts of God's intentions. According to one group, He intended to return the slaves to Africa at the conclusion of a sufficient period of training and in due time had raised up the abolitionists who fulfilled His purpose by emancipating the slaves as a preliminary to repatriation.[22] This view, however, was challenged by two rival interpretations. One of these held that God intended Negroes for perpetual servitude, which meant that abolition and emancipation were sinful acts of selfish men. The other agreed that emancipation was in God's scheme, but suggested that it had been forced prematurely by those agents of the anti-Christ, the abolitionists.[23]

In view of such opinions as these, it is not surprising that twentieth-century racists found biblical and religious sanctions for slavery. "The Bible endorses slavery, both in the Old and New Testaments," wrote John Ambrose Price, repeating the charge that Negroes were the cursed descendants of Ham and noting the fact that Abraham, Isaac, and Jacob were slaveholders. And Jesus, observed another extremist, never once denounced slavery during His sojourn on earth. On the contrary, St. Paul, His greatest apostle, specifically endorsed the institution in I Timothy 6:1–4: "Let as many as are servants under the yoke count their own masters worthy of all honor, that the name of God and the doctrine be not blasphemed. And they that have believing masters, let them not despise them, because they are brethren; but let them serve them the rather, because they that partake of the benefit are believing and beloved." [24]

---

21 Price, *The Negro Past, Present, and Future,* 42; and Bratton, "The Christian South and Negro Education," 293.

22 Bratton, "The Christian South and Negro Education," 290–97; and Bratton, "Race Co-operation in Church Work," in McCulloch (ed.), *Battling for Social Betterment,* 145–53.

23 See for example W. S. McCurley, "The Impossibility of Racial Amalgamation," *Arena,* XXI (April, 1899), 446–55; Hampton, "The Race Problem," 132–38; and John Temple Graves in *The Possibilities of the Negro in Symposium* (Atlanta, 1904), 23. Graves generally accepted the views of this latter group but drew a somewhat different conclusion. He thought the Negroes should be deported immediately.

24 Price, *The Negro Past, Present, and Future,* 32–33; and Reed, *The Brothers War,* 352.

Implicit in the biblical defense of slavery was a general religious justification for segregation and discrimination. The Bible in fact not only condoned such policies, but insisted upon them. "God Almighty knew what He was about when He established the color line dividing the races of mankind," editorialized a Mississippi newspaper in 1928, and Southerners knew better than to tamper with His work. Why He had created racial differences in the first place was something which mankind did not understand, but Southerners, at least, recognized His handiwork and accepted it in a sensible way. They agreed with Cole Blease that white supremacy was a part of the Christian religion, and they were sure that reformers who denounced segregation denounced also "the providence of God as to His purpose in the government of the world." White supremacy was "a divine law, enacted for the defense of society and civilization." [25]

Such were the implications which extremists derived from their study of the Bible. Moderates, however, who represented a more significant body of opinion, drew conclusions which, on the surface at least, were entirely different. Instead of emphasizing biblical authority for segregation and white supremacy, they stressed "the principles of Jesus" as the proper guide for racial policies. In place of the extremist's harshness, they offered the gentleness and benevolence of the Christ. "Darkened as the problem is from the standpoint of politics, social fact, and human nature," declared the Reverend Doctor Victor Irvine Masters, "it becomes bright when approached in the spirit of Jesus Christ." An official of the Home Mission Board of the Southern Baptist Convention, Masters approached race problems in much the same way as did Bishops Galloway and Bratton. For too long, he felt, the bugaboo of social equality had excited the South and prevented a realistic appraisal of racial issues. All the Negro really wanted, or needed, was Christian sympathy and help and the blessings of a pure and holy religion. But the principles of Jesus to which Masters appealed differed only in degree from the conclusions of extremists. The spirit of Jesus, like the reforms of Galloway and Bratton, demanded little alteration in the *status quo*.[26]

---

25 Laurel (Miss.) *Call*, October 16, 1928; *Congressional Record*, 70th Congress, 1st Session (April 10, 1928), 6149; Price, *The Negro Past, Present, and Future*, 139, 107; and William J. Robertson, *The Changing South* (New York, 1927), 72.

26 Victor Irvine Masters, *The Call of the South* (Atlanta, 1918), 52–53, 58–60, 70.

Masters' approach to racial problems typified the views of many Southerners. Indeed, the most important group of Southern moderates sought the solution to racial problems in fundamental Protestant Christianity. And since they were so "reasonable"—they reflected popular Christian prejudices, and their tone was lofty and idealistic without demanding alterations in traditional practices— they were an enormously influential element in anti-Negro thought. Their approach was illustrated by Robert Edwin Smith, a Texan and the author of *Christianity and the Race Problem* (1922), a work of little apparent influence but one which admirably summarized the ideas and weaknesses of moderate racism. At the outset Smith dismissed "the social status of the race question" as unworthy of attention, because "both races believe that a separate social life is most desirable and most practical." Thus, disposing of this troublesome aspect of race relations, he concentrated his thoughts upon other, more important problems. First, he explained the responsibility of whites to Negroes: to sympathize with them, to encourage them, to protect them from injustice, to express hope for their future. Second, he indicated the responsibility of white Christian ministers to Negroes: to "cry aloud against injustice, oppression, and every other evil that afflicts the land."

The irony of Smith's approach, and that of religious moderates in general, was most apparent in the solution he offered to the race problem. Here he showed, unintentionally to be sure, that pious phrases couched in the phraseology of fundamental Christianity offered little real hope for the Negro. The solution, he wrote,

is this—for both races to think, feel and act right towards each other. There is no other solution. The problem then turns on the point of right-thinking; for as we think so shall we act. The question arises then what constitutes right-thinking concerning the Negro race among us and of us? Surely we must have open minds and honest purpose to begin with. With this, we must strike out to the high hills from whence wisdom and understanding come and seek the mind and spirit of the Infinite One. "If any man lacks wisdom, let him ask of God." The mind of Christ must possess us, or we shall never think and see aright on any moral question. Deep-rooted and age-long prejudices must give place to sincere purpose to discover the truth and then follow the truth wheresoever it may lead us.

Exalted sentiments these, but their implications for the Negro included definite limitations:

Negroes must recognize the supremacy of the white man [Smith continued], and be willing to be a good second. Right-thinking people will welcome all the progress and all the good that the race may achieve. But as conditions now stand, and as far as the future can be forecasted, the Caucasian race seems destined to lead all other races. Only the shifting of the now apparent purposes of the Supreme Arbiter of Nations will make it otherwise. It is not equality of power and station that Negroes should worry about, but equality of opportunity.[27]

Moderates such as Smith sought to soft-pedal questions of social equality, but extremists never permitted them to do so. The latter constantly reminded moderates that the Christian emphasis upon toleration, brotherhood, and the Golden Rule undermined racial exclusiveness, and they charged that Christianity, "with its caste-eliminating, race-equalizing tenets" was a "mighty agency in mongrelizing the Caucasian." The doctrine of the brotherhood of man, wrote one extremist, "operating through organized religious bodies, has been, since the Negro first appeared in America, a disturbing, disorganizing influence pointing inevitably toward social equality and eventual amalgamation."[28]

Such serious charges, of course, must be refuted. The Bible and Christianity, felt moderates, must not become the preserve of bigoted extremists. It must be shown, and shown emphatically, that neither Christianity nor moderate reform based upon Christian precepts threatened white supremacy or racial purity. This task was not difficult, for religious moderates, like Southerners in general, already accepted both Christianity and Negro inferiority. "Christian men and women," declared the editor of the Richmond *Christian Advocate*, "have a desire to carry out the plan of God for all races," a plan, he hastily added, which directed them "to live together in mutual confidence and brotherliness without doing violence to the racial integrity of either race."[29] To give substance to this view, Southern churchmen often applied it to specific situations. The Reverend M. E. Dodd of Shreveport, Louisiana, for example, a vice-president of the Southern Baptist Convention, was outspokenly critical of Negro Congressman Oscar DePriest's endorsement of social equality, but he had only praise for Booker T. Washington's

---

27   Robert Edwin Smith, *Christianity and the Race Problem* (New York, 1922), 10, 34–44, 92–97, 115, 121, 138.
28   Cox, *White America*, 149, 295; Cox, *The South's Part in Mongrelizing the Nation*, 69–70; and Mallison, *Color at Home and Abroad*, 128, 117.
29   Quoted in *The Christian Index* (Jackson, Tenn.), March 11, 1926, p. 5.

advice that Negroes forego all hopes of immediate social equality.[30] Moderates felt that brotherhood and segregation, properly understood, were fully compatible.

This aspect of religious racism was a direct result of the moderate's attempt to practice his moderation. Kindly and sympathetic by nature, he was repelled by the extremist and refused to condone the latter's overt bigotry. He was certain that racial separation was the will of God, for he had already convinced himself that racial separateness was the work of God. Yet as often as not his God was a God of love who rejected the harsher, more repulsive forms of discrimination, and he faced the necessity of reconciling two divergent and contradictory ideas. His belief in Christianity led him naturally to the Golden Rule, whereas his acceptance of racism pulled him in an opposite direction. His dilemma was, to no small extent, the dilemma of the Southerner in general, and like the Southerner he equivocated. He decided that both the Golden Rule and racial exclusiveness were desirable and compatible. He sometimes gave the impression that the compromise was not entirely satisfactory, but it was surely made without conscious hypocrisy or cynicism. Its acceptance was made easy by the fact that most moderates were never aware of the inner contradiction of the two beliefs.

The extent to which organized church groups accepted the tenets of anti-Negro thought and the extent to which they practiced or condoned policies of segregation and discrimination, as indicated above, have been investigated in detail by a number of scholars, and no study of original church records has been undertaken here. Nor, indeed, is there any need to do so. There seems to be no evidence to refute the conclusion of historians and social scientists, as well as church leaders and racists, that organized Protestantism was a segregated and segregating force in the South and the nation at large. The effect of the study undertaken here has been to corroborate, by using racist literature, conclusions which Frank S. Loescher, Robert M. Miller, and others have reached from church records and the religious press. After studying policies and attitudes of major Protestant denominations toward the Negro, Loescher concluded that "far from helping to integrate the Negro in American life," Protestantism was "actually contributing to the segregation of Negro Americans.

---

30   Shreveport (La.) *Journal,* December 8, 1931.

. . . By the practices of its congregations and educational institutions," he continued, it sanctioned a caste system which stamped inferiority on a whole race. Professor Miller's conclusions were the same. "Protestant churches," he wrote of the period between 1919 and 1939, "were segregated and segregating institutions. White Protestants, while they professed to worship a God who was no respecter of persons, did their worshiping in buildings where the color of skin and not the purity of heart was the entrance test." There was also, he noted, "an unhappy correlation between Protestantism and mob violence" against Negroes.[31]

One of the chief characteristics of Protestantism's treatment of the Negro, a characteristic which Miller and Loescher noted and which was also reflected in the literature of religious racism, was a disconcerting tendency to ignore race problems altogether. Miller examined records of 117 Southern Baptist district association meetings in areas where lynchings had occurred and found only one reference to the local lynching and no resolutions of condemnation. In the religious press he found a similar situation. "Literally hundreds of editorials and articles," he wrote, "the great majority of them appearing in Southern journals, reflected the myth that a peaceful and harmonious relationship existed between the races." Nor apparently did local ministers find time for racial problems. For whatever reason, they chose to concentrate their energies upon other issues. "To judge Southern clergymen by the themes of their sermons," declared sociologist Jerome Dowd who was himself a Southerner, "one would suppose that they did not regard lynching as comparable to the sin of dancing, playing cards, or going to a theater." [32]

Behind this ostensible unconcern for race problems was the underlying fear, noted above, that segregation and discrimination did violence to basic Christian precepts. There was also the natural inclination of a conservative people to treat social problems cautiously. Accordingly, Southern religious groups developed a vague climate of opinion which reflected their wishfulness and emotions rather than "facts" or conviction. They tended to feel rather than

---

31   Loescher, *The Protestant Church and the Negro,* 15, 117; and Robert M. Miller, "The Attitudes of American Protestantism toward the Negro, 1919–1939," *Journal of Negro History,* XLI (July, 1956), 215.

32   Miller, *American Protestantism and Social Issues,* 132; Miller, "The Attitudes of American Protestantism toward the Negro, 1919–1939," 221–22; and Dowd, *The Negro in American Life,* 231.

think upon the subject, and Southern ministers who confronted this situation were unprepared to stir up trouble. The ministers sought other, less controversial sins to denounce. They accepted the advice of a Quincy, Florida, newspaper editor to forego racial questions and concentrate instead upon "constructive Christianity," that is, "preach Christ and Him crucified, the love of God and the fellowship and communion of the Holy Ghost." Ministers interested in racial issues were cautioned by Dr. C. B. Wilmer, professor of practical Christianity at the University of the South, against wasting their energies on such irrelevant and demagogic matters as social and political equality. They should put first things first, Wilmer advised, and concentrate upon "the moral and spiritual sides of the question involved." [33]

From 1900 to 1930, therefore, the Negro received little encouragement from Southern, or American, Protestantism. Sometimes excoriated in the most bigoted and demagogic language, he was more frequently patronized and urged to love God and walk uprightly in an humble—and segregated—way. At the same time non-Protestants in the South, notably Catholics and Jews, generally acquiesced in Jim Crow policies of the majority, although without giving them the Protestant's vociferous endorsement. Overstating the case perhaps, W. E. B. Du Bois declared in 1925 that the Roman Catholic Church, North and South, stood for "color separation and discrimination to a degree equalled by no other church in America." To substantiate this indictment, Du Bois noted the almost universal segregation in parochial schools and other Catholic facilities, a lack of Church supported education for Negroes above the primary level, an absence of Negro priests, and the discriminatory policies of Catholic universities and seminaries.[34]

But Du Bois did not completely overstate the matter, for the attitudes and practices of Catholics toward Negroes did not materially differ from those of Protestants. Indeed there was a substantial parallel between the two groups. Theoretically, Catholic doctrine recognized no distinctions between races, but in practice racial equality was in the sight of God only and not in the sight of man or the Church on earth. "The arbitrary exclusion of Negro Catholics

33 Quincy (Fla.) *News,* May 30, 1930; and Atlanta (Ga.) *Constitution,* October 9, 1928.
34 Letter from W. E. B. Du Bois to Joseph B. Glenn, St. Joseph's Mission, Richmond, Va., in *The Crisis,* XXX (July, 1925), 121.

from Catholic schools," one student has written, "constitutes in practice a denial of basic dogmas of the Catholic faith." But, he continues, recognition of this fact appeared very late in Catholic publications, and he might also have added that segregation was the rule rather than the exception in most Catholic facilities, including, occasionally, even a Jim Crow church and congregation.[35]

Although the above statements were made in 1948, they apply aptly to the first three decades of the twentieth century. Throughout this period, Catholic concern for the Negro was limited to a paternalism not unlike that of other whites and to occasional general appeals for interracial understanding. A few figures indicate the condition of Negro Catholics: prior to 1926 only eight Negro priests were ordained for work in the United States; the first Catholic Interracial Council was not formed until 1934; a Jim Crow seminary for training Negro priests, established in Bay St. Louis, Mississippi, graduated its first class in 1934; the number of Negro Catholics was approximately 204,000 in 1928, having increased only about 66,000 in forty years. (This lack of appeal to Negroes was due to discriminations within the Church itself, according to Father John LaFarge, S.J., a leading Catholic proponent of full equality for Negroes.) Throughout the period of this study, most Catholic schools were officially segregated, or at least had no Negro students. A survey of Catholic institutions of higher learning made in 1948 revealed that only half (76 of 154) of the Catholic colleges and universities had ever enrolled a Negro student, whereas none of those in the South had ever done so.[36]

Such statistics, however, are not the only evidence of the Negro's treatment by the Catholic church. Beginning in 1917, Negro Catholics themselves began to organize protests against discrimination within the Church. In 1930 the most important of their protest organizations, the Federated Colored Catholics, voiced the concerns of Negro Catholics:

---

35 Richard J. Roche, *Catholic Colleges and the Negro Student* ("Catholic University of America Studies in Sociology," Vol. XXVIII [Washington, 1948]), 24.

36 John C. Murphy, *An Analysis of the Attitudes of American Catholics toward the Immigrant and the Negro, 1825–1925* ("Catholic University of America Studies in Sociology," Vol. I [Washington, 1948]), 7; and John LaFarge, *The Catholic Viewpoint on Race Relations* (Garden City, 1960), 59; and Roche, *Catholic Colleges and the Negro Student*, 60–82.

We desire [they said] to educate all our boys and girls in Catholic schools, from the primary school to the university, according to each one's native ability.

We desire admission to Catholic institutions, where the denial of such admission involves the loss of tangible goods, to which, as Catholics and human beings, we may legitimately lay claim. . . .

We do not wish to be treated as a "problem," but as a multitude of human beings, sharing a common destiny and the common privilege of the Redemption of all mankind.[37]

The truth of the matter was that the Catholic church, perhaps because of its own exposed minority position, had compromised its theoretical commitment to racial equality and conformed to dominant American patterns of race relations. In some instances this conformity was achieved without demurring from Catholics; in other instances *pro forma* protests were made. A Baltimore church leader, the Very Reverend John R. Slattery complained in 1903 that

the spirit of the political party inimical to the Negro [i.e., the Democratic Party], to which for good or ill the bulk of Catholics belong, dominates many Catholics. The Second and Third Plenary Councils of Baltimore made eloquent appeals in behalf of the Negro, but not one of our orders responded. . . . Perhaps it is the wisest policy to admit frankly that because a man enters the sanctuary or a woman the cloister, he or she is still human and carries along the prejudices of his or her part of the country. No matter what Catholicism ought to do or may have done in the past, the fact is as clear as the noonday sun that many Catholics today are prejudiced against the Negro.[38]

Other Catholics, however, were even less concerned. If "the enforced granting of this inherent right to a colored Catholic threatened . . . the withdrawal of large numbers of white scholars," wrote one of them, "prudence would seem rather to dictate that the exclusion of the colored aspirant be tolerated but not sanctioned, until such time when he can be received without detriment to the school as a whole." [39]

---

37 Quoted in LaFarge, *The Catholic Viewpoint on Race Relations*, 62–63.
38 Murphy, *An Analysis of the Attitudes of American Catholics toward the Immigrant and the Negro*, 120.
39 Quoted in *ibid.*, 131.

All in all, as a leading student of the subject concludes, Catholics before 1925 did not give to the Negro and race relations the attention which those topics demanded. "Many writers," he noted, "were content merely to point out the need for improving the situation, and to criticize their fellow Catholics for their lack of interest." And, he adds, "with the exception of missionary activities, there was no organized and permanent effort on the part of the Catholic Church to assist in a comprehensive way in the social adjustment of the Negro. . . . The Catholic laity were lacking not only in interest and support, but also in charity towards the minority in their midst." [40] Finally, it should be noted that all Catholic organizations promoting better race relations were voluntary and unofficial. They were non-authoritative, which meant that they had no directive power over Catholics in general. They could advise and suggest, but not order or direct, and their approach was always gradualist. They worked on the assumption that interracial understanding could be achieved only through "the peaceful, long-term, indirect process of education," a process which called upon Negroes to accept inequality for an indefinite time. [41]

The record of Catholics, then, was not appreciably different from that of Protestants; yet there were some differences, and these were important. There was the same paternalism and the same ignoring of the Negro, but by the 1920's the Church was coming to grips with the problems of segregation and race relations, and by the thirties it was making significant strides in overcoming the evils of an earlier day.

The record of American Jewry was not above criticism on this issue either, according to a writer in *The Crisis*, official organ of the National Association for the Advancement of Colored People. "In actuality American Jews as a mass have accepted the standards of the Anglo-Saxon," wrote David H. Pierce in 1925. "No Southern rabbi has jeopardized his position or his life by running counter to the Klan's dictum that black and white must be forever separate." This was especially true of Jews in business, who felt themselves susceptible to public pressures. Jewish champions of the Negro's cause, said Pierce, were thus limited "to wealthy philanthropists,

---

40   *Ibid.*, 134–35.
41   See Thomas J. Harte, *Catholic Organizations Promoting Negro-White Race Relations in the United States* ("Catholic University of America Studies in Sociology," Vol. XXIV [Washington, 1947]), 155.

members of radical labor groups and free lance intellectuals." [42]
Such groups, however, contributed substantially to laying foundations for future advancement by the race.

The Negro then was virtually friendless. Condemned by science to a subordinate place in nature and disparaged by history for his alleged failure to contribute anything to man's civilization, he now found himself abandoned, ignored, or patronized by Christianity and the nation's religious community. To him, the brotherhood of man was no more meaningful than the fatherhood of God. The application of Christian precepts to race relations meant at best that whites would be "good" to Negroes and refrain from lynching or otherwise physically abusing them. In return the Negro was expected, indeed required for his own good, to be faithful, happy, humble, and ingratiating. In this way only could he hope for eternal salvation in heaven. As for life on earth, a servant must obey his master.

42 David H. Pierce, "Is the Jew a Friend of the Negro?" *The Crisis,* XXX (July, 1925), 184–86.

Part II

APPLICATION
OF ANTI-NEGRO THOUGHT

4

THE ISSUE
OF SOCIAL EQUALITY

> If a man really believes in equality, let him prove it by
> giving his daughter to a negro in marriage. That is the test.
>
> THOMAS DIXON (1902)

Despite their emphasis upon science, history, and religion, racists
were chiefly concerned with other, more practical things. They
believed, honestly and without reservation, that the Negro was
inferior to the white man, and their scientific, historical, and religious arguments were offered in that spirit. These, however, were
only means. Their objective was a logical and systematic justification
for Southern race policies—for policies, that is, of social segregation,
economic discrimination, and political subordination. As a rule they
gave little attention to abstract ideas of racial inequality, accepting
inequality as a proven fact. Their concern was that racial policies

reflect this fact. In their utterances, therefore, two themes were constantly repeated: socially, the races must be segregated, and politically, the whites must be supreme.

The practical application of anti-Negro thought revolved largely around these themes. Most racists, it must be remembered, had a peculiar definition of racial problems. With the Negro segregated and the white man supreme, they could not understand the reformer's alarm, for, disconcertingly, they equated racial problems with outbreaks of antipathy and violence. This fact, plus the Negro's submission to segregation and discrimination, convinced them that racial problems were nonexistent in the South, and prior to the mid-twenties their utterances reflected this conviction. Their tone was confident and self-assured, haughty and impatient of opposition. But as the agitation of reformers became increasingly effective in the 1920's, racists became more and more defensive and the tone of their writings became strident and alarmist.

Whatever their tone, however, they repeated, reemphasized, and repeated again their objections to social and political equality. The explanation sometimes advanced for this—that they themselves had doubts concerning their arguments—seems unconvincing and inadequate. Perhaps a better explanation was their realization that many Americans—including many Northerners, Republican politicians, reformers, and federal officials—were unconcerned with the practical implications of racial inequality, or were unconvinced or only half-convinced of the necessity of maintaining white supremacy. Such groups, of course, were potential integrationists, for to be unconvinced of the necessity of Southern race policies was to be a threat to the acquiescence of Americans in those policies. Yankees, reformers, and federal officials, felt Southerners, were too much inclined to stir up Negroes by sowing discontentment and dissatisfaction among them.

Like most Americans of the early twentieth century, these Yankees, reformers, and federal officials were inclined to accept the basic ideas of anti-Negro thought. The racists' task, therefore, was largely one of education. They must convince the unconvinced, appeal to the apathetic, explain to the ignorant. Did non-Southerners misconceive the Negro's place in American society? Did they misunderstand his real character, his mental and personal traits, his moral and physical proclivities? Then racists would dutifully explain them, and not once but a hundred times over. The result was a repetitiousness and a lack of originality which noticeably undermined their forcefulness, but in spite of which they were generally able to influence national opinion. Their success, however, was due in no small part to the absence of organized, articulate pro-Negro sentiment, which in turn reflected the diffidence and defensiveness of reformers on the subject of social equality. After the mid-twenties this condition changed gradually as Negroes and pro-Negro intellectuals and reformers became more vocal. Until this happened, however, the racists prevailed.

As an ideology anti-Negro thought never had a clearly recognized leader. No anti-Negro writer ever achieved the stature of Madison Grant, no anti-Negro work ever enjoyed the success of *The Passing of the Great Race,* and no single volume ever succinctly and authoritatively summarized anti-Negro ideas. Both a cause and result of the inconsistencies and contradictions of those ideas, this failure was especially apparent in discussions of social equality. Here racists never formulated a concise and well-defined argument; they turned instead to a "shotgun" approach. In every aspect of anti-Negro thought they found a justification for social segregation.

One of the fundamental contradictions of anti-Negro thought was illustrated by glowing descriptions of interracial harmony on the one hand and by desperate complaints of the ubiquitous "Negro problem" on the other. This contradiction came ultimately, perhaps, from differing views of the nature of race problems and from the different preconceptions with which different racists approached those problems. But it came also from the tendency of Southerners to concern themselves with specific incidents while ignoring general principles. Southerners, generally, and their political spokesmen, especially, were unwilling to admit that the South was plagued by a chronic racial problem, although anti-Negro theorists were under no such delusions. The latter, indeed, saw the presence of Negroes as a problem in itself, and they felt that racial antagonisms in the South were acute and pervasive. "So long as there are any races so divergent" as whites and Negroes living together, editorialized the Miami *Herald* in 1923, "there will be racial problems. The color problem is deep-seated in humanity, and always offers opportunity for friction."[1]

The problem, then, stemmed not from social, political, and economic factors, but from that innate racial antipathy which racists so frequently discussed. "The line of cleavage in Southern life," they

---

1   Miami (Fla.) *Herald,* March 17, 1923.

felt, "is the line of color," and before it all other interests, prejudices, and feelings give way. "When you ask me why I do not associate with a negro," wrote a Texan in 1911, "I do not say it is because the negro is poor and dirty and ragged and uneducated. I and all the white men I know and all I want to know object to a negro because he has a black face and other physical characteristics of the race." It was "the presence of an undue proportion of negroes in the southern States" which created troubles of enormous proportions and threatened the peace, happiness, and prosperity of the section.[2] And presumably the troubles would continue as long as the races lived together.

Upon this point the racist's perspective was colored by his conviction that the "Negro problem" was an episode in the agelong and worldwide struggle between races, a struggle which was just now turning against whites. The first portent of this reversal was the Russo-Japanese War, in which a colored nation defeated a white nation, and its most significant event so far was World War I, a civil war among Caucasians. According to one estimate this war had killed forty million whites, and colored races had benefited accordingly. The balance of world power, long held by whites, was therefore threatened and only complete unity could prevent its toppling. In this context the "Negro problem" had a new significance, and the obligations of Northern whites were much more obvious, for when the showdown comes, as come it must, American Negroes will make common cause with the colored races.[3]

Consequently, it was ironic that the Southerner welcomed Negroes to his community, and even to his home, although the welcome lasted only so long as the race was present in a servile capacity. Southerners had no objection to close personal contact with Negroes, as Thomas Pearce Bailey pointed out, provided such contact was on a well-defined basis of white supremacy. It was the Negro's "*assertion*, present or possible, of his equal worth" that irritated the white man, for assertions, said Bailey, tend to produce far-reaching acts. When Negroes are restless and impatient with subordination,

---

2 Albion W. Tourgee, *An Appeal to Caesar* (New York, 1884), 77; Chester T. Crowell, "A Message to the North," *Independent*, LXX (May 11, 1911), 990; A. S. Van de Graaff, "Unaided Solution of the Southern Race Problem," *Forum*, XXI (May, 1896), 330; and Enoch Spencer Simmons, *A Solution of the Race Problem in the South* (Raleigh, 1898), 10.

3 *Congressional Record*, 60th Congress, 1st Session (April 17, 1908), 4877; and *ibid.*, 66th Congress, 2nd Session (May 31, 1920), 8030–31.

then the white man reacts instinctively against them, but his fury subsides when the restlessness diminishes.[4] Thus, Southern race relations, though generally tranquil, were sometimes violent, but their nature at any time depended solely upon the Negro and his willingness to remain subordinate.

This theme of pessimism ran throughout the literature of Southern race problems, and it colored all discussions of social equality. "Race hatred reigns supreme," "the relations between the races is becoming more strained and acute," "the white man in the South is saturated with race hostility to the Negro," and "the Negro responds in kind"—these were opinions frequently expressed.[5] Indeed, so widespread were such sentiments that the moderate and discerning Professor Edwin Mims of Vanderbilt complained in 1926 that the South's "ever-lasting race problem" threatened to shake his confidence in the future.[6] Mims's pessimism, like that of other observers, was paralleled by the optimism and ebullience of racists who praised the interracial harmony of the South. This inconsistency, another reflection of the superficiality of anti-Negro writers, also resulted from their tendency to dwell upon incidents rather than principles. And, it should be added, they did not divide themselves into optimists and pessimists. Instead, an individual was optimistic at one point and pessimistic at another. As a group, they never decided whether to praise the South's interracial harmony or fret over its undercurrent of racial unrest.

The basic premise of social segregation was the conviction that Negroes had a definite place in American society, and the chief object of anti-Negro thought was to define that place in detail. It was, of course, subordinate and its limits were well defined, but in spite of this it was of perpetual concern to racists.

The Negro's place was, first of all, in the South. Although Southerners complained bitterly of his shortcomings and ostensibly felt that his presence was a burden to bear, they also insisted that he remain in the South. This suggests at first glance that they saw the race as an economic asset, easily exploited, and were motivated by

4 Bailey, *Race Orthodoxy in the South*, 41; and Ray Stannard Baker, *Following the Color Line* (New York, 1908), 84.
5 Price, *The Negro Past, Present, and Future*, 170; Maurice S. Evans, *Black and White in the Southern States* (London, 1915), 192, 73. The last opinion was expressed by Governor N. B. Broward of Florida in 1907.
6 Mims, *The Advancing South* (New York, 1926), 257.

that consideration. In racist literature, however, there is little evidence to support such a suggestion. Racists rarely dwelt on economic subjects. Invariably they gave more attention to factors of race—to racial purity and undefiled white maidenhood, to white supremacy and Negro disfranchisement, to the Negro's inferiority and his personal repulsiveness. They objected to Negroes not as economic competitors real or potential, but as members of an alien and inferior race, a race which was physically, mentally, and morally repugnant. This does not mean that economic factors were unimportant; for many racists, Northern as well as Southern, were consciously or unconsciously influenced by them. Despite this, other factors seem to have crystallized their attitudes toward the Negro's presence in the South and his proposed migration to the North.

Chief of these factors was the conviction that Southern whites were the only Americans who understood the Negro and knew how to cope with the problems created by his presence. Racists foresaw that the migration of·Negroes to the North and West would leave large numbers of the race in the South and would not in any fundamental sense remove their problem. On the contrary, they feared, it might actually aggravate the problem, for Northerners had little knowledge of the race and no experience in handling racial problems. They could not be trusted to restrict voting to whites only, to maintain segregated schools, and otherwise to keep the Negro in his place. Once outside the South he might be able to influence national politics, in which case the Southerner's problems would be intensified rather than ameliorated.

In addition to these practical considerations, racists had other reasons for opposing the migration of Negroes, reasons implicit in anti-Negro ideology. The race had evolved in the hot, humid climate of tropical Africa and was ill-adapted to the long, cold winters of the North. It was also unsuited, and for the same reason, to the complexities of urban, industrial civilization. To get along in Anglo-Saxon society, the Negro needed the firm, gentle paternalism of Southern whites, who understood his psychology, knew his weaknesses, appreciated his childish and disarming nature, and accepted his foibles and frailties without vexation. Outside the South he would be shamelessly exploited. Ostensibly he might be given equality, but in reality he would always be a pawn of the demagogue. In the South, however, his place was well defined and his status secure.

Implicit in this reasoning was the conviction, accepted by most Southerners, that Negroes had no desire to "go North." In other words the white man was a victim of his own ideas: having declared that Negroes should be happier in the South, he assumed that they were. "The negro remains in the South," wrote the reformer Edgar Gardner Murphy of Alabama, "because among the primary and secondary rewards of honest life, he gets more of the primary rewards at the South than at the North." He knows "that in the essential struggle for existence the spirit of the South has been the spirit of kindliness and helpfulness." [7]

So widespread was this view, especially among Southern politicians and newspaper editors, that it bears further illustration. "The very best friend the darky has ever had in this world or ever will have is the southern gentleman," said the race-baiting, Mississippi Senator John Sharp Williams, and with Williams most racists agreed. Southern whites, they believed, took care of the Negro, treated him kindly, and had a real regard for him so long as he remained in his proper place. As a result, Southern Negroes were treated with every consideration. They had equal protection of the laws, equal schools and churches, and in appreciation for this they loved the South and considered it their real home. Race relations there were friendly and harmonious, for the races understood each other, trusted each other, confided in each other, and loved each other. And nowhere else did such conditions exist.[8] Not all racists were this unrealistic, however. "The Southern white man loves the 'nigger' in much the same fashion as he does his dog or his horse," wrote William P. Pickett, reflecting the opinions of a sizeable minority of extremists. "He slaps him on the back, laughs with him, and would like to see him thrive, but he reserves the privilege of occasionally kicking him if he is 'impudent,' or shooting him if guilty of serious infraction of the law." [9]

Racists emphasized both sides of this issue. Not only were Southerners able to handle race problems and manage them effectively, but Northerners were unable to do so because of prejudice and ignorance. Northerners were interested in Negroes only in the ab-

---

7 Murphy, *The Problems of the Present South*, 184.
8 *Congressional Record*, 58th Congress, 2nd Session (April 12, 1904), 4716; *ibid.*, 66th Congress, 2nd Session (May 31, 1920), 8030; and Jacksonville (Fla.) *Times-Union*, November 11, 1930.
9 William P. Pickett, *The Negro Problem* (New York, 1909), 173.

stract, only in the mass. Their idea of the race had been gained through literature and propaganda of various kinds and was unrealistic. They believed, mistakenly, that whites and Negroes differed only in skin color and hair texture, and they were too ready to judge Negroes by their own Caucasian standards. Expecting too much from the race, they were disillusioned and disenchanted by actual contact with it. Invariably they found individual Negroes offensive and repulsive, and their reaction created a harsh, rigid, and permanent antipathy. Lacking the generations of association which produced mutual understanding and harmony in the South, they were unable to comprehend the Negro's psychology or to appreciate his personality. As a consequence race relations in the North were violent and unsettling.[10]

The Negro whom Southerners loved and understood was the "good" Negro, the "right-thinking" Negro, the Negro who recognized his place and accepted it without complaint. This, of course, was the kind of Negro which Southern paternalists wanted to develop, and they were generally convinced of their success. Except for an occasional troublemaker, Southern Negroes accepted their place voluntarily or with a modicum of coercion, and, since this was the criterion by which they were judged, they were considered by racists to be vastly superior to Negroes of the North. Whereas the latter were "arrogant, haughty, disrespectful, and insulting to the white man and his folks," the former were polite, respectful, and courteous. They were also better workers, better citizens, and better satisfied with their lot. For them life was of today, and they seldom worried about tomorrow. No sorrow or adversity ever darkened the bright hopefulness which made them nothing more than carefree children.[11]

The Negro's place, then, was humble, static, and in the South. It was also on the farm. The Southern farm, insisted racists, was the only environment which safeguarded the Negro from his own weak and credulous nature. There, he was "strengthened, encouraged and supported by close daily contact with a superior race," and there he received "the rich fruit of the Southern white man's friendship and sympathy."[12] Agricultural training, moreover, coincided with racist

10   Memphis (Tenn.) *Commercial Appeal,* March 13, 1921.
11   *Congressional Record,* 67th Congress, 2nd Session (January 18, 1922), 1368; and Robertson, *The Changing South,* 221.
12   F. M. Simmons, "The Political Future of the Southern Negro," *Independent,* LX (June 28, 1906), 1525.

ideas of the Negro's intelligence and his proper place in American society. Deficiencies of intelligence indicate that the largest element of the race will always "find its place in the field or in the lower stages of craft," declared Professor N. S. Shaler of Harvard, and others agreed with him. Eugenicists Paul Popenoe and Rowsell H. Johnson, for example, thought it likely, "as mental tests show," that agriculture offered "the best field" for Negroes.[13]

Because of his mental deficiencies, the Negro could handle only simple, uncomplicated tasks. According to Hubert Howe Bancroft, whose infrequent references to the Negro indicate an utter contempt for the race, Negro laborers are "of economic value only in certain localities and under certain conditions. The labor must be agricultural and upon a large scale" and performed in gangs under the eye of an overseer. "In plantation life alone," Bancroft concluded, could the Negro find happiness. Other writers echoed Bancroft's sentiments. "Strong muscles, hardy frames, and preference for labor in the sun," they thought, especially qualified the Negro for agricultural employment in hot climates, for "at steady, hard labor, such as chopping, splitting rails, [and] ditching," he was fully the white man's equal, if not his superior.[14]

Here as elsewhere racists explored both sides of the subject. To the extent that agricultural life was good for the Negro, city life was bad. According to this idea, which was an expression of the agrarian background and rural psychology of racists, cities brought the Negro into contact with the worst elements of both races, thus increasing his natural depravity and undermining efforts to improve him. After a few years off the farm, city Negroes lost the industriousness and diligence of the "country darky." They became shiftless and reckless, and recklessness tended naturally toward restlessness, which in turn encouraged dissatisfaction with existing conditions.[15]

---

13 N. S. Shaler, "The Negro Since the Civil War," *Popular Science Monthly,* LVII (May, 1900), 36; Shaler, "The Future of the Negro in the South," *Popular Science Monthly,* LVII (June, 1900), 149; Shaler, *The Neighbor,* 167; and Popenoe and Johnson, *Applied Eugenics,* 294.
14 Bancroft, *Retrospection, Political and Personal,* 374; Price, *The Negro Past, Present, and Future,* 132; and Randle, *Characteristics of the Southern Negro,* 38–39.
15 Phillips, "The Plantation as a Civilizing Influence," 265; Alfred Holt Stone, *Studies in the American Race Problem* (New York, 1908), 238; Odum, *Social and Mental Traits of the Negro,* 188; and E. C. Branson, "The Negro Working Out His Own Salvation," in James E. McCulloch (ed.), *The South Mobilizing for Social Service* . . . (Nashville, 1913), 389.

In other words the urban Negro was less dependent on the white man than his isolated country cousin. He was not so easily intimidated and the trouble he caused was better organized, less sporadic, and more difficult for Southerners to comprehend. The "country darky" had always been overawed by threats or occasional acts of violence, but such was not always the case with articulate and independent members of the urban Negro middle class which had emerged by the 1920's. This class was clearly a threat to the *status quo,* and racists sought desperately to block its growth.

In the view of racists a primary objection to social integration was the personal repulsiveness of members of the Negro race. They considered the Negro's personality and character traits depraved, immoral, and repugnant to the sensibility and sensitivity of civilized white men. Especially popular among extremists, this idea was a basic element in anti-Negro thought, and no discussion of racial problems was complete without it.

The Negro's strongest emotion and controlling impulse, declared racists, was an unduly exaggerated "sexual passion." Touching as it did the heart of social relations, this was not a subject for racists to ignore, and they explored in detail its sources and implications. Their explanations for it were diverse. John Moffatt Mecklin thought it probably was the result of the race's long struggle with an unhealthful environment and a high death rate—factors which favored an exaggerated development of the procreative impulse. The physician R. W. Shufeldt, an extremist, had another explanation. He insisted that the Negro's sex impulse was independent of any procreative instinct, for he had never known a Negro to have "congress with the opposite sex, having in mind the making of a child." Quite the contrary, "negroes copulate solely for the gratification of the passion—for the erotic pleasure it affords them." [16]

To buttress his views on this subject, Shufeldt included in one of his works a lengthy report by another physician, William Lee Howard, which purported to explain the Negro's sexuality in scientific terms. Its ultimate source, said Howard, was the Negro's phylogeny, his racial as opposed to his individual history. This alone explained his overabundance of "libidinous substances" and secre-

---

16　Mecklin, *Democracy and Race Friction,* 28; and R. W. Shufeldt, *The Negro, A Menace to American Civilization* (Boston, 1907), 124.

tions of the testicles, substances and secretions which entered the bloodstreams, stimulated the entire genesic system, and aroused the sex organs and the sex centers of the brain. As a result "genesic instincts" were controlling factors in the Negro's life, robbing his mind and conscience of food to administer to the strong demands of his genital organs. Even in small Negro girls lust was present "to an extent scarcely possible of belief." Howard had "never seen a negro virgin over ten years of age" and had never heard of one from his colleagues in the medical profession.[17]

The significance of this "sexual fury" was its social implications. Here was the source of the Negro's "latitudinarian ethics," his amazing lack of personal moral responsibility, and his terrible moral corruption. W. D. Weatherford, a Southern reformer and champion of interracial understanding, estimated that more than 98 percent of all Negro men were "socially impure" and that at least 95 percent had gonorrhea. Weatherford, who was by no means an extremist, thought it a fair conclusion that sexual immorality among Negroes was so debilitating that a large percentage of their children were born dead or entered the world so starved and diseased that half of them died before their first birthday. Under such conditions family life was impossible, and the race was deprived of the moral and social influences of a stable home environment. The Negro male thought no more of discarding his wife and taking another than of casting aside one suit of clothes for another, and the female was little better. She had "but dim notions of the nature or obligations of wifehood," declared the mulatto William Hannibal Thomas, for her aim in life was "to be free from parental control, to secure idle maintenance, and to indulge in unbridled sexual freedom." Fully 90 percent of them, he estimated, "are lascivious by instinct and in bondage to physical nature." In Negro homes modesty, even chastity, was impossible, and what passed for family life was hardly more than unbridled and unabashed sexual promiscuity.[18]

Not only was the Negro oversexed but his entire being was dominated by animal impulses instinctive in nature. In him, declared Hubert Howe Bancroft, the animal overbalanced the mental, and

---

17   Shufeldt, *America's Greatest Problem: The Negro*, 102–103.
18   Mecklin, *Democracy and Race Friction*, 68; W. D. Weatherford, *Negro Life in the South* (New York, 1918), 23–24, 78–79; Price, *The Negro Past, Present, and Future*, 58; and Thomas, *The American Negro*, 184, 195, 177 ff.

the individual became, in Howard Odum's phrase, "a mass of physiological reactions and reflexes." He was "volatile, without continuous, or stable form, easily disturbed, as easily quieted." He was "a strong physical organism with powerful sensuous capacity" but only feeble inhibiting power. He was a creature of the moment, for whatever feeling, desire, or passion seized him he expressed in immediate action. As a result he was sexually incontinent and had a congenital tendency to quarrelsomeness, crime, and violence.[19] He was, in short, unfit for social equality with the white man.

The weaknesses of the Negro's character were not only physical in nature, but were due in part to mental and psychical factors and reflected the race's lack of intelligence. Racists appreciated the benefits of the Negro's low intelligence—it helped him accept conditions which "a more highly organized and sensitive race would have thrown off"—but they also considered it the chief source of his racial weakness. Here was a source of his incompetence as a worker: his inability to master complex skills and follow intricate instructions, his awkwardness and sluggishness, his need for close supervision. Here was a source of his improvidence of character, his tendency to immoral conduct, his enslavement to uncontrolled impulse. Here also was an explanation for the "inveterate tendency in the Negro mind to seek safety in dependence on a superior being, [and] to shift the responsibility for coping with difficulty and danger to some power or authority outside himself." To put it bluntly, the Negro was both weak-minded and weak-willed, and he had the characteristics which inhere in such weaknesses. He was imitative, unimaginative, unreasoning, unperceptive, lacking in will power and mental discipline, and inconsequential and incoherent in his thinking. Incapable of sustained mental effort, he was aroused only by excitement, curiosity, or morbidity.[20]

These descriptions were the logical conclusions of two fundamental assumptions—that the Negro preferred an environment of immo-

---

19 Bancroft, *Retrospection, Political and Personal*, 369; Odum, *Social and Mental Traits of the Negro*, 188, 206, 239; Dowd, *The Negro in American Life*, 406; and Hart, *The Southern South*, 93–94.

20 Stone, *Studies in the American Race Problem*, 235; Walter L. Hawley, "Passing of the Race Problem," *Arena*, XXIV (November, 1900), 473; Ferguson, *The Psychology of the Negro*, 124; H. N. Hall, "Are the Various Races of Man Potentially Equal?" *Proceedings of the American Philosophical Society*, LXIII (1924), 210; and Odum, *Social and Mental Traits of the Negro*, 272.

rality, ignorance, and poverty because it encouraged his natural depravity and that his unwillingness to improve himself was causing the race to deteriorate. The latter assumption was an expression of several factors. By 1900 the mythology of the antebellum South was well developed, and by that date also a new generation of Negroes had matured. This generation was a product of the postwar era and had never "enjoyed" the discipline of slavery and the benefits of antebellum paternalism. To racists the antebellum period was the Negro's golden age, and the "darky" of that age was far superior to the Negro of the New South. They had the highest praise for "the old-time darky with his simplicity, love of the plantation, and devotion to the people of the 'big house,' " and they longed for the time "when the Negro race considered it honorable to love and protect the women and children of the white man," the time when the Negro wanted no higher privilege than being helpful and courteous to others. But now, alas, "the old time slave negro" was fast passing away, and in his place was a new Negro, who was generally "lazy, thriftless, intemperate, insolent, dishonest, and without the most rudimentary elements of morality." [21]

This contrast between the old darky and the New Negro convinced racists of the Negro's deterioration. The New Negro—who lived in town, worked for wages, received a rudimentary education, and achieved a degree of independence from white society—conformed not at all to their stereotypes. As the antebellum South grew dim in memory and fresh in mythology, the disparity between real Negroes and legendary darkies loomed larger and larger in their minds. Soon the two became completely confused, and the disparity between real and ideal was the measure of the Negro's deterioration. If one assumes the truth of racist preconceptions, moreover, the deterioration was inevitable. Without the white man's guidance, they insisted, the Negro was unable to keep pace in Anglo-Saxon civilization, and since emancipation he had been deprived of that guidance and the disciplined training which accompanied it. Thus, he was rapidly losing his ability to compete with the white man, and in his frustration was becoming lazy, boisterous, and "pushy." [22]

---

21 W. D. Weatherford, *Negro Life in the South* (New York, 1918), 11; *Congressional Record*, 67th Congress, 2nd Session (January 18, 1922), 1368; and Page, *The Negro: The Southerner's Problem*, 80.

22 For a description of the Negro with aspirations of social equality see *Congressional Record*, 67th Congress, 2nd Session (January 18, 1922), 1368.

Present patterns of racial segregation were developed or refined in the late nineteenth and early twentieth centuries. But not until after they were regularized and systematized did a body of ideas appear to rationalize them.[23] These movements—systematizing segregation on the one hand and rationalizing it on the other—were important developments in the flowering of American racism from the 1890's through the 1920's. At this time Southerners, and other Americans too, were especially receptive to racist doctrine and accepted without question the whole complex of anti-Negro ideas. As a result advocates of social equality, who were never even potentially a large number, were overwhelmed. To support political or economic equality was one thing, but to urge social equality—which racists insisted would inevitably lead to intermarriage—was something entirely different, and its advocates were few and unconvincing. Concerning social relations the Negro's friends were sensitive and defensive and frightened by the bugbear of intermarriage; they usually stopped short of endorsing social equality. Those who unequivocally accepted racial intermarriage were so few as to be insignificant.

So true was this that to note it is to repeat a commonplace. Writers who thought of themselves quite correctly as friends of the Negro went to great lengths to disassociate themselves from social integration. On this issue the race was deserted by such notable reformers as George Washington Cable, Edgar Gardner Murphy, and President Edwin A. Alderman of the University of Virginia. Cable, whose views won him the enduring enmity of Southerners and drove him to exile in the North, spoke of the Negro as an inferior race and social equality as "a fool's dream" of which he wanted "quite as little . . . as the most fervent traditionalist of the most fervent South." Social equality, he wrote in *The Silent South*, will "never exist where a community, numerous enough to assert itself, is actuated, as every civilized community is, by an intellectual and moral ambition," for no form of laws and no definition of rights can bring it about. Thus, the fear that this change or that reform will lead to social integration "ought never to be any but a fool's fear." [24]

---

23   See C. Vann Woodward, *The Strange Career of Jim Crow* (New York, 1957); Handlin, *Race and Nationality in American Life*, 46–47; and Tindall, "The Central Theme Revisited," in Sellers (ed.), *The Southerner as American*, 109 ff.

24   George W. Cable, *The Silent South* (New York, 1895), 54. See also Edwin A. Alderman, "The Growing South," *World's Work*, XVI (June, 1908), 10378; and Edgar Gardner Murphy, *The Basis of Ascendancy* (New York, 1909), 17.

National leaders in the early decades of the twentieth century held similar views. President Warren G. Harding made a notable appeal for expanded opportunities for Negroes, but at the same time he denounced social integration in emphatic terms. "Men of both races may well stand uncompromisingly against every suggestion of social equality," he declared in 1921. Indeed, "it might be helpful to have the word 'equality' eliminated from [any consideration of race problems]; to have it accepted on both sides that this is not a question of social equality, but a question of recognizing a fundamental, eternal, and inescapable difference." On this point the race issue, like politics, made strange bedfellows, for William Jennings Bryan, now in his most reactionary period, seconded the views of Harding. Anyone who will look at the subject without prejudice, said Bryan in 1923, will know that the political and social supremacy of the white man promotes the highest welfare of both races.[25] Of course Harding and Bryan were not conscious racists as were most Southern politicians, and their statements here might be taken as simply reflecting the actuality of the Negro's social inequality. Even if this is the case, the result for Negroes is the same—their status is still that of second-class citizens.

Since virtually all white men rejected social equality and racial intermarriage, racists presumed that Negroes did likewise. They were especially convinced that this was true of decent, sensible Negroes. These Negroes, they insisted, were willing to live in their appointed place and had no more desire for social equality than the white man, who had none at all. But there was a small "outlaw, stupid" element among the race which had been indoctrinated with dangerous propaganda and was unwilling "to dwell in peace, and kindly understanding with [its] white friends." This element was always a problem for white supremacists, but it was so small that they were able to dismiss its members as an unstable and radical fringe.[26]

The assertion that Negroes repudiated social equality was not so transparently false as it might first appear. On the contrary, there was significant evidence which gave it credibility. Most important

---

25 "President Harding Discourses on the Color Line," *Current Opinion,* LXXI (December, 1921), 707; and *American Forum* (San Antonio, Texas), March 31, 1923.
26 *Congressional Record,* 67th Congress, 2nd Session (January 18, 1922), 1378; *ibid.,* 70th Congress, 1st Session (January 25, 1928), 1909; Milledgeville (Ga.) *Times,* July 4, 1930; and Montgomery (Ala.) *Advertiser,* April 18, 1935, p. 4.

was the Negro's acquiescence, at least outwardly, in segregation, a passive acquiescence which racists mistook for active endorsement. More specifically, they took Booker T. Washington's Atlanta Exposition address of 1895 to mean that "intelligent" Negroes supported social segregation. They assumed, rightly or wrongly, that Washington not only accepted, but also advocated, the principles of social segregation. "In all things that are purely social," he said, "we [Negroes and whites] can be as separate as the fingers, yet one as the hand in all things essential to mutual progress." He added later, "The wisest among my race understand that the agitation of questions of social equality is the extremist folly, and that progress in the enjoyment of all the privileges that will come to us must be the result of severe and constant struggle rather than of artificial forcing." [27] There was much in such statements which racists found praiseworthy,[28] and there is considerable evidence that Washington became the leading spokesman of American Negroes because influential whites considered his social views "safe." Yet even Washington was under suspicion after his famous dinner with President Theodore Roosevelt in 1901.

Because social equality was the heart of the "Negro problem," racists were especially sensitive about it. They would have preferred to dismiss the whole subject as a snare and delusion which agitators and "white niggers" (mulattoes) kept alive for selfish and unworthy reasons, but circumstances prevented their doing so. Their reactions to breaches in social segregation were monotonously predictable. The uproar, or outrage, which followed Theodore Roosevelt's dinner with Booker T. Washington and Mrs. Hebert Hoover's tea with the wife of Negro Congressman Oscar DePriest was only a spectacular example of many such reactions.[29] To racists such incidents gave false hopes and to ignorant Negroes criminal notions and thus intensified social antipathies. The only guarantee of interracial peace was absolute white supremacy, and, in spite of isolated examples of

---

27 Quoted in Booker T. Washington, *Up From Slavery* (New York, 1901), 221, 223.

28 For representative examples of this praise see Thomas Nelson Page, "The Negro: The Southerner's Problem," *McClure's Magazine*, XXII (March, 1904), 549; Morris, *The Old South and New*, 380; and *Congressional Record*, 66th Congress, 1st Session (August 12, 1919), 4303.

29 For representative reactions see *The Crisis*, XXXVI (September, 1929), 298–99; and *Congressional Record*, 58th Congress, 2nd Session (March 16, 1904), 3341–42.

social equality or occasional outbursts of violence, racists were confident that white supremacy would endure. In the final analysis, they felt, all whites would stand together against Negroes, for no white man *really* believed in social integration or amalgamation. "If a man really believes in equality, let him prove it by giving his daughter to a negro in marriage," wrote Thomas Dixon. "That is the test. When she sinks with her mulatto children into the black abyss of a negro life, then ask him." [30]

To racists the terms *Negro problem* and *social equality* were synonymous, and efforts to treat them separately were dangerous and unrealistic. Social equality, they insisted, was but a prelude to racial intermarriage, and from intermarriage came the greatest of all evils, racial amalgamation. As a result of such convictions, they centered their attention upon social aspects of racial problems, but even here they were often confusing, contradictory, or uncertain. They were certain that racial equality and intermarriage were undesirable, and they agreed that social segregation and white supremacy must be preserved. But these were broad and nebulous terms with different implications for different individuals. Much of the confusion sprang from the fact that racist ideas were developed on different levels by different groups—by those who sought a systematic ideology, by those who dealt only with individual incidents, and by extremists, moderates, and reformers. The groups, of course, agreed upon a wide area of fundamentals, yet each was often refuted or contradicted by the others. A second source of confusion was that, in spite of repeated boasts to the contrary, racists did not in a fundamental sense understand the Negro. More often than not their contacts with the race were on a master-servant or paternal basis, and the Negroes they knew best were from the underprivileged elements of the race. They rarely knew independent, educated, middle-class Negroes, and this fact profoundly affected their thinking. A third source of confusion was their tendency to generalize from the actions of individual Negroes. Although they explicitly believed that "good" Negroes, the vast majority of the race, favored social segregation, they sometimes forgot that belief. Thus, if one Negro raped (or married) a white woman, they were prone to conclude that all Negroes were so inclined. Yet if one endorsed segregation, it was likely that they considered him a spokesman for

---

30 Dixon, *The Leopard's Spots*, 363–64.

the race. But to add to the confusion, if one spoke in favor of equality, he was generally dismissed as an individual trouble-maker.

Anti-Negro spokesmen showed little anxiety about the contradictions or perplexities which sprang from these sources. To them it was sufficient to say that both races objected to social equality because both found amalgamation repulsive. The interracial marriages which occasionally took place, usually between Negro men and white women, were due to mental derangement and temporary insanity, for "no self-respecting white woman, in the full possession of her senses, North or South, would ever be so lost to shame and love of race pride as to unite herself in marriage with a negro, to become the mother of a hybrid mulatto race." No, they insisted, no sane white man in the South, and few, if any, sane Negroes condoned intermarriage.[31]

If this were true, it might be asked, how could any real danger to racial purity exist? If Negroes preferred segregation, if they had no desire to intermarry with whites, if thoughts of "mixing" never entered their minds unless planted by agitators, were social equality and promiscuous mingling really imminent? Although the premises of the question were correct, replied racists, the answer was "yes." Most Negroes, they explained, were naturally docile and readily accepted their place in society. But they also possessed a spark of animalism which was easily ignited by promises of equality. They were, in short, too easily aroused, and to relax social controls over them was to invite disaster. Years of bondage and subordination had made them contemptuous of their race, and they were strangers to the instinct of race purity. Their fondest desires were to marry white women and to reappear in a blended race with their kinks straightened, their odor dispelled, and their color bleached.[32]

Thus, racists had things both ways. The Negro had no desire for social equality—but demagogues and agitators might create such a desire by exciting his baser animal instincts. In those instincts, they felt, was the potential for destroying racial purity, and to restrain them was the chief object of Southern race policy. The instincts were psychological as well as physical and outsiders who knew nothing of

---

31   Simmons, *A Solution of the Race Problem in the South,* 30; and Weather-ford, *Negro Life in the South,* 7.

32   Dowd, *The Negro in American Life,* 453; and John J. Vertrees, *The Negro Problem* (Nashville, 1905), 19.

the Negro were unable to understand them. There was no danger in the Negro revolting, for the race was weak, disorganized, and easily intimidated. The danger lay in Negroes questioning their place and in whites agreeing that the questioning was legitimate and justified. Racists, therefore, pleaded for a united front against the race. Division would be the beginning of the end. One concession would lead inevitably to another, and full equality would eventually produce complete amalgamation. The problem, as Ernest Sevier Cox indicated, "is not black warriors, but colored brothers-in-law." [33]

To racists the consequences of racial amalgamation were horrible to contemplate, yet few of them were especially troubled that a vast amount of miscegenation had already taken place in the South. To be sure, they denounced such miscegenation, but their greatest strictures were reserved for wholesale racial intermarriage, which they alleged to be imminent. In effect, then, they attacked the imaginary danger and ignored the actual one. The truth was that they saw little danger in amalgamation as long as intermarriage was avoided and mulattoes were relegated to the "inferior" race, but equality even of a superficial sort tended to elevate mulattoes more rapidly than pure Negroes. In addition to the social objections to racial mixture, there were also important physical objections, the chief of which was the conviction that amalgamation inexorably reduced the superior race to the level of the inferior. Intermixture of similar stocks, e.g., closely related "races" of Caucasians, was sometimes beneficial, for the qualities of one tended to complement those of the other, but the mixture of dissimilar races was universally harmful, for, like water, inherited racial qualities seek the lowest possible level. Thus, the mixture of a highly specialized race and a coarsely generalized one, of Caucasians and Negroes in other words, would produce an offspring approximating the latter. The offspring, however, might inherit disharmonic combinations of physical characteristics. A large frame, for example, might be combined with small kidneys or a small heart, and large teeth might be crowded in a small jaw. Such disharmonies of course meant physical frailty, and when combined with a similar mental frailty they made the mulatto a decidedly inferior creature.[34]

In this fashion racists justified their opposition to "this rotten,

33 Cox, *White America,* 259.
34 Glenn Frank, "The Clash of Color," 98; and H. S. Jennings, *The Biological Basis of Human Nature* (New York, 1930), 287, 281.

indecent doctrine of marriage between the white and African races."
Social necessity, they believed, far outweighed the individual's right
to choose his own spouse, for marriage was a social institution and
must be governed by social conventions. It was, in John Moffatt
Mecklin's words, "society's legitimatised method for the perpetua-
tion of the race in the larger and inclusive sense of a continuous
racial type which shall be the bearer of a continuous and progressive
civilisation." Thus, when two races of such widely divergent physical and psychic characteristics that their blending would destroy the
purity of both dwelt together, society had the right, indeed the duty,
to forbid their intermarriage. The Southern states therefore were
fully justified in prohibiting white-Negro marriages, for such unions
would contaminate the purity of its stock and jeopardize the integrity of its social heritage.[35]

The mulatto, the person of mixed white and Negro ancestry, was
an object of racist scorn. (Narrowly defined, a mulatto had one
parent who was a pure white and the other a pure Negro; however,
the term was popularly used to include all persons of mixed ancestry
and is so used here.) In the opinion of racists the mulatto was
inferior for several important reasons. Not only was he the progeny
of basically different racial stocks, but he descended from the most
depraved elements of those stocks as well, from coarse, impure,
degenerate white men and grossly immoral and lascivious Negro
women. Inferior and debilitated themselves, such parents could
beget only inferior and debilitated offspring. Environment, too,
contributed to the mulatto's inferiority. "All skilled in the science of
procreation," wrote a Southerner around the turn of the century,
"tell us that the best specimens of manhood are produced in wed-
lock, where there is mutual affection and mutual respect, as well as
ease of mind and peace of conscience on the part of the mother
during the period of gestation." But such conditions rarely accompanied the birth of a mulatto child, especially when his father was
white and his mother Negro. In such cases there was "a certain
disgust on the part of the white parent, a knowledge of inequality on
the part of the colored parent, the illegal act, [and] the sin and
remorse of unlawful cohabitation, weighing upon the minds of the
parents." These factors, of course, adversely affected the child in the
womb, who was from birth an unnatural production. And he grew to

---

35 Mecklin, *Democracy and Race Friction*, 147.

maturity in the environment in which he was conceived and delivered—in poverty, vice, and depravity and without the restraints of family life and Christian morality. The result was a "fungus growth," "a miserable mess of motley mongrels," belonging to neither race but possessing the vices and low character of the Negro rather than the vigor and virtue of the Caucasian.[36]

To substantiate these assertions, anti-Negro spokesmen described the mulatto in detailed and derogatory terms. Their object was to prove him physically inferior to whites and Negroes, even though some racists considered him intermediate between the two. He was usually described as a random mixture of white and Negro characteristics, but as a crossbreed of discordant stocks he was said to have the "weakness and infertility" common to hybrids. Professor N. S. Shaler, for example, was convinced that the average mulatto was much shorter lived and much less fertile than the race of either parent, although he lacked reliable statistical data to prove his assertion. Shaler did, however, have the testimony of his father, "an able physician, who had been for nearly all of a long life in contact with negroes , . . . that he had never seen a halfbreed who was more than sixty years old." [37]

Not everyone, however, was satisfied with hearsay evidence. To confirm the impression which Shaler had offered, other spokesmen gathered an exhaustive array of statistical evidence, generally in the form of anthropometrical statistics which they derived from meticulous measurements of the mulatto's physical features.[38] Lung capacity, chest mobility, head shape, cranial capacity, muscular development, nervous system—indeed his entire physical make-up—were measured and remeasured from every conceivable vantage point, and with predictable results. Invariably they "proved" the mulatto inferior; however, as techniques improved he was generally placed between Negroes and whites.

Despite their differences over the relative physical ability of

---

36 *American Forum* (San Antonio, Texas), June 20, 1923; Alfred H. Stone, "The Mulatto Factor in the Race Problem," *Atlantic Monthly*, XCI (May, 1903), 576, and McCurley, "The Impossibility of Racial Amalgamation," 454.

37 N. S. Shaler, "Our Negro Types," *Current Literature*, XXIX (July, 1900), 45.

38 See C. B. Davenport and Morris Steggarda, *Race Crossing in Jamaica* (Washington, 1929); and Hoffman, "Race Traits and Tendencies of the American Negro," 164 ff., 184 ff.

Negroes and mulattoes, racists agreed that the latter was more intelligent than the former. Professor Samuel J. Holmes of the University of California summarized their opinion when he suggested in 1923 that mulattoes were probably superior to Negroes in mental capacity and definitely superior in intellectual achievement. This, of course, would be the logical result of the intermediate cranial capacity which resulted from the infusion of white blood. The mulatto tended to approximate the Caucasian in cerebral structure and exhibited more of the Caucasian temperament than did Negroes. He had more nervous energy, was more alert and deft in movement, more energetic, more ready to perceive and to take advantage of opportunities, and more adaptable to Caucasian civilization.[39] He was also the recognized leader of Negroes in America, a "fact" which racists repeatedly emphasized. Every distinguished leader of American Negroes had been part white, declared William Joseph Simmons of the Ku Klux Klan, expressing the view of most racists. "In fact a majority of the most distinguished have contained only a small infusion of Negro blood." Negroes of accomplishment, added another extremist, were in reality white men with an infusion of African blood. Their capability was due to white blood, their weakness and instability to the diluting and neutralizing effects of black blood.[40] The race could take no credit for the achievement of many of its foremost leaders.

But whatever his accomplishments, the mulatto was a product of discordant and dissimilar heritages. He had two souls, two temperaments, two sets of opinions, and was unable to think or act strongly and consistently in any direction. Mentally and spiritually he was attuned to the traditions of neither race, and his soul was the scene of perpetual conflict of inharmonious tendencies. To such a person life could be nothing but tragedy. Restless and dissatisfied, he forever protested his station in life, but his protest, said racists, was not that of a Negro, for no Negro ever protested his place or race. Rather, the mulatto's protest was the desperate rebellion of "a forceful Aryan in soul-entanglement with an utterly strange being," a Caucasian spirit imprisoned in the forbidding circle of mongrel blood, inimical inheritance, and pernicious environment. And as if to

---

39   S. J. Holmes, *Studies in Evolution and Eugenics* (London, 1923), 221, 223; Tillinghast, "The Negro in Africa and America," 121; and Ferguson, "The Mental Status of the American Negro," 540.

40   Simmons, *The Klan Unmasked*, 157; and Pickett, *The Negro Problem*, 287.

intensify his sense of tragedy and protest, the mulatto was often educated and given a glimpse of the possibilities of life in the white man's world.[41] Drawn thus between conflicting inheritances and wistfully longing for the white man's society, he was brutally relegated to the status of a Negro. No wonder he was dissatisfied! Sensitive and self-conscious to an extraordinary degree and possessing a tragic sense of loneliness and isolation, he was perpetually discontented. He was a man without a race, and the realization of this created the morbid psychosis and despairing bitterness which explained his fanatical determination to smash the color line.[42]

Perhaps this idea, that mulattoes were the principal agitators for racial equality, was the cause of their calculated disparagement. "The negro problem in this country," said racists, "is essentially the problem of the mulatto, especially the near-white mulatto." It was he who embittered race relations, and his longing for amalgamation with the white race was the explosive element in the race problem. If he were given equality with the white man, the race problem would be largely settled, for he had no interest in Negroes as a race. He was, in fact, more prejudiced against pure Negroes than were whites. The latter had a strong paternalistic interest in the Negro and conscientiously sought his improvement. Mulattoes, however, merely used him, exploiting his grievances as a means of achieving their own equality with the white man. Racists, of course, were ostensibly alarmed by anyone who exploited the Negro, and they took it upon themselves to expose the mulatto's designs. In doing so, however, they also sought to destroy his self-confidence and self-respect and undermine his usefulness as a leader of the Negro race.

In the final analysis, the race problem stemmed from the Negro's desire for "sexual equality," a desire expressed in his innate fondness for white women and his disposition to commit the crime of rape. Or such at least was the opinion of racists, and to many of them this was the fundamental fact of anti-Negro thought. No discussion, diatribe, or treatise was complete without noting it, and every idea, action, and policy was examined in light of it. In bluntest form it said simply

---

41 Stoddard, *The Rising Tide of Color*, 258–59; McDougall, *The Group Mind*, 133; Baker, "The Tragedy of the Mulatto," 582–98.
42 Stoddard, *Re-Forging America*, 303; and Robert E. Park, "Mentality of Racial Hybrids," *American Journal of Sociology*, XXXVI (January, 1931), 545.

that the object of racial policy was to protect pure and undefiled white maidenhood from the nameless and unspeakable crimes of brutal black assaulters.[43]

This preoccupation with sex and womanhood was deep-seated and complex, and to explain it adequately is a major task in itself. It was the stock in trade of such popular racists as Southern politicians and newspaper editors, but to assign it completely or even primarily to these groups is misleading. It was a concern of all racists at all levels of education and sophistication—of patricians such as Thomas Nelson Page, of historians such as Philip Alexander Bruce and Claude Bowers, of female writers such as Myrta Lockett Avary, of politicians such as Representative James P. Buchanan of Texas, of extremists such as E. H. Randle.[44] Bruce, for example, thought there was "something strangely alluring and seductive to the negro in the appearance of a white woman," something which "aroused and stimulated" him by its "foreignness" to his "experience of sexual pleasures" and moved him to gratify his "lust at any cost and in spite of any obstacle." Page likewise felt that Negro men did "not generally believe in" female virtue, and he suggested that they were dominated by an uncontrollable passion for white women.[45] Less careful writers were proportionately more outspoken.

Anti-Negro writers, in short, were universally concerned with the sexual aspects of racial problems. On few other subjects, all relating to sex and social equality, was there such general agreement, and for such a condition no glib explanation will suffice. Perhaps a psychological or psychoanalytical approach, as offered by Oscar Handlin and Wilbur J. Cash,[46] is most fruitful. In any event the racists' preoccupation with sex and womanhood was a part of the South's engrossment in the same subjects. It began long before 1900, continued uninterrupted after 1930, and manifested itself in a variety of ways—in the social, political, and economic degradation of Negroes, in the despoliation of Negro women, in the idealization of white

43   *Congressional Record,* 67th Congress, 2nd Session (January 25, 1922), 1703; Thomas, *The American Negro,* 65.
44   For representative expressions see Page, *The Negro: The Southerner's Problem,* 112; Bowers, *The Tragic Era,* 308; Myrta Lockett Avary, *Dixie After the War* (New York, 1906), 377; *Congressional Record,* 67th Congress, 2nd Session (December 17, 1921), 468.
45   Hoffman, "Race Traits and Tendencies of the American Negro," 231 (for quotation by Bruce).
46   Handlin, *Race and Nationality in American Life,* 111–28; and Cash, *The Mind of the South* (New York, 1954), 124–27, and *passim.*

women, in the matriarchal aspects of Southern society, and in an exalted but artificial sense of chivalry. An explanation of such a phenomenon based solely on the anti-Negro literature of a thirty-year period can be at best only tentative.

Whatever its explanation, its relevance to anti-Negro racism between 1900 and 1930 was real and vivid and was nowhere more evident than in discussions of rape. This crime, said racists, was caused by agitators who stimulated the Negro's innate but usually dormant desire for white women. It had been unknown to the antebellum South, but in the abnormal atmosphere of Radical Reconstruction Negroes got a glimpse of social equality, coeducation, and intermarriage; and, as a consequence, their animalism was aroused. At that time, also, the discipline of slavery was removed and the freedman confused freedom with license. For the first time he cast lustful, lascivious eyes on white women, and the seeds for later race problems were sown. The harvest, said racists, had been abundant and grim.

Rape, "the foul daughter of Reconstruction" to use Claude Bowers' phrase, at once became a common crime in the South. Southern women soon found themselves, in the words of Ben Tillman, "in a state of siege," in constant danger from Negro rapists. They dared not travel alone upon the highway out of sight of white men or remain alone at home except on necessity. When they did so, they gathered their helpless little children inside the solitary farmhouse and shuddered with nameless horror at any knock upon the door. Always the fear existed that lurking in the dark was a black brute, a "sooty desecrator," a monstrous beast crazed with lust. Thus, rape became sometimes a daily occurrence in the Southern states. "In countless communities," declared Congressman John N. Tillman of Arkansas in 1924, "no mother is safe for an hour unless guarded by watchful husband or son." [47]

To meet this threat to the South's greatest treasure, "her priceless jewel of beautiful, splendid, and spotless womanhood," racists condoned extreme measures, including violence and lynching. But in justifying violence they invariably pictured it as the white man's response to the Negro's outrages. They thought it fairly proven that

---

47 Bowers, *The Tragic Era*, 308; Page, *The Negro: The Southerner's Problem*, 84; George T. Winston, "The Relation of the Whites to the Negroes," *The Annals*, XVIII (July, 1901), 108–109; and *Congressional Record*, 68th Congress, 1st Session (June 7, 1924), 11304.

lynchings in the South were not the result of race antipathy, but were due instead "to crimes which meet the summary justice in cases of whites and blacks alike." As Congressman James F. Byrnes pointed out, rape was "directly and indirectly [responsible] for most lynchings in America." Byrnes, of course, ignored conclusive evidence that only a small percentage of lynchings was actually caused by rape or suspicion of rape. According to a study made in 1942, only 17 percent of Negroes lynched between 1889 and 1941 were even accused of rape.[48] Yet, as Byrnes's statement indicates, this belief was accepted as a truism by racists, and it illustrated their disposition to take an idea which was partially true—some lynchings *were* caused by rape—and convince themselves by constant repetition that it was generally valid.

In spite of this conviction, however, lynchings were usually justified on grounds of expediency: a drastic situation demanded drastic remedies. In 1902, for example, a coroner's jury in Wayne County, North Carolina, found that one Tom Jones, a Negro lynched for allegedly raping a white woman, had come "to his death by gunshot wounds, inflicted by parties unknown to jury, obviously by an outraged public acting in defense of their homes, wives, daughters, and children." Because of the enormity of Jones's crime, said the jury, the outraged public "would have been recreant to their duty as good citizens had they acted otherwise." Other spokesmen specifically delimited this newly recognized right to lynch. Congressman Thomas Spight of Mississippi did "not think that lynchings for any other crime than the nameless one against womanhood ought ever to occur." And the Confederate Veterans of Grenada, Mississippi, resolved in 1904 that they were "unalterably opposed to the lynching of a human being, save, perhaps, for the one unmentionable crime." [49] Such statements ignore the fact that mob violence is a volatile matter which is rarely concerned with evidence and proof or which, when unleashed, has little regard for distinctions between rapists and other offenders. But they were the logical conclusions of other racist assumptions, and in their own curious way they combined the Southerner's paternalism with his determination to preserve white supremacy.

---

48 *Congressional Record*, 67th Congress, 2nd Session (December 19, 1921), 544. On lynching see the brief discussion in Gossett, *Race*, 269–72.

49 James Elbert Cutler, *Lynch-Law* (London, 1905), 381; *Congressional Record*, 58th Congress, 2nd Session (March 16, 1904), 3340; and *ibid.* (March 28, 1904), 3827.

Other, more specific justifications for lynchings were also offered. The white man's law, said many racists, was unsuited to Negroes, who were adapted by racial experience to the ways of the jungle. Due process, trial by jury, even imprisonment, were meaningless to them, for they saw no connection between crime and punishment unless the one was immediately followed by the other. Courts and trials offered no real deterrent to Negro crime, even when conviction was certain. And if the rapist were tried, the pure and helpless victim, already robbed by the Negro's hellish lust of "that which is prized above all else on earth," would be further humiliated by having to repeat on the witness stand the horrible incidents of the fiendish outrage.[50]

Whereas most racists justified lynching as an expediency, an extremist fringe approved it on the broader grounds of principle. According to Charles E. Woodruff, an Army surgeon, lynch law was merely an expression of democracy, for it was "the highest prerogative of the sovereign democracy to make and execute their own laws." Since Southern lynch mobs sometimes "constitute all the sovereigns" in a community, there could be no objection to them as undemocratic. Tom Watson, once the Negro's greatest champion among Southern politicians, expressed similar ideas in his later life. Lynch law, he felt, was a good sign, a sign that a sense of justice yet lived among the people.[51] To such extremists lynching or the threat of lynching was the *sine qua non* of keeping the Negro in his place. Therefore, it had its own justification. Morally and legally Southerners were justified, yes even obligated, to eliminate any Negro who was so senseless and depraved as to attack a white woman.

Because of their attitude toward lynching, racists agreed that mob violence was a problem to be handled by state and local governments. There must be no interference by federal authority or Yankee theory. Especially dangerous were efforts to enact federal antilynching legislation. Several times between 1900 and 1930, most notably in 1921 and 1922, Northern liberals made serious efforts to enact such legislation, and in each effort Southern Congressmen reached new heights in denouncing federal interference in local problems and in fulminating against those who supported such interference. Not only was federal legislation unnecessary, they declared, but it was unwise

---

50 Cutler, *Lynch-Law*, 224–25; and *Congressional Record*, 60th Congress, 1st Session (February 22, 1908), 2349.
51 Charles E. Woodruff, *Expansion of Races* (New York, 1909), 371; and C. Vann Woodward, *Tom Watson: Agrarian Rebel* (New York, 1938), 432.

in the highest degree. Ignorant and vicious Negroes would interpret it as a concession to social equality, and racial problems would be aggravated rather than diminished. Congressman John Rankin of Mississippi suggested that the Dyer antilynching proposal of 1921–22 be retitled "a bill to encourage rape," for such, he predicted, would be its chief result.[52] The solution to lynching, said Rankin, rested with those whose actions provoked the mob, with Negroes rather than with whites; and outsiders who really desired to be helpful should encourage the Negro to refrain from attacks upon white women. Not until the danger of such attacks was eliminated would lynchings come to an end.

The engrossment of the racist mind in social equality had many ramifications. Here as elsewhere there were all shades of opinion, but only the extremist explored the full implications of social segregation. Only he realized the truth—that Negroes *did* desire social equality and could not be bought off indefinitely with the platitudes of moderation. Social relations were, paradoxically, the subject of chief concern to racists and also the subject upon which they were most close-minded. Whites who were proud of their moderation and toleration on other issues endorsed strict segregation in all things social and blinded themselves to the difficulties of their position. Even the leading spokesman for the Negro race before 1915 advised his people to accept social segregation at least temporarily. Social segregation and racial purity were truths which friends as well as enemies of the Negro accepted.

By the 1920's, however, as W. E. B. Du Bois and the National Association for the Advancement of Colored People replaced Booker T. Washington as the chief spokesman for Negroes, and as intellectuals, liberal religious leaders, and reformers redefined their attitudes, the situation began to change. To be sure, few concrete gains had been made in social integration before 1930, but that a new era was dawning in this most sensitive area of race relations was already apparent. Indicative of the change was the appearance in Washington of Oscar DePriest, the first Negro Congressman since 1901. Even more indicative was an invitation to Mrs. DePriest to sip tea at the White House.

---

52 *Congressional Record*, 67th Congress, 2nd Session (January 19, 1922), 1426.

5

THE ISSUE
OF POLITICAL EQUALITY

White supremacy is not oppressive tyrannical supremacy,
but is compassionate, God-like supremacy exercised for the
good of our nation, the happiness of the human race, and
the civilization of the world.

REPRESENTATIVE WILLIAM C. LANKFORD (D-GA.)

In spite of their deep concern with social equality, racists were
more immediately concerned with combating political equality and
the efforts of reformers to give the Negro a voice in Southern politics.
The issues of social and political equality, however, were inextricably interwoven, so inextricably in fact that those who foresaw
imminent social integration usually based their fears upon the
danger that Negroes were winning political equality. Alarmists who
warned of the dangers of social equality usually felt that those
dangers could be indefinitely circumvented, but they had no such
confidence concerning political equality, for upon this issue the

Negro's friends were vocal and racists divided. Most Southerners and all extremists wanted to remove the race from politics altogether, whereas moderates and reformers wanted to enfranchise "qualified" Negroes. The division was important. On no other issue of significance was there such substantial disagreement.

During the late nineteenth and early twentieth centuries, from the end of Reconstruction to America's entry into World War I, political aspects of the race problem were more important than social aspects. In spite of occasional interracial marriages and a few instances of racial coeducation and in spite of the fact that a considerable amount of illicit amalgamation took place, there was never any prospect of Negroes achieving social equality. Whatever the danger to white supremacy, and it seems to have been minute, it came not from social integration but from the fact that Negroes retained a modicum of political power long after "redemption" had destroyed their hopes for social, educational, and economic equality. Until the end of the century they continued to vote or to be voted in limited numbers and occasionally to be elected or appointed to public office even in the deep South. To racists all this was baleful in the extreme, and around 1900 they made politics the center of their attention.

In retrospect, however, it seems clear that they overestimated the Negro's political power, both real and potential. After Reconstruction his influence was rarely more than nominal, and political currents in the new century were discouraging. The progressive movement produced many meaningful reforms in political, economic, and social realms, but it ignored the Negro altogether or, as happened in several instances, actually furthered his subordination. In some cases the two movements—progressivism and the subordination of Negroes—were actually one, for as C. Vann Woodward remarks, progressivism in the South was "generally progressivism for white men only, and after the poll tax took its toll not all white men were included." [1] Southern progressives frequently led movements to disfranchise the Negro and make social segregation total and legal. Hoke Smith, reform governor of Georgia, was perhaps the best example of this, but other examples abounded—Carter Glass of Virginia, Charles B. Aycock and Josephus Daniels of North Carolina, and even John Sharp Williams and James K. Vardaman of Mississippi were progressives in important particulars. But it must be

---

1   Woodward, *Origins of the New South,* 373.

remembered that progressivism had another side which worked in the opposite direction and which ultimately undermined the authority of racist spokesmen. Progressives emphasized democracy and environmentalism and rejected the determinism which was so important to racists. "The democratic, environmentalist outlook adopted by most of the leading social scientists and historians of the Progressive era," writes John Higham, "weakened the intellectual respectability of the confused, ill-defined concepts of race prevalent in the nineteenth century."[2]

The political nadir of American Negroes lasted roughly from 1890 to 1920, from the beginning of legal and constitutional disfranchisement until the emergence of an emboldened Negro leadership which exchanged its traditional supplication for a new and effective militancy. In 1890 Mississippi commenced the long, dreary process of constitutional amendments and statutory enactments which disfranchised the Negro and made his segregation virtually complete. Before 1900 South Carolina and Louisiana followed suit, and by 1910 Oklahoma and the remaining states of the old Confederacy had done likewise.

It was from this movement that traditional twentieth century patterns of segregation and disfranchisement emerged. Areas or practices in which the races had previously permitted considerable integration were now segregated. In 1904 Berea College in Kentucky, an interracial institution of long standing, was required by state law to discontinue its policies of integration in favor of newly developing patterns of segregation. Throughout the South the color line was made more rigid as contact between the races became more formalized and impersonal, and Jim Crow became the central fact in the Negro's life. Ubiquitous and inflexible segregation was now the practice in all public and private facilities—in schools, on railroads, in hotels, restaurants, and theaters. To be sure, the Supreme Court insisted in 1896 that all Jim Crow facilities be equal, but in practice the South, and the North also, ignored this dictum. And the Negro had no redress. His loss of political power had destroyed his ability to influence public policy.

Indirect as well as direct means were employed in disfranchising the race. Literacy and property qualifications and tests of character

---

2 Higham, *Strangers in the Land*, 148–49.

and reputation were imposed, as were poll taxes, payable months before election and for several consecutive years. Military service, the "grandfather" clause, and ability to interpret the state constitution were also used against the Negro. Voting registrars were permitted to exercise personal discretion in evaluating an applicant's qualifications, especially concerning the nature of his reputation and his proficiency in interpreting the state constitution. As a result, the laws were applied unevenly and the pattern of disfranchisement varied. Most registrars disqualified all Negroes under their jurisdiction, although a few allowed a nominal number to vote even in the deep South. Their voting, however, was restricted to meaningless general elections; rigorously excluded from membership in the Democratic party, the Negroes were unable to vote in the election-determining white primary.[3] To supplement these legal means of disfranchisement, Southerners sometimes found it necessary to intimidate Negroes who attempted to register. In the early twentieth century the Negro's economic dependence upon the white man was virtually complete, and white landlords, employers, and merchants found economic reprisal an effective instrument against "uppity" Negroes who wanted to vote. The reprisal, moreover, was sometimes reinforced by the subjection of politically minded Negroes to mental anguish, physical harassment, and in extreme cases, mob violence. Precisely how many Negroes were disfranchised by these threats and how many by statutory or constitutional measures is impossible to determine. It is sufficient to say that by 1910 the race had lost its influence in national, state, and local politics.

In that year Judge Gilbert T. Stephenson, a North Carolinian, published a survey of the anti-Negro legislation enacted during the preceding decades. Entitled *Race Distinctions in American Law,* his work was a spirited defense of that legislation as well as an attempt to prove that it was not, or at least it need not be, discriminatory. Endorsing the separate-but-equal doctrine, Stephenson condemned racial discrimination but he insisted that whites and Negroes be segregated by law. The effect of his work, which was a detailed examination of both state and national laws, was to document the Negro's lowly legal and political status. Occasionally, a judge ruled

---

3 On the disfranchisement movement see Gilbert T. Stephenson, *Race Distinctions in American Law* (New York, 1910); "Disfranchisement," *The Crisis,* XXX (June, 1924), 62–63; and Woodward, *Origins of the New South,* 321 ff.

against segregation and discrimination but the presumption was always to the contrary. Hostile courts, laws, and public opinion made the Negro's rights tenuous and nebulous at best. In 1910 he was completely segregated and disfranchised in the South and ghettoized, though not disfranchised, in the North.[4]

Like other racists Stephenson believed that segregation and disfranchisement would ensure interracial amity by removing the major sources of interracial friction. The belief, however, was unfounded and reflected a basic misunderstanding of race relations. In fact, as C. Vann Woodward has remarked, "in place of the improvement in race relations promised by the disfranchisers as a result of their work, there occurred a serious deterioration in almost all departments." Disfranchisement campaigns were invariably accompanied by systematic propaganda for white supremacy, and as a result "race hatred, suspicion, and jealousy were whipped to a dangerous pitch" and inflammatory atrocity stories were widely circulated by politician and press.[5] Between 1900 and 1910 an average of more than ninety Negroes was lynched each year in the South, and race riots frequently accompanied disfranchisement. The disintegration of race relations reflected the deterioration of the Negro's legal and political status.

From this background racists approached the issue of political equality. No sooner had the Negro been disfranchised than he began the long and difficult struggle to regain the vote, and from 1900 to 1930 the struggle was a source of chronic uneasiness for racists. Endorsed by important reform elements, it was the most meaningful effort to solve the race problem during these decades. Its potentialities were underscored by Republican orators who attacked disfranchisement as a violation of the Fifteenth Amendment and who reminded Southerners that the Fourteenth Amendment authorized the reduction of congressional representation for states which denied the vote to Negroes. To meet such threats as these, racists needed a well-reasoned and effectively articulated defense of their position, but none was ever developed. Instead, they again resorted to a broadside approach. Their justifications for disfranchising the Negro were so numerous and varied that one is today more impressed by their number, variety, and emotion, and frequency of repetition than by their forcefulness, clarity, or logic.

---

4 Stephenson, *Race Distinctions in American Law*, 351, 361.
5 Woodward, *Origins of the New South*, 350.

The weakness of anti-Negro thought upon this point was the result of several factors. Racists accepted the Negro's alleged inferiority as self-evident and, thus, gave him no credit for political ability or potential. In their opinion Radical Reconstruction had demonstrated his civic incapacity and proved that political equality was incompatible with white civilization. Hasty and superficial in their reasoning, they never questioned the assumptions which led to these conclusions. That the Negro's participation in Reconstruction politics was artificial and contrived never occurred to them, nor did they stop to think that his gullibility and excesses were products of ignorance, inexperience, and economic distress rather than innate racial incapacity. Unwilling to concede any formative influence to environment, they never understood that education, political training, and economic self-sufficiency are the means by which political independence are achieved. By exaggerating the ill effects of Black Reconstruction, they strengthened the Southerner's prejudice against political equality. Men of singular purpose, they used history as they used everything else. But by misinterpreting the history of Reconstruction they seriously miscalculated the political future of the Negro and the South.

The chief objection to political equality was the conviction that it would, as "every schoolboy knows," lead directly to social equality. A suffrage based upon individual and personal qualifications alone would destroy racial integrity, pollute the white race, and undermine Anglo-Saxon civilization. It was the first step toward racial amalgamation and the destruction of the white man's priceless racial heritage. To prevent such eventualities it was a small matter to sacrifice the Negro's alleged right to vote.

Not all racists, however, accepted the contention that political equality was a prelude to social equality. Many moderates thought the two subjects were entirely separate. Such national leaders as Theodore Roosevelt and such moderate Southerners as George Washington Cable actively supported the Negro's right to vote while strongly denouncing efforts at social integration. Both Roosevelt and Cable were convinced that Negroes had no desire for social equality and they rejected the Southerner's fear of amalgamation as an argument against enfranchising the race. "While the colored people always did and still do accept with alacrity an undivided enjoyment of civil [i.e., political] rights with the white race wherever cordially offered," wrote Cable, "they never mistake them for social privileges, nor do they ever attempt to use them to compel social intercourse." [6]

But whether they endorsed Cable's view or not, racists agreed that Negro voting was a major element in the South's race problem. They were convinced that disfranchisement was the way to interracial harmony, and they urged the Negro to cease his agitating and to accept political subordination voluntarily. "At present," wrote Professor N. S. Shaler in 1904, "the main point is to make an end of the unhappy frictions which have come to separate the races. To do this it is necessary to take the mass of the Negroes for a time out of politics, for so long as the dominant whites are kept in fear of being despoiled of their property and the blacks in hope of gaining power, class ill-will is certain to become greater and there is danger that it be made permanent." Disfranchisement thus promised a truce in race hatreds. As if to confirm Shaler's observations, a Mississippi Congressman in the same year surveyed the effects of disfranchisement in his state. "For more than ten years," said Thomas Spight, "the negroes of Mississippi have understood that they were not to be allowed to participate in State or county governments, and as a result we have had but little trouble with them, and they have been better satisfied and more prosperous than at any time since their emancipation." [7]

The way then to interracial peace was obvious. The Negro's participation in politics was irritating and unsettling. Originating in the partisanship of Reconstruction, it reflected the Yankee's ignorance and was an injustice and injury to both races. A natural consequence of the Radicals' egalitarian propaganda, it had convinced the Negro that he had certain inalienable rights the circumscription of which caused him frustration and resentment, and these in turn were irritants to racial peace. To remedy this uneasy situation, racists wanted to disabuse the Negro of his misconceptions and enact federal guarantees of white supremacy. Endorsed by such divergent spokesmen as John Moffatt Mecklin, Charles Francis Adams, James K. Vardaman, and Professor Charles H. Brough of the University of Arkansas, who was president of the University Commission on Southern Race Questions, this view represented an im-

---

6 Cable, *The Silent South*, 73.
7 Shaler, *The Neighbor*, 158; and *Congressional Record*, 58th Congress, 2nd Session (March 16, 1904), 3340.

portant element in anti-Negro thought.[8] It emphasized the unpleas-
ant results of past experiments in Negro voting, not only in the
postbellum South but also in Haiti and Santo Domingo. As described in such works as James Anthony Froude's *The English in the
West Indies* and Lothrop Stoddard's *The French Revolution in San
Domingo*, the consequences of Negro suffrage were dire indeed.
Occasionally cited by racists, these works described Haiti and Santo
Domingo as mired in a morass of mongrel ineptitude and depravity
and as object lessons in the consequences of political equality. They
offered "proof" that the Negro could destroy a civilization but could
not build a new one in its place. This was, said racists, the real
reason they opposed political equality.

In the broadest sense their opposition stemmed from their conviction that races are unequal. If the Negro was innately inferior, as
they insisted, he was perforce incapable of exercising or even comprehending the responsibilities of citizenship. This idea, of course,
was the ultimate source of racist thought on political questions and
originated in the conviction that social, cultural, and political institutions were expressions of racial capabilities. "Political institutions," wrote Alfred P. Schultz, summarizing the view, "are the
products of a race and change with the race." Thus, no system of
government was innately superior to another. A race deserved—no,
it required—the system which best reflected its political capacity
and evolutionary development. In white society the Negro would
always be politically inept, for he had not experienced the racial
struggles from which the white man's political institutions had
evolved.[9]

There was little wonder then that the Negro was a failure in
American politics. Giving him the franchise had suddenly projected
him forward into a stage of civilization many generations in advance
of his natural development. Until recently his ancestors had lived by
the laws of the jungle, and it was no reflection upon him that he
could not formulate laws and administer governments as well as the

---

8   Mecklin, "The Philosophy of the Color Line," 343–57; Charles Francis
    Adams, *The Solid South and the Afro-American Race Problem* (Boston,
    1908), 17–19; Harry Earl Montgomery, *Vital American Problems* (New
    York, 1908), 330; and Charles Hillman Brough, "Work of the Commission
    of Southern Universities on the Race Question," *The Annals*, XLIX (Sep-
    tember, 1913), 55.
9   Schultz, *Race or Mongrel*, 265.

white man. He must undergo those hundreds of years of development, struggle, and sacrifice which are necessary for political maturity, but while doing so he must remain politically subordinate. To
give him civic responsibilities beyond his natural capacity would
disrupt his evolutionary development and undermine the white
man's efforts to promote interracial goodwill.[10]

Among popularizers these ideas appeared in the conviction that
Negroes had no inherent capacity for self-government and could not
be trusted with the ballot until they demonstrated a capacity to use
it with due intelligence and patriotism. The simple mind of the
average Negro, ran this view, saw no connection between conscientious voting and good government, but rather regarded the ballot as
merely a saleable commodity. Negroes judged public issues by a
single criterion, racial self-interest, and always voted as a bloc. But,
paradoxically, they placed no substantial value on the right to vote,
and the great bulk of them did not greatly resent being deprived of
it. Since Redemption they had come to realize that political equality
was not essential to their happiness, and they had gradually withdrawn themselves from politics. Thus, disfranchisement had been
largely a voluntary process and the present clamor for Negro
suffrage had no support among Negro masses.[11]

The paradox in these views is apparent. On the one hand the
Negro was castigated as incapable of comprehending political processes, while on the other he was criticized for using the ballot for
racial self-interest. If he judged political issues by racial criteria he
was voting as a bloc, but if whites did likewise they were exercising
intelligence and independent judgment. And although the Negro
had no desire to participate in politics, it was necessary to take
extreme measures to prevent him from doing so.

To understand these paradoxes one must also understand the
political milieu in which they were uttered. Following the Negro's
disfranchisement, Southern politicians were in a predicament of
their own creation. Having made race relations the chief issue in

---

10 William H. Fleming, *Slavery and the Race Problem in the South* (Boston,
    1906), 41; and Oscar W. Underwood, "The Negro Problem in the South,"
    Forum, XXX (October, 1900), 218.
11 See Simmons, "The Political Future of the Southern Negro," 1523; James
    Bryce, "Thoughts on the Negro Problem," *North American Review*, CLIII
    (December, 1891), 649; and *Congressional Record*, 66th Congress, 1st Ses-
    sion (August 25, 1919), 4305.

politics during the disfranchisement campaign, they now found themselves victims of their own designs. Instead of easing tensions, eliminating demagoguery, and encouraging political division among whites, disfranchisement had intensified tensions, encouraged the demagogue, and made unity among whites more essential than ever. Every politician, however earnest and capable, now became a potential victim of bigotry and prejudice. A premium had been placed on intolerance and extremism, and Southern political campaigns became struggles for new heights, or depths, of race-baiting and deceit. Like the Negroes whom they criticized, whites now measured political issues by the single criterion of race, and as a result the level of politics and the caliber of public officials declined noticeably. Tillman and Vardaman, Blease and Heflin, Cotton Ed Smith and Tom Watson, like the sterility of the one-party system which nurtured them, were but spectacular results of the South's enslavement to the monomania of race. Interested only in their personal fortune, they carried the South down the dead-end street of intolerance and bigotry, and from the resulting impasse they were unable to extricate the section. Their efforts to do so, in fact were few and languid and proposed no alteration of racial policies. The source of extrication would ultimately come from other directions—from Negroes, Yankee reformers, Northern and Southern moderates, the federal government, and others of whom Southern politicians were so scornful.

But to return to arguments against political equality. Unlike most moderates, extremists sometimes felt that disfranchisement was only a partial solution to the Negro problem. In their opinion the two races were so unequal that each should be governed by a separate code of laws especially adapted to its ability. The two races could never be successfully governed by the same laws any more than children and adults could be controlled by the same rules. Like a child the Negro needed a governing hand in every detail; the white man, however, throve best in an atmosphere of freedom and daring. Nor must the child be allowed to interfere with the adult's freedom, for to do so would jeopardize the advancement of civilization. "It may be said," declared Oscar W. Underwood, "that we have no right to deny the privileges of a free government that we have won for ourselves to the inferior races with whom we come in contact. This may be true when it does not jeopardize our own free institutions; but when it does, our first duty is to ourselves and to the free government created for us by the wisdom and courage of our ancestors." [12]

Upon these and similar premises racists based their defense of Southern policies which disfranchised the race. Such policies, they felt, were the only realistic response to the stupendous solecism of Negro suffrage. Of the possible alternatives—repeal of the Reconstruction amendments or continuing mass Negro voting—the former was blocked by Yankee intransigence and the latter was contradictory to Southern experience. Repeal of the amendments was the only real solution, for the problem would endure as long as they remained in the Constitution. Yet disfranchisement was a workable though not an ideal alternative. It neutralized immediate dangers, but the seeds of potential trouble remained.

Disfranchisement, said racists, should not be judged by abstract theories of civil rights and democracy, but by the purposes of its enactment, the evils it eliminated, and its tranquilizing effects upon race relations. The Negro had not been disfranchised merely "for political or race advantage, but . . . for his good and the country's good, and, speaking broadly, for our own salvation," declared Senator Furnifold M. Simmons of North Carolina in 1906. And although "the manner of his disfranchisement, in some instances at least—as in the cases of Louisiana and North Carolina—may seem harsh and inequitable, as a matter of fact, it is neither. Properly interpreted, these apparently discriminating provisions simply declared, what experience had conclusive proven"—that the Negro has no inherent capacity for self-government. Disfranchisement was thus a blessing in disguise. "The restriction of suffrage in Mississippi was the wisest statesmanship ever exhibited in that proud Commonwealth, and its results have been . . . beneficent and far-reaching," said Congressman Eaton J. Bowers in 1904. "We have disfranchised not only the ignorant and vicious black, but the ignorant and vicious white as well, and the electorate in Mississippi is now confined to those, and to those alone, who are qualified by intelligence and character for the proper and patriotic exercise of this great franchise." Even the moderate Edwin A. Alderman believed that disfranchisement was "the chiefest [*sic*] political constructive act of Southern genius in reference to the Negro," for it had the effect of "removing the blacks from politics, and centering their thought on industrial life, removing

---

12 Underwood, "The Negro Problem in the South," 218.

frightful temptations from the politics of the white people, and, in a large way, placing the whole idea of suffrage on the highest plane possible in a republic." [13]

Like other phases of anti-Negro thought the defense of disfranchisement was affected by the limitations of the racist mind. Like other Americans racists venerated the Constitution and boasted of their adherence to its principles. To be able to do this they were sometimes forced to resort to tortured and legalistic interpretations of the Reconstruction amendments. In this manner they were able to ignore the fact that their actions nullified the spirit as well as the letter of the Constitution. They declared emphatically that their actions and policies were consistent with the guarantees of the Constitution, including the Reconstruction amendments, and that their laws were impartially administered. Disfranchisement was not a result of racial discriminations, as commonly alleged, but of the Negro's ignorance, immorality, proneness to crime, and failure to pay a nominal poll tax. In 1926 Governor William W. Brandon of Alabama assured critics of his state's election laws that Negroes were disfranchised "merely because they fail to qualify by registering, or because they fail to comply with the laws of the state," laws which were impartially applied to whites as well as Negroes. Both the constitution and statutes of Alabama prescribe voting qualifications, he continued, and neither permits discrimination on account of race, color, or previous condition of servitude.[14] In view of the Southerner's preoccupation with race, this conclusion was perhaps unexpected, but it illustrated the tendency of racists to enhance their plausibility and reasonableness by rationalization and by underplaying factors which their critics found objectionable. Intensely conservative, they were unwilling to admit (or unable to understand) that by their actions they were openly flouting the Constitution. It was essential that Caucasian civilization and the Southern way of life be preserved by legal and constitutional means, and for this reason it was necessary that racists be convinced of the con-

13   Simmons, "The Political Future of the Southern Negro," 1522–23; *Congressional Record*, 58th Congress, 2nd Session (April 8, 1904), 4536; *ibid.*, 70th Congress, 1st Session (January 23, 1928); and Alderman, "The Growing South," 10377.
14   Atlanta (Ga.) *Constitution*, February 21, 1926.

servatism and orthodoxy of their policies. This was not, however, a difficult task.

In anti-Negro thought there was an inherent denial of basic democratic principles. Implicit in the idea of innate racial inequality, this denial was made explicit in the various discriminations imposed upon Negroes. Yet racists, especially those who reflected the anti-Negro views of the South, were ostentatious champions of democracy, and they seem never to have realized that their racial policy denied the political philosophy which they so loudly championed. In their own minds they were democrats, and the fact that they restricted democracy to whites only, and not even to all whites, was not to them a contradiction. Conscious of the American democratic heritage, of which they considered themselves perpetuators, and aware that defenders of Americanism must pledge allegiance to democratic forms, most racists were unwilling to criticize the principles of democracy. Defining these principles as the precepts of the Constitution and the Declaration of Independence, they assured themselves that neither document required or even permitted racial equality. Southern policies were, thus, completely constitutional and "American," and assertions to the contrary misrepresented the attitudes and actions of the founding fathers.

A minority of anti-Negro spokesmen, however, did denounce democracy in principle as well as in practice. Composed largely of intellectuals whose chief interest was racial theory rather than the Negro, this minority had no faith in democratic principles and said so in no uncertain terms. Such representatives of this group as Lothrop Stoddard, Madison Grant, and Henry Fairfield Osborn, as well as Thomas Dixon and Ernest Sevier Cox, were alarmed by the nation's failure to base its policies upon Stoddard's "iron law of inequality." This failure, complained Stoddard and Grant, sprang from the widespread and fatuous delusion that environment, education, and opportunity could improve inferior races, and its chief result was a misguided attempt to uplift those races rather than a conscientious effort to define their place in society and keep them there. This generation, wrote Osborn in 1921, "must completely repudiate the proud boast of our fathers" that they acknowledged no distinction of race, creed or color. It must also remember, added Dixon, that in spite of all the high-sounding phrases of our Declaration of Independence, the United States was not a democracy but had been from the beginning an aristocratic republic founded squarely on African slavery.[15]

As abstract subjects democracy and political theory received little attention from anti-Negro spokesmen. Neither was discussed except in relation to specific issues or events—Negro suffrage, poll taxes, or voting qualifications—and without concern for general principles. Nevertheless the discussions followed a recognizable pattern. The cornerstone was the contention that democracy is suited only to racially homogeneous societies. "True democracy and a considerable citizenship of a people considered non-assimilable by the dominant majority" were felt to be essentially contradictory and should be recognized as such. The founding fathers had ignored factors of race differences because their political ideals were for the most part inherited from a people which had attained ethnic homogeneity in the insular atmosphere of England. Their ideals presupposed a uniform background of race instincts and traditions, and efforts to apply them to a society which lacked this uniformity were singularly unrealistic.[16]

A further illustration of this view of democracy was the contention that Southern race policies were perfectly compatible with the Declaration of Independence, provided it was properly interpreted. Assertions to the contrary were figments of the imagination of biased and willful theorists. "The phrase in our Declaration of Independence, that all men are created equal," wrote sociologist Jerome Dowd, was never "understood as meaning anything more than that all the white men composing the population had inalienable right to equal opportunity in this new country." The founding fathers "so generally understood that citizenship in this country was for Caucasian only that the question was not even discussed, and all of the original declarations of equality in our organic laws must be interpreted as having reference to the white population only." Other spokesmen, however, disagreed somewhat with Dowd. They interpreted both the Declaration of Independence and the Constitution as guaranteeing theoretical equality to *all* men, but, they hastened to

---

15   Chicago (Ill.) *Blade,* November 11, 1922; Grant, *The Passing of the Great Race,* 16, xxxiii; Thomas Dixon, *The Victim, A Romance of the Real Jefferson Davis* (New York, 1914), 75; and Cox, *White America,* 321 ff.

16   William W. Gregg, "The Mulatto—Crux of the Negro Problem," *Current History,* XIX (March, 1924), 1067–68; and Mecklin, *Democracy and Race Friction,* 20.

add, equality of rights in the abstract did not presuppose equality of exercise of those rights in the concrete. The Declaration, explained William Jennings Bryan, meant only that everyone should have equality before the law and equal protection in their rights, and these guarantees were fully compatible with segregation and disfranchisement.[17]

Accepting this narrow interpretation of political equality, racists agreed that the right to vote was not an absolute natural right which existed for the benefit of the individual. Instead it was a great civil and political privilege, conferred or withheld for the benefit of and in the interest of society and good government. It was not conferred by the Constitution, nor was it an attribute of citizenship. It was instead a right conferred by the states and they alone had the power to prescribe its qualifications. The disfranchisement of Negroes was thus an exercise of state power and of no concern to the nation as a whole.[18]

A final criticism of democracy was implied in the assumption that race rather than personal quality was the measure of individual ability. It mattered not that some Negroes excelled some whites in ability, for it might very well be, as Professor William Benjamin Smith of Tulane pointed out, that some dogs are superior to some men. "Preposterous, indeed," said Smith, "is this doctrine that personal excellence is the true standard," for regardless of the character of individual Negroes, it was inexpedient for the South to treat them individually. The lowliest white man is still higher than the highest Negro, observed Professor Thomas Pearce Bailey of Mississippi, and to change this attitude would be to invite racial amalgamation.[19]

There was, then, nothing undemocratic about segregation and disfranchisement. Such policies in no way contradicted the truth that governments derive their just powers from the consent of the governed. Quite the contrary. Most Southerners supported segregation and disfranchisement and to attack them was to attack the principle of majority rule. In large areas of the South, including the states of South Carolina and Mississippi, a majority of the popula-

17 Dowd, *The Negro in American Life*, 486; and *American Forum* (San Antonio, Texas), March 31, 1923.
18 *Congressional Record*, 58th Congress, 2nd Session (January 27, 1904), 1277; *ibid.*, 67th Congress, 1st Session (July 12, 1921), 3625; and *ibid.*, 58th Congress, 2nd Session (April 12, 1904), 4715.
19 Smith, *The Color Line*, 15–16; and Bailey, *Race Orthodoxy in the South*, 88–89.

tion was Negro, but this detail was of little interest to racists. It was sufficient for them that most Southerners were whites, for a Southern white, they felt, was *ipso facto* a segregationist. Such reasoning led inevitably to one conclusion: outside efforts to interfere with Southern policies were themselves the antithesis of democracy, and violations of the American system of states' rights and local self-government. Senator Tom Heflin urged the establishment of segregated streetcars in the nation's capital on the grounds that segregation was a basic principle of democracy. All men, he said, were guaranteed the right of pursuit of happiness, but the guarantee was violated unless the white man was free to select the company in which his pursuit took place. The Negro had no guaranteed right to pursue happiness in an integrated society, but the white man had every right to choose his own associates. It was one of the basic privileges of democratic society. If he perchance chose white associates only, the Negro had no choice but to accept the workings of democracy.[20]

By 1900, as previously noted, the North and the federal government had abandoned the Negro. Efforts to protect the race were now sporadic, half-hearted, and ineffectual, and as long as this condition persisted white supremacy was safe. Southern politicians, of course, realized this, and their jeremiads on the subject were designed to improve their chances for reelection rather than to solve a racial problem which was advantageous to many of them. It should be noted, however, that many Northerners who loudly condemned Southern race policies were also guilty of partisan insincerity. More vocal than sustained in their condemnation, these Northerners succeeded in embarrassing the South and enhancing their own political prospects without any corresponding benefits to the Negro. Unmindful of Southern intransigence and Northern apathy, they were unwilling to compromise their principles and work for half-measures which might have ameliorated the Negro's condition. They sought such "reforms" as reducing the South's congressional representation under section 2 of the Fourteenth Amendment, enacting punitive and unenforceable antilynching laws, securing the appointment of Negroes to important federal offices in the South, and harassing Southerners with threats of force bills and federal control of

---

20   Tillman, "Causes of Southern Opposition to Imperialism," 443; and *Congressional Record*, 60th Congress, 1st Session (February 22, 1908), 2340.

elections. The results were negative. The Negro benefited not at all, whereas the alarm of Southern politicians was given an ostensible basis of fact.

This condition was altered in important respects by World War I. Increasingly sensitive to discriminations and beckoned by broadening economic opportunities, Negroes were now migrating northward in larger and larger numbers. Freed there from Southern political restrictions and protected by the anonymity of urban life, they began at once to influence the politics of Democrats and Republicans alike. Encouraged, they initiated other changes which soon began to alter the traditional pattern of race relations. Interracial organizations, now stronger and more vocal, shifted their emphasis from the improvement of race relations within segregation to achieving equality through complete integration. Reflecting the emergence of the National Association for the Advancement of Colored People, most militant and best organized of these groups, the shift was another evidence of the rise of a new and substantial Negro middle class. Better educated, more independent economically, and more accomplished intellectually than "old time darkies" had been, this class was dissatisfied with subordination and was able and self-confident enough to further its own improvement. Its efforts, moreover, were not unaffected by wartime propaganda for democracy and the role of Negroes in achieving the allied victory. The results of these efforts were so substantial that even the intensification of racial intolerance in the early 1920's failed to diminish their vigor. The Negro's sense of race consciousness, noted the *Wesleyan Christian Advocate* of Atlanta in 1924, was increasing markedly. Agitation for racial advancement, long and vigorously prosecuted by leaders of the black race and encouraged by leaders of the white race, was bearing bitter fruit. "The Negro has become race-conscious," complained the *Advocate*, "which is another way of saying race-assertive." [21]

As a result of the war and its aftermath, the Negro's role in politics and the political uses of the race issue were altered. Organized opposition to Southern race policies increased notably and was made more effective by new and bolder leadership. Southern protestations that Yankees and Negroes were plotting racial equality now had a basis in fact, and the plausibility of extremists was accordingly

---

21 *Wesleyan Christian Advocate* (Atlanta, Ga.), February 1, 1924, p. 1.

enhanced. More important than this, however, was the fact that a substantial foundation was being laid for later advancement by the Negro.

Like most Americans concerned with racial problems, anti-Negro spokesmen were frequent advocates of the educational, economic, and social improvement of Negroes. Racial difficulties, they maintained, stemmed in no small part from the ignorance, immorality, and indigence of Negroes, and the elimination of these deficiencies was a prerequisite to solving the race problem. To their chagrin, however, as these deficiencies were gradually overcome, the emergent Negro middle class demanded further advancement, including the beginnings of racial equality. As a result racists, especially moderates and reformers, were in a quandary. Having urged the Negro to take the initial step toward independence, they were unwilling to see him take a second. Indeed they never understood why he desired to do so. Ignoring the fact that education and economic independence would increase rather than diminish the Negro's desire for equality, they sowed seeds which from their point of view bore a bitter harvest indeed. "This is a new day and we have what is called a new negro and he seems to be somewhat of a problem," editorialized the Greenville *Enterprise* in 1929, reviewing recent developments in race relations. "He is a product of our making, we have sent him to school, to college, trained his mind, given him a degree, or musical training at any rate, and as a result we have a problem with which to deal. He has lived no doubt in an atmosphere of culture, training and refinement, and he comes out of school a polished, finished, product and we lament because he does not fit in our old scheme." [22] This was, Southerners came to realize, a major factor in the shifting pattern of race relations in the 1920's.

Postwar changes appeared in various forms. In the early years there was a decided increase in racial violence. "The Red Summer" of 1919 ushered in "the greatest period of interracial strife the nation had ever witnessed. From June to the end of the year," wrote John Hope Franklin, "approximately 25 riots were held in American urban centers." At the same time, the "Protestant fraternity known as the Ku-Klux Klan"—the description is Tom Heflin's—increased in strength and spread throughout the nation.

22　Greenville (S.C.) *Enterprise,* March 30, 1929.

Even the Klan, however, was unable to stem the rise of socialism and bolshevism around the world, and those "isms," feared racists, boded ill for the future of interracial peace. Not only were they alien and un-American, but their propaganda for equality was antiracial and its diffusion an earmark of racial degeneracy.[23] Clearly they were threats to white supremacy and racial purity.

Among postwar developments the most conspicuous was the migration of Negroes to urban centers in the North. As previously noted, this movement was condemned by Southerners upon several grounds. For present purposes the most relevant of these was the friction and danger caused by "ignorant young negroes who go to northern cities and get their heads filled with social equality ideas" by reading Northern newspapers, edited by Negroes intensely prejudiced and hostile to the South. They then return to their home town, declared a North Carolina newspaper in 1925 "with their minds filled with bitterness towards the whites and the feeling that they are deprived of their liberty and freedom. They have associated with a certain class of white women in the north and then resent their inferiority [*sic*] status in the south." This situation, continued the newspaper, would remain a major source of race friction as long as Negroes were free to migrate where they pleased.[24]

Another unsettling effect of the war was the resentment which returning Negro soldiers sometimes had for established racial practices. On hindsight it would appear that this influence was more apparent than real and except for isolated incidents existed only in the minds of racists. "The uniform has been permitted to give [Negroes] . . . an unprecedented degree of protection and consideration," complained the Houston *Chronicle* in 1919, giving voice to Southern fears. "High wages and allotments have made them shiftless and irresponsible." Senator William F. Kirby of Arkansas, repeating the *Chronicle*'s complaints, said, "The Negro on the whole is well disposed, industrious, peaceable, and law-abiding, and makes a good farm laborer and farmer, but when he is given military training

---

23 John Hope Franklin, *From Slavery to Freedom* (New York, 1948), 472; Thomas Dixon, *Companions* (New York, 1931), 29; and Stoddard, *The Rising Tide of Color,* 220.

24 Hickory (N.C.) *Record,* November 4, 1925.

it changes his disposition and he becomes idle and arrogant, a troublesome element in the rural districts."[25] When the war had begun Southerners had been understandably reluctant to allow the Negro to fight. Only the grudging realization that the racial consequences of his *not* fighting were worse than those of his fighting had convinced them that he should serve in the army at all.

After the war racists were increasingly alarmed over the rising tide of color. The Negro problem, they now realized, was an integral part of the restiveness among colored races around the world. Despite the realization of this, they continued to concentrate upon immediate problems, especially the growing agitation for racial equality among reformers and Negro leaders. In August, 1919, James F. Byrnes, then a young South Carolina Congressman, admirably summarized their concern with this problem. Speaking in the wake of increased racial violence, Byrnes blamed the decline of racial goodwill on "the incendiary utterances" and ultraradical tendencies of the "would be leaders of the race," notably W. E. B. Du Bois. Already, he complained, the philosophy of Booker T. Washington, "who preached conservatism to the race," was challenged by a "crowd of radicals" who appealed to the passions of Negroes and incited them to deeds of violence. Among these radicals Byrnes singled out the Industrial Workers of the World (I.W.W.), "the Bolsheviki of Russia," and "the misguided theorist of the North."

If the two races are to live together in this country [Byrnes said] it may as well be understood that the war has in no way changed the attitude of the white man toward the social and political equality of the negro. If as a result of his experience in the war he does not care to live in this land without political and social equality, then he can depart for any other country he wishes, and his departure will be facilitated by the white people of this country, who desire no disturbing factor in their midst. If by reason of his experience he seeks social and political equality with the white man, but refuses to consider leaving for parts where it will be willingly given to him, and cherishes the hope that by violence it can be gained here, he can not too quickly realize that there are in this country 90,000,000 white people determined not to extend political and social

---

25 "What the South thinks of Northern Race-Riots," *Literary Digest*, LXII (August 16, 1919), 17; and *Congressional Record*, 66th Congress, 2nd Session (April 8, 1920), 5319.

equality to the 10,000,000 negroes, and a resort to violence must inevitably bring to the negro the greater suffering.[26]

Brynes's impassioned alarm was a standard element in the anti-Negro literature of the 1920's. Throughout the decade Southerners pleaded with Northerners for sympathy, and when it was not forthcoming they resorted to bluster. But Northerners were now less willing to appease anti-Negro opinion, and Southerners as a result became frustrated and irritated. Gradually they came to realize that in the eyes of the non-Southerner their treatment of the Negro was anachronistic. With the passage of time they saw their principles as well as their threats and boasts betrayed or disproved. Contrary to the predictions of some racists, the migration of Negroes to the North did not produce political unity among whites there. Instead of diluting the race problem by scattering the Negroes, it intensified the problem, at least from the Southern point of view. Instead of creating sympathy and understanding among Northerners, it increased the Negro's political power and enhanced his ability to pressure the federal government. It also promoted integration in federal employment in Washington, and in 1928 a Negro Congressman from Chicago. The edifice of racial inequality which had been so carefully constructed from fact, myth, and wish fulfillment was now buffeted on all sides, and cracks, though at first only minute, began to appear on the surface. The structure, however, was hearty and well constructed and Southerners were resourceful antagonists. But they were now on the defensive, and in their plight they cast around for signs of hope. They sought another Booker T. Washington to lead the race back to conservatism, but none appeared. What did appear was the pompous, mysterious, and alluring Marcus Garvey leading a movement to repatriate Negroes in Africa.[27]

Garvey, however, was too absurd even for racists, who fell back upon the white primary as the chief defense for white supremacy. But events soon proved that even this was a stopgap, as both national parties began to glance less furtively at the growing Negro vote in the urban centers of pivotal Northern states. Should competi-

---

26 *Congressional Record,* 66th Congress, 1st Session (August 25, 1919), 4304–4305.

27 For racists' attitudes toward Garvey see Edmund David Cronon, *Black Moses, The Story of Marcus Garvey and the Universal Negro Improvement Association* (Madison, 1955), 188 ff.

tion for this vote become active, the North would openly oppose rather than passively accept the cruder forms of segregation and disfranchisement. As this began to happen in the 1920's the white primary became chiefly a holding action, designed to prevent Negroes from voting in the South. Thus the paradox. As the Negro gained political leverage in the North he was less and less influential in the South. In the North politics provided the chief means for his emancipation. In the South it was the chief instrument of his subordination.

The Negro was a chief stock-in-trade of Southern politicians, as Tom Watson astutely observed in his Populist days. "The politicians keep the negro question alive in the South to perpetuate their hold on public office," Watson had said then. "The negro question is the joy of their lives. It is their very existence. They fatten on it. With one shout of 'nigger!' they can run the native Democrats into their holes at any hour of the day." And, he might have added, they treated all political innovations in the same manner. They supported prohibition as a means of keeping the Negro sober, but denounced woman suffrage as an underhanded means of doubling the number of Negro voters. Eventually anything to which they objected was labeled as an instrument for subverting racial purity.[28]

Based largely on expediency and opportunism, this approach to politics was not without its difficulties. Fearful of federal action in the field of race relations, Southern politicians since Calhoun had endorsed the principles of states' rights and limited government. Throughout the nineteenth century they opposed measures to enlarge federal authority at the expense of the states. In the early twentieth century, however, confident at last that Yankees had acquiesced in Southern race policies, they relaxed their opposition. During Wilson's administration they gave their support as well as their names to measures enlarging the scope and function of federal authority—the Glass-Owen Act, the Clayton Act, the Smith-Lever Act, the Smith-Hughes Act, the Adamson Act. In the wave of patriotism which accompanied the world war, they zealously supported measures which restricted individual freedom and gave government an expanded economic role, such as the Overman Act, the Lever Food Act, the espionage and sedition acts, and measures to benefit

28   Hart, *The Southern South,* 160; *Congressional Record,* 66th Congress, 1st Session (May 21, 1919), 90; and *ibid.,* 65th Congress, 2nd Session (September 20, 1918), 10775.

organized labor and cotton farmers. As a consequence of these measures the federal government assumed a responsibility which it had previously exercised only by indirection—the protection of special interest groups.[29]

In view of later developments, the Southerners' support for these measures was extremely shortsighted. If the federal government was legitimately concerned with problems of cotton farmers, veterans, or labor unions, might it not also be concerned with those of Negroes? This question was asked with increasing urgency in the twenties and was a source of continuous embarrassment to Southerners. Their inability to ignore it or to answer it was a measure of their dilemma. At the root of the dilemma lay their failure to take a long-range view of politics. Concerned chiefly with protecting white supremacy, but also with keeping the race issue agitated, they never evolved a clear and concise political ideology. Their politics was a strange mixture of constitutional and social conservatism and agrarian radicalism and was filled with inconsistency. Many Southerners supported prohibition as consistent with the principles of states' rights and local self-government and then objected to woman suffrage as a violation of those same principles. They allowed immediate considerations of patriotism, patronage, or federal aid to entice them into supporting measures which were detrimental to their long-range ends. Under the impact of progressive reform and wartime emergency the status of state and local governments declined noticeably and the individual's relationship to the national government was altered accordingly. And no postwar reaction to normalcy could reverse the situation completely. The degree to which Southerners had abetted this trend, and it was substantial, was the extent to which they contributed to their own difficulty.[30]

For this difficulty, however, they blamed Yankee politicians and the latter's efforts to protect Negroes by federal legislation. Aware now that appeals to Northern opinion were futile, they attempted to

---

29 On the support of Southern Congressmen for Wilsonian measures see Dewey W. Grantham, Jr., "Southern Congressional Leaders and the New Freedom, 1913–1917," *Journal of Southern History*, XIII (November, 1947), 439–59; Richard M. Abrams, "Woodrow Wilson and the Southern Congressmen, 1913–1916," *Journal of Southern History*, XXII (November, 1956), 417–37; and Anne Firor Scott, "A Progressive Wind from the South, 1906–1913," *Journal of Southern History*, XXIX (February, 1963), 53–70.

30 See I. A. Newby, "States Rights and Southern Congressmen During World War I," *Phylon*, XXIV (Spring, 1963), 34–50.

discredit reform by smear, ridicule, and indignation. Every action in any way favorable to Negroes or critical of the South was described as part of a conspiracy to further social integration and amalgamation. This was their response to antilynching legislation, to the integration of federal employees in Washington, to the seating of black and tan delegations by Republican national conventions, to appeals for expanded economic and educational opportunities for Negroes. The seating of a black and tan delegation from Georgia at the Republican National Convention in 1920 led the Atlanta *Constitution* to declare that a Republican victory in the upcoming elections would in effect place Negroes on a plane of equality with the whites. This attitude also lay behind the calculated disparagement of Southern Republicans by Southern Democrats. Southern Republicans, declared John Sharp Williams, are "generally radicals and fanatics upon political questions without the ordinary common hard sense that leads a man to know the difference between a nigger and a white man." But the difference, explained Williams, was obvious. "The niggers are Republicans and the white men are Democrats." [31]

During the 1920's a new element was injected into American politics, an element which boded ill for defenders of white supremacy. During this decade Northern Democrats first became willing to court Negro votes at the expense of Southern whites, and by 1928 the courtship had already begun to bear fruit. In the presidential election of that year, both parties gave at least a modicum of deference to Negro voters, thereby establishing a pattern which has since become a routine in national politics.

In discussing this election, historians frequently note the bitter cleavages it produced in the South. Aware of the Southerner's traditional loyalty to the Democratic party, they explain these cleavages by the Southerner's objections to Al Smith's Catholicism, urban background, and opposition to prohibition. Of course a wet Catholic from New York City had little appeal to dry, Protestant, rural Southerners, but many of the latter objected to Smith because they saw him as an advance agent for total racial integration. Others, however, and this is equally important, were convinced that white supremacy was imperiled only by Herbert Hoover and the Republicans. From this disagreement a bitter, name-calling contest devel-

---

31   Atlanta (Ga.) *Constitution,* June 9, 1920, p. 8; and *Congressional Record,* 67th Congress, 1st Session (November 22, 1921), 8120.

oped to determine which candidate was the greater threat to white supremacy. Whether they supported Hoover or Smith, however, many Southerners agreed with a Florida newspaper editor that white supremacy was the most vital issue of the campaign.[32]

If white supremacy was the end to be defended, the fundamental question was that of means. A large and influential element believed that by nominating Smith the Democratic party had betrayed the South and forfeited all claim to its support. Smith's nomination, they felt, had signaled the demise of the historic Democracy and the rise in its stead of a new and alien mobocracy directed by a polyglot of forces whose interests were opposed to the South. "By virtue of a startling metamorphosis unparalleled in history," declared a Florida newspaper following Smith's nomination, "this so-called 'Democratic Party' of today HAS SUDDENLY BECOME THE PARTY OF THE NEGROES—and they are all flocking to it in all parts of the country—A COALITION OF BLACKS AND UN-AMERICANIZED FOREIGNERS UNDER TAMMANY LEADERSHIP, ARRAYED AGAINST WHITE, PROTESTANT AMERICA!"[33]

To many Southerners, then, Smith was a greater lover of the Negro than his Republican opponent and a much stronger advocate of social equality. Among the evidences offered to substantiate this belief none was more often repeated than the fact that a Negro member of the New York State Civil Service Commission had a white female secretary assigned to him, and his duties involved interviewing white female applicants for civil service jobs. "Don't you know," asked one Southern newspaper, "that black buck's nostrils swell with animal passion and pride every time he hauls a pretty white girl before him and examines her application for a Tammany Hall or city job—and breathes his hot breath into the face of his unfortunate Caucasian Private Secretary lady?"[34]

The most outspoken Southern opponent of Smith's nomination was the Senator from Alabama, Tom Heflin. Waging a personal vendetta which aroused religious prejudices as well as racial animosities, Heflin described Smith as a man who would destroy white supremacy and "undo all that we have done to protect the white

---

32 Gainesville (Fla.) *Sun*, October 24, 1928.
33 Winter Haven (Fla.) *Times*, September 28, 1928.
34 *Yellow Jacket* (Moravian Falls, N.C), November, 1928 (exact date not noted on clipping).

women of the South from the lust and carnality of brutal negroes." [35]

Heflin's views, however, were not shared by most Southerners. The largest and most influential segment of Southern opinion was that of loyal Democrats who denounced Hoover and the Republicans in terms as disparaging as those Heflin used against Smith. The Republican party, said loyal Democrats, had always been the antagonist of white supremacy. It was born of hostility to the South and was still loyal to its original purpose. Historically the party had stood for social equality and 1928 was no exception, for now it was led by "this Englishman" Herbert Hoover, who was "in favor of making young white girls use the same water closets as negro men" and whose Quaker faith denied all distinctions of race. The Democratic party, however, the party of white supremacy, was racial before it was political, and a vote for Smith was a vote for the South, for an old-fashioned South which was determined to preserve a white man's civilization at all hazards.[36]

The average Southern politician treated the race problem with both realism and hypocrisy. Not only did he realize that race prejudice was primarily emotional, but he also knew that inflamed emotions were a less likely source of political embarrassment to himself than candid inquiries into social and economic problems. To the politician the race issue was a benefaction, potential if not always real, and inasmuch as his success at the polls was frequently in proportion to the vehemence with which he employed it, he represented the chief obstacle to reforming racial policies.

Despite this, politicians invariably insisted that their only concern was the welfare of Negroes and the elimination of racial friction. They disclaimed any desire to use the Negro as a stepping stone for political advancement. On the contrary, their actions were deliberately misinterpreted by critics who misunderstood the Negro and misrepresented the proportions of the race problem. Even Negroes themselves understood the situation better than did these critics, and except for a disgruntled few they held Southern politicians in high esteem. Should the Negro be given the vote, the politicians ironically suggested, their election majorities would be greatly enlarged. But, alas, the Negro had no desire to vote and the politician was left to take his chances with an all-white electorate.

---

35 *Congressional Record*, 70th Congress, 1st Session (May 19, 1928), 9151–52.
36 *Ibid.* (May 21, 1928), 9300; and Eatonton (Ga.) *Messenger*, November 2, 1928.

Such illogic was typical of politicians like John Sharp Williams, who in his own words was "popular with darkies" and glad of it. "I never belonged to the nigger-hating and nigger-baiting class of the South," he told the Senate in 1918. "Nobody can make a nigger baiter out of me; nobody can make a nigger hater out of me; and nobody in Mississippi can ever make out of me a man who gained, or would gain, office by 'cussing' negroes [*sic*]." Williams' fellow Mississippian, Congressman John Rankin, whose demagogic use of race prejudice was remarkable even in Mississippi, reflected the same attitude. "I have no antipathy for the Negro as a race," he said. "I have no prejudice against him because he is a Negro. . . . But I understand him; I know his weaknesses, his shortcomings, and his limitations. I want to see him protected in the enjoyment of life, liberty, and the pursuit of happiness." This could best be done, Rankin thought, by remanding the race question to the South and its political leaders, who were far better friends of the Negro than were Northern demagogues or reformers.[37]

Before World War I, Northerners had accepted such statements at face value. National political leaders during the Progressive era had rarely questioned Southern assurances of goodwill and sincerity in handling the Negro problem. Since they had little interest in the race, they had abandoned it, rationalizing their action by statements that only Southerners understood the Negro and the problems created by his presence. President Wilson, describing himself as "a Southern man," told members of the University Commission on Southern Race Questions in 1914 that he knew how sincerely Southerners desired "the good of the Negro and the advancement of his race on all sound and sensible lines," and he applauded the commission's efforts in that direction. President Taft had likewise reminded a delegation of Southern Negroes that their greatest hope lay in the sympathy and the help of the "noble, earnest, sympathetic white men in the South." "I thank God," Taft said, "that in the South there is developing fast evidence of a stronger and stronger sympathy with the effort to uplift the race among the white men of the South, who feel themselves responsible for the whole of Southern civilization."[38]

---

37 *Congressional Record*, 65th Congress, 2nd Session (October 1, 1918), 10982; and *ibid.*, 67th Congress, 2nd Session (January 19, 1922), 1428.
38 *Minutes of the University Commission on Southern Race Questions* (n.p., n.d.), 17; and William H. Taft, *Political Issues and Outlooks, Speeches*

This view, which was also held by Theodore Roosevelt,[39] was as widely believed by Northern politicians of the prewar period as it was by Southern. It was admirably summarized by George Harvey, editor of *Harper's Weekly* and one of Wilson's early political mentors:

There is in the community in which I live but one disposition toward the South [Harvey told an audience in Charleston, South Carolina, in 1904] and that is, not to interfere, but to help. We do not believe that your great problem of reconciling perfect justice for all with the absolute supremacy, social and political, of the white race is insoluble. We cannot believe that God in His wisdom ever placed before His civilizing, Christianizing people an obstacle which they should be incapable of removing.[40]

In the postwar years, the fondest hope of Southern politicians was to lead Northern opinion back to this position. The changed times, however, had produced a changed situation, and as a consequence the Negro had made noticeable political gains by 1930. He had elected a Congressman from Illinois, and an increasing number of Northern politicians felt the pressure of his political strength. After 1928 he was a permanent issue affecting both major parties and the federal government. In 1930 his opposition contributed significantly to the Senate's rejection of John J. Parker, whom Hoover had nominated to the Supreme Court.[41] Parker, a North Carolinian, was unacceptable to Negro leadership because of anti-Negro statements he had made in the past, and he was thus the first important victim of the Negro's newly won power. It was in politics, then, that the Negro made his first advances toward equality. During the decades following 1930 he would continue to make such advances, and his success would be in proportion to his ability and willingness to exert political pressure.

Delivered Between August, 1908 and February, 1909 (New York, 1909), 242.

39 See Theodore Roosevelt, "The Progressive and the Colored Man," *Outlook*, CI (August 24, 1912), 910; and Roosevelt, *American Problems* (New York, 1926), 344–46.

40 George Harvey, *The Power of Tolerance* (New York, 1911), 127. For similar attitudes by Senator William E. Borah see *Congressional Record*, 66th Congress, 1st Session (June 3, 1919), 563.

41 See Richard L. Watson, "The Defeat of Judge Parker: A Study in Pressure Groups and Politics," *Mississippi Valley Historical Review*, L (September, 1963), 213–34.

6

SOLUTIONS OF THE
"NEGRO PROBLEM"

> Mr. Lincoln said that this nation could not exist "half slave
> and half free." I think it is equally true that this nation can
> not exist *half white* and *half black.*
>
> REPRESENTATIVE FRANK CLARK (D-FLA.)

Anti-Negro thought was always essentially negative. Racists
were against social and political equality, against "uppity" Negroes
dissatisfied with discrimination, against reformers seeking to alter
the *status quo.* They emphasized the Negro's racial incapacity, his
social inferiority, his personal deficiency, his inability to adjust to
white society. They supported policies of discrimination, subordination, and repression. And despite the weakness inherent in a negative approach, they usually found themselves in the role of opposition. Recognizing the disadvantages of their position, they
undertook to convince the public that their principle objectives were

positive—that they sought to preserve racial purity, to maintain Caucasian civilization, and to secure for the Negro maximum benefit from a civilization in which he would forever remain a misfit. Always, they emphasized, they had the best interest of the race at heart. Their sole motivation was a desire to promote interracial harmony and goodwill.

For reasons such as these, anti-Negro spokesmen after 1900 offered a multitude of specific proposals for solving or removing the race problem, a problem which in their opinion stemmed from the presence of Negroes in large numbers in the South. So numerous and varied were their proposals that they constituted a major segment of racist thought. In the final analysis they represented the logical conclusions and long-range thinking of persons who gave little attention to either logic or long-range thought. But to understand the racist mind, one must understand not only its analysis of race problems but also its suggestions for solving them.

One of the keys to this understanding is a recognition of the racists' inveterate, almost irrational, hatred for anyone whom they considered an outsider, a reformer, or a friend of the Negro—anyone, that is, who proposed to alter race policies in the Negro's favor. Heirs to the Southerner's distrust of those who would meddle with internal or peculiar institutions, they rejected offhand all assertions that Northerners, reformers, moderates, the federal government, even the Negro himself, had any proper concern with race relations in the South.

In defending this view, racists found support from an unlikely source—from William Graham Sumner, the nation's foremost exponent of the immutability of social mores and the immunity of social customs from the tamperings of reformers, legislators, or humanitarians. Before the Civil War, Sumner wrote, Southern whites and Negroes "lived in peace and concord, and each one grew up in the ways which were traditional and customary." The war, however, abolished established patterns of race relations and new ones had to be developed, a process which had been retarded by Radical attempts to control the new order by legislation. The results, of course, had been detrimental, proving again that legislation cannot make mores.

It is only just now [wrote Sumner in 1911], that the new society [in the South] seems to be taking shape . . . [though] it is not at all what the humanitarians hoped and expected. The two races are separating more than ever before. . . . Some [reformers] are [still] anxious to interfere and try to control. They take their stand on ethical views of what is going on. . . . But it is evidently impossible for anyone to interfere. We are like spectators at a great national convulsion. The results will be such as facts and forces call for. We cannot foresee them. They do not depend on ethical views any more than the volcanic eruption on Martinique.[1]

Thus, assured that reform was futile if not dangerous, racists turned their guns upon reformers. Their first impulse was to ignore reformers altogether, but, unable to restrain their considerable talents for invective and vituperation, they launched a campaign of calculated disparagement and ridicule. The nature of their efforts was reflected in colorful and opprobrious epithets: "lunatics and visionaries," "howlers," "malignant agitators" seeking "office, or notoriety, or bribes," "seasonal agitators and philo-negrists," peddlers of "vicious advice or ill-considered philanthropy," "blatant demagogues," "non-resident theorists," "aspiring Mulattoes . . . purblind philanthropists, and . . . designing politicians," "a few long-haired negrophilists . . . and a lot of short-haired white women who disgrace both their race and sex."[2]

More important than uncomplimentary language were charges that reformers were insincere, that they were uninformed or misinformed on the nature and scope of race problems, and that their meddlings constituted a major source of racial unrest in the South. A favorite tactic was to charge reformers with hypocrisy, however moderate or inane the reforms they espoused. Believing that any moderation of Southern race policies would ultimately lead to social equality, racists thought it hypocritical that advocates of moderation did not practice social equality. The failure to do so, however, merely reinforced the belief that reformers, like Northerners in general, cared for the Negro only in the abstract, only as a far-off persecuted minority. "The white man's zeal for the inalienable rights of the Negro," wrote a Georgian in 1931, "continues to augment substantially with the square of intervening distance" between himself and the Negro.[3]

To racists there was a direct correlation between the reformer's

1   William Graham Sumner, *Folkways* (Boston, 1911), 77–78; and Sumner and Albert Galloway Keller, *The Science of Society* (New Haven, 1927), III, 2215 ff.

2   These descriptions are gleaned from a general reading of racist literature. For one good account see Arthur Styron, "A Southern View of Northern Reformers," *North American Review*, CCXXXVIII (August, 1934), 149–57.

3   Lawrence W. Neff, *Race Relations at Close Range* (Emory University, 1931), 21.

ignorance and his enthusiasm for the Negro, and in this fact lay one of the principal sources of racial troubles in the South. "If selfish and mischievous agitators will only cease inculcating in the negro mind fancied wrongs," stated Congressman (later Senator) Tom Connally of Texas, "if white encouragement be withdrawn from negroes in northern cities, who live on funds fleeced from trusting negroes of the South and give them in return evil counsel and impossible hopes, we shall draw nearer to racial adjustment." To Southern politicians this constant prating by breeders of race hatred was the greatest cause of the outrages by Negro men and thus the chief source of lynching, race prejudice, and race riots. In their opinion "theorists and agitators"—"carrion maggots who engender, create, and live on the stench of race hatred"—were instilling incendiary ideas into the minds of the Negroes from which the South would harvest a whirlwind of disorder, chaos, and bloodshed.[4]

After World War I racists increasingly held Negro leadership responsible for this agitation. By the early twenties the National Association for the Advancement of Colored People, "an organization of Negro men with white wives," was already an object of invective. This "notorious organization," editorialized the Memphis *Commercial Appeal* in 1921, consists of "uplift negroes and uplift white men" and "a few so-called philanthropists (white) of northern birth who are just as busy as are our negro fakirs in this race problem." It had to its credit, added the Jackson *Daily News* in the same vein, not "a single achievement for the advancement of colored people." Its guiding spirit was W. E. B. Du Bois, "a Northern Negro who hates the South and everything Southern. He is brilliantly educated but has a warped mind. He is perhaps the most vicious, vindictive, volatile, and uncompromising hater of the Southern white man who ever lived." [5]

In condemning reformers, racists again reversed logic. They sought to demonstrate that reformers, and not racists themselves, were the real enemies of the Negro, and they insisted that reform was detrimental to their efforts to improve the race. The Negro "cannot be coddled into civilization by an overplus of sympathy

4 *Congressional Record,* 67th Congress, 2nd Session (January 25, 1922), 1730–31; and Odum, *Social and Mental Traits of the Negro,* 141.
5 *Commercial Appeal* (Memphis, Tenn.), March 13, 1921; and *The Crisis,* XXXV (April, 1928), 130.

from friends far or near, North or South," wrote a Georgia educator. He must be kept in tutelage until his advancement had been earned. And anyway, as historian Holland Thompson pointed out, the Negro suffered much less from segregation and discrimination than did his "sometimes too sympathetic" white friends, who judged racial policies by Caucasian rather than Negro standards. Actually, Thompson suggested, segregated Negroes were generally contented with their position. They recognized the white man's superiority and their own inferiority and had nothing but contempt for whites who preached or practiced equality.[6]

Having disposed of reformers, racists offered their own proposals for reform. In doing so they were chiefly concerned with demonstrating their recognition of the "realities" of race and the frictions created by different races living together in the South. "Reality" dictated the abandonment of theoretical humanitarianism and sentimental enthusiasm, and recognition of this fact was a preliminary to understanding the race problem and devising a workable solution of it.

The realism of which racists were so proud was their acceptance of social Darwinism, a cluster of ideas which formed the core of their social philosophy. Again they took their cue from William Graham Sumner, whose *The Science of Society* was an attempt "to make it possible for re-formers to understand the methods by which and the limits within which human efforts can realize human hopes." In his opinion these limits were narrow. "The existence of the human race on earth, and of human society, is conditioned by forces in nature and in society," he wrote. "It is subject to law. If men could do what they chose to do, there could be no laws and so no chance for the development of science. The power of man to control the forces that play about his little life is extremely limited and consists in the skill which he develops in adjustment. . . . Any interference to prevent the survival of the fittest" would tend "only to promote the survival of the unfittest."[7]

These ideas were readily applicable to the Negro and race relations in the South.

---

6 Branson, "The Negro Working Out His Own Salvation," in McCulloch (ed.), *The South Mobilizing for Social Service,* 388; and Thompson, *The New South* (New Haven, 1919), 144.

7 Sumner and Keller, *The Science of Society,* 2216, 2215, 2220.

Wherever there are great masses of an inferior race closely associated with a superior [wrote Edward Eggleston of Virginia], the fittest must survive and exercise supervision and control over the unfit. This is an inflexible and irrevocable decree of mankind in all ages and in all lands, reinforced and uniformly supported by natural law throughout the entire kingdom of living things; a law superior to ordinary interpretations of justice. . . . The development of political institutions and the growth of mankind are under the operation of law, as controlling as the laws of the natural world around us, and no interference of any power can permanently put "the bottom rail on top." [8]

More often than not the efforts of reformers ignored these truths, and it was this fact which led racists to accuse them of misunderstanding the nature of race and racial problems. There was in nature a ceaseless struggle for survival which applied to races today just as it applied to the evolution of mankind.

The implication here was that racial improvement is a matter of evolution and heredity, not environment and education. It could not be hastened or molded, however well-intentioned the efforts to do so. "History and science tell us," wrote James Bryce, "that social and moral advancement is an extremely slow process, because it issues from a change in the physical as well as mental nature of a race." Since the Negro was well behind the white man in evolutionary development, many generations and thousands of years must pass before he would reach "the pinnacle of wisdom and knowledge upon which the Caucasian stands to-day." Nor was this an isolated opinion. Raymond Patterson, a Northerner whose study of the Negro was prefaced by President Taft, believed that "the adjustment of relations between the black race and the white in America cannot be a matter of years, or even of generations, but of centuries." [9]

The Negro then must remain a few centuries longer the white man's dependent, cognizant of his own inferiority and submissive to a superior will and guidance. Then, "perhaps in a few thousand years," both races "will have reached a higher plane of civilization, and a different or better justice may be possible." In the meantime, as Theodore Roosevelt observed, "the [Negro] race cannot expect to get everything at once. It must learn to wait and bide its time; to prove itself worthy by showing its possession of perseverance, of thrift, of self-control. The destiny of the race is chiefly in its own

8 Eggleston, *The Ultimate Solution of the American Negro Problem,* 236.
9 Bryce, "Thoughts on the Negro Problem," 643; and Raymond Patterson, *The Negro and His Needs* (New York, 1911), 9.

hands, and must be worked out patiently and persistently along these lines." [10]

Other spokesmen, however, denied the efficacy of evolution. They felt that the Negro could expect no improvement, or at least no absolute improvement, from this source. For while he was improving himself, the white man, who was already fifty generations ahead, according to H. L. Mencken, would likewise evolve upward. He would never catch up and the races would always be unequal. "When time shall have gone on," declared John Sharp Williams, "and the negro race shall have developed to the level on which we stand now, if it ever does . . . the white race will be even then just as far in advance of him as it is today, because the real progressive race of the world is not going to cease to progress. While we help him up, rung by rung, we shall go ahead of him rung by rung." [11]

In discussing solutions to the Negro problem, racists often turned their attention to education. To reformers education was the most likely means of improving the Negro's character, and it was of considerable importance to them. Extremists, however, who considered evolution and heredity the only sources of racial improvement, had no such faith in education. Whether Southern whites were also influenced by the cost of public education for Negroes is problematical. It is certain, though, that racists would limit the Negro's education to the rudiments of the three R's and to basic agricultural and mechanical skills. A reflection of their anti-intellectualism, this attitude also reflected their fear that education would plant strange and disquieting ideas in the Negro's mind and undermine the appearance of racial tranquility in the South.

To be of value, they insisted, the Negro's education must suit his racial peculiarities and capabilities. It must differ fundamentally both in quality and content from that of the Caucasian. "The same amount of educational effort," noted sociologist Franklin Henry Giddings, "does not yield equal results when applied to different stocks." Formal education was a recapitulation of racial experience. The system and techniques evolved by the white man were products of his racial history and from them the Negro could benefit little.

---

10 Avary, *Dixie After the War*, 392; Letter, John W. Wilson, of Leesburg, Va., to Editor, *The Nation*, CXXXVIII (January 17, 1934), 75; and Roosevelt, *American Problems*, 354.

11 *Men Versus The Man*, 116; and *Congressional Record*, 58th Congress, 2nd Session (April 12, 1904), 4716.

Nor could education create new traits of character or personality. At best it could do no more than mold and train innate traits. Thus, the educated Negro would remain a Negro. "Education expands whatever kind of mind the individual being educated has," wrote the South Carolinian William P. Calhoun, "but you cannot by cultivating the mind of the ass make a horse out of him; nor can the negro be made a white man by cultivating his brain, since they [*sic*] are what God made them and will remain so." The Negro's education must be designed to enhance whatever was desirable in his nature and inhibit whatever was not.[12]

The implications of this are apparent. Racial differences necessitate different educational programs. But since the American system was adapted to the ability of the average white students, it was unreasonable to expect Negroes as a group to make satisfactory progress in it. Perhaps, suggested psychologist George Oscar Ferguson, they should be allowed an extra year or two to complete the program.[13]

Other writers stressed curriculum adjustment and character training as the best method of adapting the system to the Negro. "On account of economics and psychological differences in the two races," declared members of the Southern Educational Association in 1907, "we believe that there should be a difference in courses of study and methods of teaching, and that there should be an adjustment of school curricula as shall meet the evident needs of negro youth." The curriculum, however, should not be merely an attenuated version of that of white schools. It should de-emphasize book learning and stress the attributes of good character and citizenship—"honesty, truth, chastity, industry, and respect for the Sabbath." It should "introduce *lessons in industry* and *morality* and place them on an equality with *reading, writing,* and *arithmetic.*" William Hannibal Thomas wrote, "The end and aim of the race's education should be to inculcate self-respect, self-restraint, prudent forethought, careful industry, honesty, courage, the grace of patience, the purity of maidenhood, the continence of youth, the nobility of manhood, the chastity of womanhood." [14]

12   Giddings, *The Principles of Sociology,* 328; Calhoun, *The Caucasian and the Negro,* 20, 79.

13   Ferguson, "The Mental Status of the American Negro," 542.

14   Weatherford, *Negro Life in the South,* 111; Charles H. Smith, "Have American Negroes too much Liberty?" *Forum,* XVI (October, 1893), 177; Charles N. Otken, *The Ills of the South* (New York, 1894), 209; and Thomas, *The American Negro,* 115–16.

Compared to these aims, the development of the mind was insignificant indeed, especially in light of the fact that the aims were best achieved by industrial and agricultural training. "Manual training is the true basis of the negro's education," felt racists, "whether he intends to become a mechanic or not," for the purely moral influence of such training was genuine and profound. "Negroes are in less need of literary education than of practical knowledge and genuine wisdom," wrote Ulrich Bonnell Phillips. "They need to become well-developed men and women, and not half-baked scholars." [15]

In addition to being ill adapted to the racial and character traits of the Negro, literary education had specific detrimental effects upon individual Negroes and through them upon race relations in general. An excess of education had proved the ruin of many Negroes, for when "advanced to higher mathematics and composition," they became dudes and vagabonds and lost their respect for the white man. "In the vast majority of cases," wrote one Southerner, "the higher culture of 'coloured universities' . . . merely spoils a ploughhand or housemaid." As a result, wrote another, "we have thousands of negro men and women roving the streets, looking impudent and avoiding work." [16]

This view of Negro education was summarized by Howard W. Odum in 1910 in a volume in the "Columbia University Studies in History, Economics, and Public Law":

The young educated negroes are not a force for good in the community but for evil [wrote Odum]. They feel that manual labor is beneath their dignity; they are fitted to do no other. They sneer at the idea of work, and they thus spread dissatisfaction among the members of their race. They imitate the whites and believe themselves thereby similar to them. They love only the show of apparent results and do not care for the details of attainment. They have not rejected vicious practices in their own lives nor condemned them in theory; on the contrary they have chosen to practice them and to condone the vices which are increasing in the race to its rapid deterioration. They uphold immorality and wish to ostracize any who assist the white man contrary to their own notions, thinking all the while that they are manifesting a spirit of race loyalty. It is clear that their moral natures are miserably perverted.[17]

---

15   Philip Alexander Bruce, *The Rise of the New South* (Philadelphia, 1905), 163; and Phillips, "The Plantation as a Civilizing Influence," 265. See also Washington, *Up From Slavery*, 127.
16   Calhoun, *The Caucasian and the Negro*, 69; Smith, *The Color Line*, 160; and Price, *The Negro Past, Present, and Future*, 145.
17   Odum, *Social and Mental Traits of the Negro*, 41–42.

Among the criticisms of literary education, none was more interesting than the charge that it increased criminality in the Negro. Especially popular among extremists, including many Southern politicians, this view accepted the "irresistable" conclusion that the more you educate the Negro the more criminal he becomes. Increased Negro criminality and decreasing Negro illiteracy, it held, were "linked together like Siamese twins." Thus, James K. Vardaman was convinced that literate Negroes were more criminal than illiterates, and Governor William Dorsey Jelks of Alabama believed that Negro schools were "turning out thieves and vagrants in companies, battalions, and armies." Jelks stated that "for the most part, the negro teacher . . . has either taught the beauty of idleness and the decency of theft, or has, at least, made no impression to the contrary on the plastic mind of the child." It is far better, he suggested, "to have a citizenship which is honest than one which can read." [18]

More serious than the linking of education and criminality were charges that education discontented the Negro with his proper place in white society. This view was rejected by most moderates, a fact which indicated that extremists had a better understanding of the Negro's aspirations for equality. It also contradicted earlier statements that the race was incapable of benefiting from a literary education. The contradiction, however, was partially sidestepped by asserting that education, instead of improving the Negro, perverted his sense of values and aroused in him desires which could be gratified only by social equality and intermarriage. "Education increases the power of the human brain to think and the heart to suffer," wrote novelist Thomas Dixon, and "sooner or later . . . educated Negroes feel the clutch of the iron hand of the white man's unwritten laws on their throats." As a result they become arrogant and assertive and dissatisfied with white supremacy. Some of them in turn become sullen and brooding and violate the unwritten laws, and race hatreds and mob violence are the result. "If you educate the Negroes," stated one Southerner bluntly, "they won't stay where they belong." [19]

---

18   "Governor Vardaman on the Negro," 270; and William Dorsey Jelks, "The Acuteness of the Negro Question," *North American Review*, CLXXIV (February 15, 1907), 391, 393, 394.
19   Dixon, *The Leopard's Spots*, 265; Guild, "A Plea from the South," 485; and Baker, *Following the Color Line*, 85.

Among the proposed solutions to the Negro problem, none was more unrealistic than the suggestion that all Negroes be returned to Africa. Obviously such suggestions never received much support even in the South, and they illustrated the extent to which intellectual, book-writing racists sometimes lost touch with public opinion.

Deportation, or repatriation to use a popular racist euphemism, did not originate with twentieth-century racists. On the contrary, it was a standard ingredient of anti-Negro thought throughout the nineteenth century. Receiving its first significant expression in the American Colonization Society, it had at one time or another been endorsed at least abstractly by Jefferson, Madison, Monroe, Clay, Lincoln, and other leading Americans.[20]

Attracted by this long and honorable history, twentieth-century racists sought to identify their colonization schemes with those of the founding fathers and pre-Civil War leaders. In detail, however, their proposals more closely resembled those of post-Reconstruction writers. After the Negro was emancipated and made a citizen, deportation lost whatever semblance of reality it might once have had, and it was abandoned by responsible political leaders. Among extremists, however, the idea persisted throughout the late nineteenth century, and they advanced numerous schemes for the removal of Negroes from the United States. Among these were proposals by H. S. Fulkerson of Mississippi, a latter-day Hinton Rowan Helper; Charles H. Otken, an apologist for Southern race policies; Enoch Spencer Simmons, a North Carolina lawyer; Carlisle McKinley, editor of the Charleston *News and Courier*; and W. Laird Clowes, an Englishman who toured the South in 1890. In addition no less a political leader than Wade Hampton of South Carolina endorsed deportation as an ideal solution for the race problem.[21]

Finally, a small number of Negro leaders, most notably Bishop Henry M. Turner in the late nineteenth and early twentieth cen-

20 On early deportation projects see Walter L. Fleming, "Deportation and Colonization, An Attempted Solution of the Race Problem," in *Studies in Southern History and Politics Inscribed to William Archibald Dunning*, 3–30; and Henry N. Sherwood, "Early Negro Deportation Projects," *Mississippi Valley Historical Review*, II (March, 1916), 484–508.
21 H. S. Fulkerson, *The Negro; As He Was; As He Is; As He Will Be* (Vicksburg, 1887), 106 ff.; Otken, *The Ills of the South*, 253 ff.; Simmons, *A Solution of the Race Problem in the South*; [Carlisle McKinley], *An Appeal to Pharaoh, The Negro Problem, and Its Radical Solution* (New York, 1890); W. Laird Clowes, *Black America* (London, 1891), 180 ff.; and Hampton, "The Race Problem," 138.

turies and Marcus Garvey in the 1920's, also advocated deportation as the only lasting solution of the Negro's problems in this country. Turner and Garvey's support of deportation was an expression of the pessimism and hopelessness with which some Negroes viewed their race's future in America.[22]

Twentieth-century racists who advocated or endorsed deportation were surprisingly numerous and varied. Among them were William P. Pickett, a New York extremist; William Archer, an Englishman who toured the South around 1910; Ernest Sevier Cox of Virginia, the South's leading race theorist between World Wars I and II; William McDougall, the British-born social psychologist and member of the Harvard faculty; A. H. Shannon, a Mississippian chiefly concerned with preserving racial integrity; John Temple Graves, the elder, a Georgia newspaper editor and frequent inciter of racial antipathies; Joseph P. Widney, a California race theorist; Clinton Stoddard Burr, a leading nativist; Thomas Dixon, the novelist; and Lawrence W. Neff, a Georgia Methodist minister.[23]

These writers, and many others, developed detailed schemes for removing Negroes from the United States. To be sure, their proposals differed substantially in details, but they generally agreed on fundamentals. Negroes must eventually be eliminated from the nation, and they must voluntarily accept repatriation. Constitutional and legal objections must be swept aside, and the federal government must finance and direct the movement. Those who benefited by the Negro's presence in America, e.g., Yankee reformers and Southern exploiters of Negro labor, must be ignored. Strangely, however, Africa was not the only location to which Negroes might be deported. Central and South America, the Caribbean islands, the Philippines, and New Guinea were also suggested. In selecting a location, two criteria were important: it must be a tropical area and undesirable for European habitation.

---

22 On Negro attitudes toward deportation see August Meier, *Negro Thought in America, 1880–1915* (Ann Arbor, 1963), 63–68, 272–73. On Garvey see Cronon, *Black Moses.*

23 Pickett, *The Negro Problem,* 337 ff.; Archer, *Through Afro-America,* 233 ff.; Cox, *White America,* 329 ff.; McDougall, *The Group Mind,* 176; McDougall, *The Indestructible Union,* 162–63; A. H. Shannon, *The Negro in Washington* (New York, 1930), 250 ff.; *The Possibilities of the Negro in Symposium,* 23; Widney, *Race Life of the Aryan Peoples,* II, 171; Burr, *America's Race Heritage,* 156; Thomas Dixon, *The Clansman, An Historical Romance of the Ku Klux Klan* (New York, 1905), 46–47; and Neff, *Race Relations at Close Range,* 16–18.

Having selected locations for the resettlement of Negroes overseas, racists developed detailed plans for deporting the race. They sought to be as specific as possible and to anticipate all criticisms. They strove for flexibility, plausibility, and reasonableness. Among the multitude of these proposals, those of William P. Pickett and Ernest Sevier Cox were representative.

Pickett's plan for the gradual removal of Negroes from this country was developed in *The Negro Problem, Abraham Lincoln's Solution,* a book which reflected little of Lincoln's compassion for the Negro but which made much of his anti-Negro utterances. Believing the Negro an alien, inferior, and unassimilable race whose mere presence was an impediment to national progress, Pickett urged the adoption of a national policy for gradual removal "not in a spirit of hostility to the negro, but as a measure necessary for the permanent welfare of both races, and in which each will co-operate in carrying the project into execution." To implement this policy he proposed the adoption of a constitutional amendment declaring Negroes born after 1925 ineligible for national citizenship. He urged in addition the repeal of all civil rights laws, the abolition of interracial marriages, and the absolute exclusion of Negro immigrants from the country. Following these initial measures, Congress would adopt "a carefully devised and generously assisted plan to induce the voluntary emigration of all persons of African blood." Toward this end the nation would acquire "one or more tracts of territory suitable for the purposes of colonization, and, if found necessary and feasible," would assume "a protectorate for that purpose over the Island of Hayti or perhaps Liberia, provided, of course, that the consent of either or both of those countries could be obtained." The plan would be the exclusive responsibility of the federal government and would be administered by a new cabinet officer, the Secretary of Emigration. Congress would be given the necessary authority to finance the project. Total cost, Pickett estimated, would be $100,000,000 per year for forty years, or $200,000,000 per year for nineteen years.

Success in any scheme of deportation, he thought, depended upon its attractiveness to Negroes. Not particularly concerned with where Negroes should go, but only that they should leave, he suggested a variety of inducements. Not only would he furnish transportation to the emigrants, but every effort would be made to make them self-sufficient in their new home. The federal government, moreover, might attempt to create jobs for Negroes outside the United States, in Cuba, Puerto Rico, and Panama, for example, irrespective of any general plan of deportation, and agreements might be made with Mexico for the settlement of Negroes there. Whatever the attractions, however, not all Negroes could be induced to leave voluntarily, and Pickett, who understood this clearly, did not propose forcibly to deport them. He suggested instead that they be herded onto reservations and there ruled and cared for as wards of the nation.

Like other advocates of deportation, Pickett saw the Negro's removal as a boon for blacks as well as whites, for North as well as South. Separation from the white man, he declared, would give the Negro a separate nation and a distinct nationality. It would permit him political freedom, intellectual advancement, economic opportunity, and spiritual development. It would also expedite the development of Africa, hasten rehabilitation of the South, and regenerate the nation as a whole.

Despite his enthusiasm Pickett made no effort to win popular support for his proposals. In this respect he differed from Ernest Sevier Cox, whose activities on behalf of repatriation as he preferred to call it were unique among race theorists. Cox's plans for removing the Negro were similar in many respects to Pickett's, though they differed in several important details.[24] Like Pickett, he assumed that only the federal government had sufficient authority and adequate resources to undertake the project. Also, he expected opposition from "certain negroid [i.e., mulatto] professors," from whites who profited by Negro labor, and from "bigoted negrophilist[s] whose program for the equalization of the races cannot but end in amalgamation." He did not, however, have any concern for the wishes of individual Negroes. "The question of the repatriation," he wrote, "should not be left to the Negro's adverse decision, any more than the question of the removal of the Indian was left to the choice of the Indian." With the exception of only the aged, Negroes who refused voluntary repatriation would forcibly be deported, and they would be sent exclusively to Africa. But since Liberia was too small to accommodate the entire American Negro population, settlements might be made in the Belgian Congo, the former German colonies, or French or Portuguese Africa. Perhaps certain of these areas might

---

24 Cox's plans are outlined in *White America*, 329 ff.

be taken by the United States as payment for European war debts. Cox rejected all proposals that Negroes be resettled in a separate state within the United States, or that they be dispersed throughout Latin America and the Caribbean. A separate Negro state would probably be located along the Gulf of Mexico and would "deprive the white race of the most desirable portion of the Union." Resettlement in Latin America would interfere with the white man's preemption of the Western Hemisphere. Eventually, he wrote, the Western world must become a Caucasian world.

In detailing his plans, Cox was even more specific than Pickett. "We would not return our Negroes en masse," he wrote, "*but only those of breeding age,* and be as much as a generation in placing them in their new homes." Financing the plan would be the responsibility of Congress. Real property of emigrants would be confiscated and the emigrants reimbursed with transportation to Africa, a homestead, and basic living expenses during a transition period. During the initial stages of removal, emigrants would be selected for their skills and physical fitness, but once the project was functioning Negroes would be sent indiscriminately. At first the "Ideal Negro State" would be governed by the white man, who would rule in the name of the United States but in the interest of the Negro. During this time the white man would encourage "and, in some instances, . . . enforce beneficial measures upon the Negro." If the Negro refused to work he would be compelled to work, not for the white man's profit but for his own welfare. At the same time, he would be given a compulsory and universal system of practical education, confined to those lines which promote material well-being. He was to be taught, guided, and advised by the white man, and prepared for independence. As a result he would be able to work out his own destiny and Africa would be civilized and Christianized.

Despite the professed concern with human factors and the insistence that deportation would not produce individual hardships or unhappiness, racists never recognized the implications of their proposals. To them the Negro was an alien, not an American, and they mistakenly assumed that he had the same view of himself. They failed to recognize the attachments which the race had developed for America, and they were unable to understand its rejection of a forced movement which would have been in many respects as shattering as the transportation of slaves to America. Nowhere was the heartlessness of anti-Negro thought more apparent or the delusions of racists more obvious. Nowhere was their estrangement from popular opinion more striking. Happily, few Americans, or Southerners for that matter, took deportation seriously, and no such scheme had the faintest possibility of adoption. Americans generally accepted the idea of innate racial inequality and they usually demanded that Negroes be segregated and subordinated, but they rejected deportation as impracticable and undesirable.

Negro support of deportation is more difficult to evaluate. To the extent that such a movement was completely voluntary, it could not be objected to. Yet Negro support of deportation was a product, at least in large part, of the same pressures which led whites to endorse it. It appealed to Negroes who despaired of their race's ability to compete with the white man or to those who were inclined toward black nationalism or black racism. Thus, it had some of the aspects of a movement to encourage Negroes to flee the country before the country deported them.

To proponents of deportation the chief obstacle to success was not the cost or impracticability of the project or even the unwillingness of Negroes to be repatriated. It was, rather, the mulatto. Not only was the mulatto opposed to deportation, but even racists admitted that Europe as much as Africa was his "ancestral homeland." Yet whatever his proportion of white blood he was always regarded as a Negro and without his removal deportation would be incomplete. Consequently, most plans for deportation gave him special consideration.[25] Through some system of tortured reasoning, racists did not insist that he be sent to Africa. Only partly Negro, he would go only part of the way to Africa—to the West Indies, perhaps, (Haiti and Santo Domingo were favorite designations) or to Central or South America.

Not all racists regarded deportation as a solution to their problem. Such Southerners as John Ambrose Price, William Benjamin Smith, and Bishop Charles B. Galloway rejected it outright. Price thought the removal of Negroes would be "unjust, unchristian, [and] un-American," whereas Galloway felt "their coerced colonization would be a crime, and their deportation a physical impossibility." Racists who accepted this point of view, however, meant no compliment to

---

25 See for example Gregg, "The Mulatto—Crux of the Negro Problem," 1069; and Sayers, *Can the White Race Survive?*, 171 ff.

the Negro. They were simply convinced that, removed from the white man's supervision, the race would degenerate into the jungle savagery from which it sprang. "To remain a human being, and to be subservient to human use," wrote Price, the Negro must remain with the white man and under his control.[26]

A variation of the suggestion that Negroes be deported was the proposal that a separate Negro state be created within the United States. Southerners suggested that such a state might be created within the territories of Arizona or New Mexico or other sparsely settled areas in the West. Non-Southerners, though, usually favored carving a Negro state out of the deep South, perhaps along the Gulf of Mexico from Louisiana to western Florida. Such a location, they felt, would minimize the cost of the project and simplify problems of transportation and rehabilitation.

A detailed plan for creating a Negro state was offered by William P. Calhoun, who rejected deportation as "to chimerical" and "too stupendous to be considered at all." Disavowing any inclination "to deprive the negro of his constitutional rights or drive him from the United States," Calhoun proposed to allow the race to "remain in the United States and enjoy perfect political freedom without interference from" Caucasians. To accomplish this the Negro would be placed "where he will have his own State government; where he can vote and his vote will be counted, and WHERE HE WILL BE SEPARATED FROM THE WHITE MAN ABSOLUTELY; where it will be a crime for any white man to live in the same State with him; where he can prove his right to be a free man and where, untrammelled, he can show his ability to govern himself, improve his morals and show that he is the equal of the white man." The nation, felt Calhoun, had ample room to establish a separate Negro state, and the race, facing either colonization or extermination, would eagerly accept the former. The new state would be located on those millions of acres of public domain "beyond the Mississippi River," and the cost of transportation and a homestead for each settler would be borne by the federal government. But to prevent individual hardship, the project would be completed over the period of a generation. There would be no necessity to remove all Negroes at one time, wrote Calhoun. "State

26 Price, *The Negro Past, Present, and Future*, 233; Smith, *The Color Line*, 79; and Galloway, *The South and the Negro*, 8.

by State could be taken in turn. . . . To land millions of people with limited means in a houseless country, with no fields cleared for farming purposes would not be justice to them." [27]

In the Negro state envisaged by Calhoun and others, no white man would be allowed to settle permanently, to vote, or to own property. Initially government would remain in the hands of whites and might be patterned after western territorial governments, but eventually Negroes would be given control of their own affairs. Such a state would substantially benefit both whites and Negroes, but its greatest benefits would accrue to the South. With the Negro's departure the section would "awaken, as from a nightmare, to the realization of its splendid destiny." No longer would "one of the richest and most beautiful sections of the world be hampered in its material and spiritual development by a legacy of ancestral crime." [28]

Frustrated in their desire to deport the Negro, racists turned to other solutions, generally less extreme but frequently no less unsatisfactory. The range of proposals was broad, from moderate to extreme, from uplifting the Negro to sterilizing or emasculating him, and they were suggested by persons of all ranges of opinion. Moderates concentrated on two proposals: application of the principles of fundamental Christianity, and self-improvement by the Negro.

In many respects moderates were in no better position to solve the race problem than were extremists. They too accepted the "fact" of racial inequality, and they also accepted the South's denial of social equality to Negroes. Thus, they condoned racial segregation and its attendant evils and rejected any independence of action on the part of Negro leaders. They always spoke in the most glittering of generalities, and herein lay their weakness. They offered enthusiasm, pious phrases, and uplifting as substitutes for realistic reform. Unable to understand that Negroes had aspirations for racial equality, they were unsuited to lead an effective movement for reform. As a result, they abdicated their proper role of mediating between extremes, and Negroes turned to themselves or to Northern whites for aid and guidance. Therefore, the Southern extremist—the Ku Klux Klansman, the politician, and others who recognized that Negroes would be satisfied with nothing less than equality—became the South's chief defenders against Negro encroachments.

---

27 Calhoun, *The Caucasian and the Negro*, 145 ff.
28 Archer, *Through Afro-America*, 243.

Yet the moderates' approach to the Negro problem was not unsympathetic. Unwilling to resort to methods which they considered bigoted or demagogic, they accomplished their ends by other and quieter means. Within the framework of segregation they sought to aid and improve the Negro; they emphasized the obligations of whites to Negroes, marveled at the race's accomplishments since emancipation; and to the extent that they were influenced by religion, which was usually large, they accepted the Bible as a fixed and final standard for conduct in racial affairs.

Although preoccupied with Christianity, moderates never lost sight of their other solution to the race problem—their insistence upon self-improvement by the Negro. This approach, which blamed racial prejudice on ignorance, immorality, and poverty among Negroes, urged the race to improve itself by education and by social and economic discipline. The Negro must drop his longing for social equality, accept the place assigned him in American society, and cultivate the goodwill of whites, especially those in the South. Above all, the race must disassociate itself from reformers and radical leaders.[29]

The attractiveness of this approach lay in the fact that it removed from whites, and thus from racists, all responsibility for the existence of race problems. As a means for rationalizing segregation and discrimination it was of considerable value. The Negro was to blame for race problems. He was inferior and degenerate, and the white man was forced for his own protection to separate the races and subordinate the Negro. The condition, moreover, must continue until the Negro became substantially equal to the Caucasian. The latter might aid the former in the upward struggle but the major task was the Negro's.

Some proponents of this view were more exacting than others. Convinced that Negroes were capable of improvement only under close and constant supervision, they advocated a system of race relations based on rigid yet gentle paternalism. As Henry M. Field, a lesser known brother of David W., Cyrus W., and Stephen J. Field, wrote in 1894,

---

29 See for example Murphy, "The Task of the Leader," 1–30; Montgomery, *Vital American Problems*, 214–76; Odum, *Social and Mental Traits of the Negro*, 277 ff.; and Lydia Hardy Hammond, *In Black and White* (New York, 1914). For similar views see Booker T. Washington, *The Future of the American Negro* (Boston, 1899).

the negro is not an abnormal specimen of humanity; he is simply a child, and to be treated as a child. If you have a child that is rather dull and slow of improvement, you do not beat him, but teach him, and have long patience with him, till finally you make a man of him. So these Americans of African descent are but children in understanding, and are to be treated like children, not with severity on the one hand, nor fond indulgence on the other.[30]

Among many Southerners the most realistic solution to the Negro problem was to maintain the *status quo.* Segregation and disfranchisement seemed to them to be working reasonably well and they saw no reason for experimenting with such volatile matters. Closely attuned to public opinion, they realized that current race policies were acceptable to most Southerners and Americans and that public opinion was dubious of any proposal for altering those policies. Unconcerned with carrying their thoughts to a logical conclusion, they gave little attention to theoretically ideal or permanent solutions to the race issue. Like death and taxes the Negro was always with us, they reasoned, and they were resigned to suffer the problem as one of the burdens of life to which there was no final solution. Thus, they accepted the statement of Congressman John Rankin that "segregation, or a separation of the races" was "the only immediate, reasonable, humane, [and] sensible" system under which different races could live together.[31]

As suggested solutions to the race problem, each of the above proposals received considerable attention. Other suggestions, which received little attention and less popular support, were also advanced and are significant as indications of the excesses to which racists sometimes drove themselves. Clinton Stoddard Burr suggested the establishment of a series of reservations, after the manner of South Africa, upon which all Negroes would be forced to live. The American Communist party proposed that a separate state for Negroes be created within the heart of the Black Belt in the South. And Winfield H. Collins of Maryland suggested that "Negroes be encouraged to distribute themselves equally over the country." [32]

The lunatic fringe among racists offered more extreme solutions.

---

30   Henry M. Field, *Bright Skies and Dark Shadows* (New York, 1890), 154.
31   *Congressional Record,* 67th Congress, 2nd Session (January 19, 1922), 1428, 1703.
32   Burr, *America's Race Heritage,* 153; James S. Allen, *The Negro Question in the United States* (New York, 1936); and Winfield H. Collins, *The Truth about Lynching and the Negro* (New York, 1918), 142.

R. W. Shufeldt thought "it would doubtless be a capital thing, if it could be done, to emasculate the entire negro race and all of its descendants in this country, and effectually stop the breed right now, and thus prevent any further danger from them, and the horrors of their crossing continually with the Anglo-Saxon stock." The Southern extremist James Denson Sayers, who favored deportation of all Negroes, would allow those who objected to remain. However, "in order that the mongrel and Negro who insists on remaining may not reproduce any more," he would force them to submit to sterilization. In time, he wrote, "this must come to be as legitimate as sterilization of the venereally diseased and other constitutionally unfit parents." Finally, Congressman James M. Griggs of Georgia broached the ultimate solution. Noting an increased amount of racial agitation among Negroes, he warned in 1908 that "the utter extermination of a race of people is inexpressibly sad, yet if its existence endangers the welfare of mankind it is fitting that it should be swept away." [33]

In the final analysis racists contributed nothing to the solution of the race problem. The sheer multiplicity of their solutions reflected the absence of a clear and consistent anti-Negro philosophy. Among themselves they disagreed widely as to the most desirable or effective method of solving the race problem, and even those who agreed upon a certain solution were frequently at odds on how best to attain it. The result was a lack of direction which made impossible a concerted effort to achieve a permanent solution.

Despite their inability to solve the problem, however, they could and did prevent others from solving, or at least ameliorating, it. Consequently, race relations in the South drifted from crisis to crisis and problem to problem, with each crisis or problem producing whatever expediency local conditions dictated. In one instance a lynching or race riot would occur. In another a threat of force was sufficient. In a third economic or social reprisals were invoked. Yet, since extremists, moderates, and reformers alike rejected social equality, the drift took place within a framework of rigid social segregation. With few exceptions those who proposed new departures in race relations did so with an air of confidence that their

33   Shufeldt, *The Negro, A Menace to American Civilization*, 145; Sayers, *Can the White Race Survive?*, 171–72; and *Congressional Record*, 60th Congress, 1st Session (April 17, 1908), 4876.

suggestions were worthy of serious consideration and were likely to receive such consideration. But they expended little energy organizing public support for their proposals.

For these reasons the conclusion—that the principle deficiency of anti-Negro thought was its inability to offer a satisfactory solution to the problem which it found so engrossing—is inescapable. Yet given the nature of anti-Negro thought such a failure was inevitable. Despite the vast amount of time and energy devoted to analyzing the Negro and his racial characteristics, racists had no real insight into the Negro and the problems of race relations. In fact they basically misunderstood both, and even when their proposals were acceptable to whites they were unacceptable to Negroes. In the long run they clouded rather than clarified race problems and generated more prejudice than understanding. Eventually they fell back upon segregation and disfranchisement—solutions which had developed with a minimum of philosophical justification and which were largely based upon "the way things have always been." Their chief contribution was not to solve the problem, but to provide an ideological rationalization for a makeshift that had developed from prejudice and expediency. They thereby strengthened that makeshift and made its overthrow more difficult.

THE PERSISTENCE
OF RACISM

> This [second world] war was not fought to change one
> whit the definition or meaning of true democracy and true
> Americanism. We fought to preserve what we already
> had. . . . If some overzealous person or persons . . . left
> colored Americans under the impression that a victory in
> this recent war meant the breaking down of the color line
> in the South or social equality and intermarriage with the
> white race, then I am sorry.
>
> THEODORE G. BILBO

The years from 1930 to 1954 were years of transition for both the
Negro and anti-Negro thought. By 1930 the popularity and respectability of racist ideas in intellectual circles were noticeably diminish-
ing. Scientific and scholarly authority was now distinctly against the
racist, and the appeal of extremists diminished even in the South.
Popular opinion in the North continued to be largely indifferent to
the Negro, but where Northerners had once condoned the repressive
policies of an earlier period, they now accepted, at least indirectly,
the moderately pro-Negro changes wrought by the New Deal. In the
process racists lost not only their intellectual authority but also the

191

apathy or indifference of the federal government and public opinion outside the South. The shifting, of course, was a long, slow process and one of frustration and disappointment for the Negro. Eventually, however, it would produce significant changes in the attitudes and practices of white Americans.

The forces which initiated this change in the 1920's were strengthened by events of the thirties and forties. The Depression, the New Deal, the Nazi's treatment of Jews, World War II—each had a definite influence upon American attitudes toward the Negro. As perhaps no other event could have done, the Depression laid bare the discriminations and handicaps under which Negroes lived, but the poverty and hardships of the thirties made race seem somehow less important than immediate economic problems. For this and other reasons the New Deal included a better deal for Negroes as well as whites, although equality, to be sure, was still a long way off. The Negro's struggle was also affected by the racial excesses of Nazi Germany. Indeed, for the first time in recent history, racists were embarrassed by the actions of extremists, and they went to great lengths to disassociate themselves and their ideas from Nazism. Their problems were further complicated by World War II and the wartime propaganda for democracy and freedom. For the second time in a generation Negroes were called upon to make the supreme sacrifice, and the racial unrest during the war indicated that they were becoming less and less willing to remain in their "place." The threatened march on Washington in 1940 had inaugurated a new phase of Negro militancy.

Yet in the middle forties the Negro could point to few concrete gains. Some progress had been made. His spokesmen were received with more and more deference in national political councils and were increasingly successful in getting their views before the public. Their role in community life outside the South and their educational and economic opportunities were expanding, even if not spectacularly. But in vital areas of racial policy Southern intransigence was still a match for Northern apathy; and equality, even theoretical equality, remained a distant dream.

In this atmosphere of hope and disappointment, of progress and frustration, the Swedish economist Gunnar Myrdal undertook his comprehensive and thoughtful analysis of the American race problem. Published in 1944 under auspices of the Carnegie Corporation, Myrdal's work *An American Dilemma* admirably summarized both the Negro's status in America and the major ideas and emotions which determined his status. At a time when democracy was under heavy attack, Myrdal chided Americans about the most glaring failure of their own democracy and in so doing reminded them of the possibilities of the democratic faith. Nor was his message in vain, for in the next decade the Negro's struggle for equality began at last to fructify. President Truman integrated the armed forces, sought the enactment of fair employment practices legislation, and committed the national Democratic party to equal rights for Negroes. Finally, in 1954 the Supreme Court issued a second emancipation proclamation by destroying the legal basis for racial segregation in public schools, and soon this most important bastion of racial discrimination began slowly to give way. Under the impetus provided by these actions and spurred by the Negro's new militancy, the race's advancement since 1954 has been beyond the expectations of all but the most sanguine. And although this advancement has been sporadic and piecemeal, it has already begun to quicken its pace.

It has also stimulated a resurgence of anti-Negro racism and has helped to revitalize and repopularize ideas which had been almost forgotten. This is, of course, a relative statement, for the ideas of racism have never entirely disappeared. Several important racist works did not appear until after 1930, among them Robert Bennett Bean's *The Races of Man* (1932), Madison Grant's *The Conquest of a Continent* (1933), Lothrop Stoddard's *Clashing Tides of Colour* (1935), and Samuel J. Holmes's *The Negro's Struggle for Survival* (1937). These works, however, clearly belong to the racist tradition of an earlier day, as did Charles A. Lindbergh's "Aviation, Geography, and Race," which appeared in the November, 1939, *Reader's Digest*. Aviation, wrote Lindbergh, is an achievement of the white man's racial genius, a genius which is seriously imperiled by such interracial squabbles as World War II. This "is a war within our family of nations," he told his fellow Caucasians,

a war which will reduce the strength and destroy the treasures of the White race. . . . It is time to turn from our quarrels and to build our White ramparts again. . . . Our civilization depends on a united strength among ourselves; on a strength too great for foreign armies to challenge; on a Western Wall of race and arms which can hold back either a Genghis Khan or the infiltration of inferior blood. . . . [We must] guard ourselves against attack by foreign armies and dilution by foreign races.[1]

---

1   Charles A. Lindbergh, "Aviation, Geography, and Race," *Reader's Digest,* XXXV (November, 1939), 66.

The success of resurgent racism in postwar America has been limited. Latter-day racists have been especially troubled by their inability to reconcile the language of democratic equality with the practice of segregation and discrimination. They are aware of the dwindling appeal of overt anti-Negro ideas, even in the South, and they have come, albeit reluctantly, to accept the unpopularity of their position, and have reconciled themselves to a minority status in American society. As a result the tone of their literature is less confident and assured than that of a generation ago. It is more blustering, bellicose, and self-righteous. It is also, as they themselves realize, manifestly anachronistic, for its major ideas have changed little since the beginning of the century. The thunderings of Southern politicians continue in Theodore G. Bilbo's *Take Your Choice: Segregation or Mongrelization* (1947) and Herman Talmadge's *You and Segregation* (1955). Grand racial theory reappears in Ira Calvin's *The Lost White Race* (1945) and Nathaniel Weyl and Stefan Possony's *The Geography of Intellect* (1963). The plight of the white South is restated in Judge Tom P. Brady's *Black Monday* (1955) and W. E. Debnam's *Then My Old Kentucky Home, Good Night* (1955). Historical racism is continued in Nathaniel Weyl's *The Negro in American Civilization* (1960) and W. E. Michael's *The Age of Error* (1957). Religious racism reappears in T. Robert Ingram's *Essays on Segregation* (1960), and patrician paternalism in William Alexander Percy's *Lanterns on the Levee, Recollections of a Planter's Son* (1946).

The most important expression of anti-Negro thought today is the effort of Southern whites to prevent racial integration in public schools. Though largely unorganized, this campaign has staved off massive integration. It has, however, been forced to accept a token amount of integration, and this integration in turn has led to periodic and sporadic efforts to organize Southern forces. So far the most significant result of these efforts has been the formation of the Citizens Councils of America, an organization of extremists who oppose any meaningful improvement in the Negro's status and who are apparently willing to go to almost any limits to win their point. The councils embody in important respects the strength as well as the weakness of Southern efforts against integration. Despite the name, they exist as effective organizations only in Mississippi, but there they are well organized, apparently well financed, and wield considerable political power. Through its official publications, originally *The Citizens Council* and now *The Citizen*, the Mississippi council provides an organ of expression for anti-Negro extremists. It also publishes and distributes a sizeable literature, including speeches, pamphlets, and books; sponsors a radio program; and supplies speakers for Southern and non-Southern audiences. By these means it has attempted to make itself the official spokesman for "the Southern point of view." And though it has not gone unchallenged by Southerners, especially more moderate and respectable elements such as the Virginia Commission on Constitutional Government, its efforts have not been without success. Today it is easily the most important dispenser of extremist views and the most articulate defender of a Southern way of life which has been slowly disappearing for several decades.

The most curious and perhaps unexpected result of the councils' endeavors has been the revival of scientific racism. Like other facets of racist thought, scientific racism never entirely disappeared after 1930, but in the middle of the twentieth century it would seem that any attempt to resurrect its old and discredited arguments would be immediately laughed aside. But such it seems is not the case at all. In 1962 Dr. Wesley C. George, formerly chairman of the department of anatomy of the University of North Carolina medical school, "proved" again that whites and Negroes are biologically unequal; and only four years before, Dr. Audrey M. Shuey, chairman of the psychology department of Randolph-Macon College, had similarly "proved" that Negroes are intellectually inferior to whites. Dr. Shuey's findings were endorsed by Henry E. Garrett, professor emeritus of psychology and former chairman of the psychology department of Columbia University, former president of the American Psychological Association, and author of numerous authoritative works in the field of psychology; and Dr. Frank C. J. McGurk, professor of psychology at Villanova University has reached similar conclusions. The list of scientists and pseudo scientists who continue to give comfort to racists is still long.[2]

Fortified by this authority the new scientific racism has been taken up by a host of popularizers. It has been accepted uncritically by such writers as William D. Workman of South Carolina, a newspaper columnist and a leading spokesman for conservative Republi-

---

2 See George, *The Biology of the Race Problem;* Audrey M. Shuey, *The Testing of Negro Intelligence* (Lynchburg, Va., 1958); Frank C. J. Mc-

canism in his state; by Nathaniel Weyl, a New Yorker whose studies of the Negro convinced him of the inferiority of the race; and James Jackson Kilpatrick, editor of the Richmond *News Leader,* reviver of the doctrine of interposition, and one of the South's most articulate and effective defenders of segregation.[3] Probably the best known of the recent statements of scientific racism is that of Carleton Putnam in *Race and Reason: A Yankee View.* A Northern businessman turned biographer and social critic, Putnam is today perhaps the South's most effective interpreter of racial extremism. He is a forceful writer and speaker and a vocal champion of the Citizens Councils, which act as distributors of his speeches and writings, including his "masterful analysis of the U.S. race problem" on a fifty-minute long-playing phonograph record retailing for five dollars.

Putnam's views center around his conviction that "modern anthropology," which he traces to the researches and influence of Franz Boas, is based upon a series of equalitarian myths which disregard an overwhelming body of objective evidence contradictory to its prejudices and preconceptions. The races, he believes, are innately and obviously unequal, not only in intelligence but in relative ability to create and absorb civilization, to understand and exercise the responsibilities of citizenship, and to live by acceptable moral and social codes. And this, he says, is grounds aplenty for segregation and white supremacy.[4]

With Putnam, a circle has been completed. The twentieth century began with reputable scientists and scholars as the chief authorities for racist ideas. During the 1920's and 1930's, however, these groups changed their minds and came to see environment as the source of racial inequality. Southern politicians and extremists, who in the thirties and forties were the chief defenders of segregation and white supremacy, were not inclined to pursue the intellectual and scientific bases for their views. In the fifties and sixties, however, under stress of the social revolution which integration is producing,

Gurk, "Scientist's Report on Race Differences," *U.S. News and World Report,* XLI (September 21, 1956), 92–96; and McGurk, "Negro vs. White Intelligence," *Harvard Educational Review,* XXIX (Winter, 1959), 42–62.

3   See W. D. Workman, Jr., *The Case for the South* (New York, 1960), 211–47; Nathaniel Weyl, *The Negro in American Civilization* (Washington, 1960), v–vi, 159–214; and James Jackson Kilpatrick, *The Southern Case for School Segregation* (New York, 1962), 72–93.

4   See Putnam, *Race and Reason;* and Putnam, "Evolution and Race: New Evidence," 7–10.

racists have been obliged to invoke again the old authorities. But this time, despite a few notable exceptions to the contrary, it has been the extremists themselves, and not scientists and scholars, who have supplied the evidence.

Between the two world wars, both the nature and influence of anti-Negro thought changed profoundly. The changes, however, are more easily described than explained. The division between cause and effect was rarely clear, and to interrelate them is an elusive yet engaging task. Perhaps the changes are too recent to be explained finally and definitively, but it would seem to be a part of the historian's responsibility to suggest tentative explanations.

Ideas, to repeat a commonplace, do not exist in a vacuum. They are expressions of social forces, and explanations or rationalizations of observed phenomena. Apparently there is and has always been a close relationship between the status of Negroes in this country and the attitudes of whites toward them, a fact which applies equally to scientific, academic, and popular opinion. As long as the Negro was a slave or menial, whites assumed that that was his natural place in society. As he elevated himself by acquiring property, becoming educated, and achieving an air of middle-class responsibility and stability, whites, both intellectuals and others, re-examined their attitudes toward him. That this is the case is indicated by the fact that changes in scientific and academic opinion did not occur significantly earlier than changes in popular opinion. The changes, moreover, occurred chiefly in the North where the Negro's advancement was most substantial and noticeable and where whites had had less reason to form fixed views of the race on the basis of a long tradition in which the Negro was apparently inferior. In other words the race was *believed* to be inferior as long as it *was*—ostensibly—inferior, and one can expect Southern attitudes to change as the Negro elevates himself in Southern society. As he asserts and wins his right to equal educational, economic, political, and social opportunities the plausibility of racist ideas will be lost and that of racial equality will be enhanced proportionately. In this light it would seem that the recent resurgence of interest in systematic racism is a temporary phenomenon merely indicating that some Southerners are slow to reconcile themselves to the social revolution in which they are living. This is not to say that these two forces—the status of Negroes and the white man's attitude toward them—are simply cause and effect.

Of course they are interrelated and each is dependent upon the other. It appears certain, however, that changes in the Negro's status have in the past produced the only lasting changes in anti-Negro thought. As long as the Negro was a slave, for example, the Bible was thought to defend slavery, but when he was segregated it was segregation that the Bible defended. When he achieves equality, one hopes, the Bible will then defend equality.

Improvement of the Negro's status, however, is not a complete explanation for changes in racist thought. It was itself the result of a broad pattern of events which benefited the Negro: the democratic, environmentalist emphasis of twentieth-century liberal reform; the American's inclination to discuss problems in the language of democracy and to insist upon the form of democracy in settling those problems; the decline of interest in racism in the North after passage of restrictive immigration legislation in the early twenties; the national reaction against the Ku Klux Klan and other extremist groups in and after the middle twenties; the economic and political consequences of the migration of Negroes from the South; the growing realization that racial discrimination gives the nation a black eye in world opinion; the improved organization and increased effectiveness of Negro and interracial groups; the increasing unwillingness of the New Negro to accept his traditional place in American life; and the shift of Negro voters from the Republican to the Democratic party.

The mere passage of time also produced a softening of attitudes toward the race. By the 1920's Reconstruction and the disfranchisement campaigns had become dim historical memories rather than personal reminiscences, and it was difficult to get the younger generation worked up over them. Even more significant, perhaps, was the tendency of whites, even in the South, to view the Negro problem with ambivalence. They were, as Gunnar Myrdal has emphasized, torn between a desire to maintain white supremacy on the one hand and devotion to the American creed of democracy, equality, and New Testament Christianity on the other. Thus, they were never able to follow a logically consistent policy toward the Negro as white South Africans have toward their racial "minorities." But whatever the cause, by the outbreak of World War II there were few reputable Americans outside the South who still openly held the racist views of the early twentieth century.

Complexity and contradiction, paradox and diversity, make anti-

Negro thought of this period extremely difficult to evaluate and even more dangerous to generalize about. It existed in all sections of the nation and in all strata of society—it was by no means a monopoly of the poor white—but there was always significant disagreement between extremists, moderates, and reformers, and this fact impaired their effectiveness. Anti-Negro ideas, moreover, never completely dominated American thought, for there was always a substantial body of dissent. Moderates never developed their ideas as completely as did extremists; as a result the latter were able to dominate anti-Negro thought. But as the appeal of racism dwindled after World War I and as attacks upon it became more persistent and direct, anti-Negro spokesmen became further and further alienated from popular American opinion. Thus, they lost their ideological hold on the American people long before the people were prepared to abandon race policies which anti-Negro ideas had justified. But as this paradox becomes more and more apparent, Americans are less and less willing that those policies should endure.

BIBLIOGRAPHY

GOVERNMENT PUBLICATIONS

The files of the *Congressional Record*, 1900–1930, provided valuable material.

NEWSPAPERS

Clippings collections at Atlanta University and Tuskegee Institute libraries were used. These collections contain clippings from daily and weekly, Southern and non-Southern, white and Negro newspapers. They are especially extensive for the period after World War I.

BOOKS

Adams, Charles Francis. *The Solid South and the Afro-American Race Problem*. Boston: n. p., 1908.

Allen, James S. *The Negro Question in the United States.* New York: International Publishers, 1936.

Allen, Marilyn R. *Alien Minorities and Mongrelization.* Boston: Meador Publishing Co., 1949.

Archer, William. *Through Afro-America, An English Reading of the Race Problem.* London: Chapman and Hall, 1910.

Armistead, W. S. *The Negro is a Man, A Reply to Professor Charles Carroll's Book "The Negro is a Beast or In the Image of God."* Tifton, Ga.: Armistead and Vickers, 1903.

Avary, Myrta Lockett. *Dixie After the War.* New York: Doubleday, Page and Co., 1906.

Bailey, Thomas Pearce. *Race Orthodoxy in the South, and Other Aspects of the Negro Question.* New York: Neale Publishing Co., 1914.

Baker, Ray Stannard. *Following the Color Line.* New York: Doubleday, Page and Co., 1908.

Ball, Frank P. *Divine Creation versus The Theory of Evolution.* No imprint, 1925.

Bancroft, Hubert Howe. *Retrospection, Political and Personal.* New York: Bancroft Co., 1912.

Bean, Robert Bennett. *The Peopling of Virginia.* Boston: Chapman and Grimes, 1938.

―――. *The Races of Man, Differentiation and Dispersal of Man.* New York: University Society, 1932.

Bilbo, Theodore G. *Take Your Choice: Separation or Mongrelization.* Poplarville, Miss.: Dream House Publishing Co., 1947.

Boas, Franz. *The Mind of Primitive Man.* New York: Macmillan, 1911.

Bowen, Trevor. *Divine White Right.* New York: Harper and Brothers, 1934.

Bowers, Claude G. *The Tragic Era.* Cambridge: Literary Guild of America, 1929.

Bradbury, John M. *The Fugitives.* Chapel Hill: University of North Carolina Press, 1958.

Brady, Tom P. *Black Monday.* Winona, Miss.: Association of Citizens Councils, 1955.

Bratton, Theodore DuBose. *Wanted—Leaders! A Study of Negro Development.* New York: Department of Missions and Church Extension, 1922.

Brigham, Carl C. *A Study of American Intelligence.* Princeton: Princeton University Press, 1923.

Brodie, Fawn. *Thaddeus Stevens, Scourge of the South.* New York: Norton, 1959.

Brown, William Montgomery. *The Crucial Race Question or Where and How Shall the Color Line Be Drawn.* Little Rock: Arkansas Churchman's Publishing Co., 1907.

Bruce, Philip Alexander. *The Rise of the New South.* Philadelphia: George Barrie and Sons, 1905.

Bryce, James. *The American Commonwealth.* New York: Commonwealth Publishing Co., 1908.

Bryce, James. *The Romanes Lecture 1902: The Relations of the Advanced and the Backward Races of Mankind*. Oxford: Clarendon Press, 1902.

Burbank, Luther. *The Training of the Human Plant*. New York: Century Co., 1908.

Burch, Henry Reed, and Patterson, Howard. *American Social Problems*. New York: Macmillan, 1920.

Burge, Lorenzo. *Pre-Glacial Man and the Aryan Race*. Boston: Lee and Shepard, 1887.

Burgess, John W. *The Civil War and the Constitution*. New York: Charles Scribner's Sons, 1901.

————. *Reconstruction and the Constitution*. New York: Charles Scribner's Sons, 1902.

————. *Sovereignty and Liberty*. Volume I of *Political Science and Comparative Constitutional Law*. Boston: Ginn and Co., 1913.

Burr, Clinton Stoddard. *America's Race Heritage*. New York: National Historical Society, 1922.

Cable, George W. *The Silent South*. New York: Charles Scribner's Sons, 1895.

Calhoun, William P. *The Caucasian and the Negro in the United States*. Columbia, S.C.: R. L. Bryan, 1902.

Calvin, Ira. *The Lost White Race*. Brookline, Mass.: Countway-White Publications, 1945.

Carroll, Charles. *The Negro A Beast or In the Image of God. . . .* St. Louis: American Book and Bible House, 1900.

————. *The Tempter of Eve*. St. Louis: Adamic Publishing Co., 1902.

Cash, Wilbur J. *The Mind of the South*. New York: Doubleday and Co., 1954.

Caucasian (ps.). *Anthropology for the People, A Refutation of the Theory of the Adamic Origin of all Races*. Richmond: Everett Waddey Co., 1891.

Chamberlain, Houston Stewart. *Foundations of the Nineteenth Century*. New York: John Lane Co., 1913.

Clowes, W. Laird. *Black America*. London: Cassell and Co., 1891.

Cohn, David L. *God Shakes Creation*. New York: Harper and Brothers. 1935.

Collins, Charles W. *Whither Solid South?* New Orleans: Pelican Publishing Co., 1947.

Collins, Winfield H. *The Truth about Lynching and the Negro in the South*. New York: Neale Publishing Co., 1918.

Commander, Lydia Kingsmill. *The American Idea*. New York: A. S. Barnes and Co., 1907.

Commons, John R. *Races and Immigrants in America*. New York: Macmillan, 1915.

Conklin, Edwin Grant. *The Direction of Human Evolution*. New York: Charles Scribner's Sons, 1922.

Coody, Archibald, IV. *Chapter Number Six, The Race Question*. Vicksburg: Mississippi Printing Press, 1944.

Coon, Carleton S. *The Origin of Races*. New York: Knopf, 1962.

Coon, Carleton S. *The Story of Man.* 2nd ed. rev. New York: Knopf, 1962.

Coulter, E. Merton (ed.). *The Course of the South to Secession.* New York: Appleton-Century, 1939.

———. *The South During Reconstruction, 1865–1877.* Baton Rouge: Louisiana State University Press, 1947.

Count, Earl W. (ed.). *This is Race, An Anthology Selected From the International Literature on the Races of Man.* New York: Henry Schuman, 1950.

Cox, Ernest Sevier. *The South's Part in Mongrelizing the Nation.* Richmond: White America Society, 1926.

———. *Teutonic Unity.* Richmond: n. p., 1951.

———. *White America.* Richmond: n. p., 1923.

Cram, Ralph Adams. *The Nemesis of Mediocrity.* Boston: Marshall Jones, 1921.

Cronon, Edmund David. *Black Moses, The Story of Marcus Garvey and the Universal Improvement Association.* Madison: University of Wisconsin Press, 1955.

Crookshank, F. G. *The Mongol in Our Midst.* New York: E. P. Dutton, 1924.

Cruden, Robert. *James Ford Rhodes, The Man, the Historian and His Work.* Cleveland: Western Reserve University Press, 1961.

Cutler, James Elbert. *Lynch-Law.* London: Longmans, Green, 1905.

Darwin, Charles. *The Descent of Man.* New York: Burt, 1874.

Davenport, C. B., and Steggerda, Morris. *Race Crossing in Jamaica.* Washington: Carnegie Institution, 1929.

Davis, Allison, *et al. Deep South, A Social Anthropological Study of Caste and Class.* Chicago: University of Chicago Press, 1941.

Davis, William Watson. *The Civil War and Reconstruction in Florida.* New York: Columbia University Press, 1913.

Debnam, W. E. *Then My Old Kentucky Home, Good Night.* Raleigh: n. p., 1955.

Dixon, Roland B. *The Racial History of Man.* New York: Charles Scribner's Sons, 1923.

Dixon, Thomas. *The Clansman, An Historical Romance of the Ku Klux Klan.* New York: Grosset and Dunlap, 1905.

———. *Companions.* New York: Cleveland, Otis, 1931.

———. *The Leopard's Spots, A Romance of the White Man's Burden, 1865–1900.* New York: Grosset and Dunlap, 1902.

———. *A Man of the People, A Drama of Abraham Lincoln.* New York: Appleton and Co., 1920.

———. *The Southerner, A Romance of the Real Lincoln.* New York: Appleton and Co., 1913.

———. *The Traitor, A Story of the Invisible Empire.* New York: Doubleday, Page, 1907.

———. *The Victim, A Romance of the Real Jefferson Davis.* New York: Appleton and Co., 1914.

Donald, David. *Lincoln Reconsidered.* New York: Vintage Books, 1961.

Douglass, H. Paul. *Christian Reconstruction in the South.* Boston: Pilgrim Press, 1909.

Dowd, Jerome. *The Negro in American Life.* London: Jonathan Cape, 1927.

Dunning, William Archibald. *Reconstruction, Political and Economic, 1865–1877.* New York: Harper and Brothers, 1907.

East, Edward M. *Heredity and Human Affairs.* New York: Charles Scribner's Sons, 1938.

————. *Mankind at the Crossroads.* New York: Charles Scribner's Sons, 1938.

Eckenrode, H. J. *Bottom Rail on Top, A Novel of the Old South.* New York: Greenberg Publishers, 1935.

————. *Jefferson Davis, President of the South.* New York: Macmillan, 1923.

————. *Rutherford B. Hayes, Statesman of Reunion.* New York: Dodd, Mead, 1930.

Eggleston, Edward. *The Ultimate Solution of the American Negro Problem.* Boston: Richard G. Badger, 1913.

Evans, Maurice S. *Black and White in the Southern States.* London: Longmans, Green, 1915.

Fairchild, Henry Pratt. *People, The Quantity and Quality of Population.* New York: Henry Holt, 1939.

Ferguson, George Oscar. *The Psychology of the Negro, An Experimental Study.* New York: Science Press, 1916.

Field, Henry M. *Bright Skies and Dark Shadows.* New York: Charles Scribner's Sons, 1890.

Fitzhugh, George. *Sociology for the South, or the Failure of a Free Society.* Richmond: A. Morris, 1854.

Fleming, Walter L. *Civil War and Reconstruction in Alabama.* New York: Columbia University Press, 1905.

————. *The Sequel of Appomattox.* New Haven: Yale University Press, 1919.

Fleming, William H. *Slavery and the Race Problem in the South.* Boston: Dana Estes, 1906.

Fletcher, John Gould. *The Two Frontiers.* New York: Coward-McCann, 1930.

Franklin, John Hope. *From Slavery to Freedom.* New York: Knopf, 1948.

————. *Reconstruction After The Civil War.* Chicago: University of Chicago Press, 1961.

Froude, James Anthony. *The English in the West Indies.* New York: Charles Scribner's Sons, 1892.

Fulkerson, H. S. *The Negro; As He Was; As He Is; As He Will Be.* Vicksburg: Commercial Herald, 1887.

Fuller, Edgar I. *The Visible of the Invisible Empire.* Denver: Maelstrom Publishing Co., 1925.

Gaines, Francis Pendleton. *The Southern Plantation, A Study in the Development and Accuracy of a Tradition.* New York: Columbia University Press, 1925.

206   *Bibliography*

Galloway, Charles B. *The South and the Negro.* New York: Southern Education Board, 1904.

Galton, Francis. *Hereditary Genius: An Inquiry into its Laws and Consequences.* London: Watts and Co., 1950.

Garner, James W. *Reconstruction in Mississippi.* New York: Macmillan, 1901.

Garth, Thomas Russell. *Race Psychology.* New York: McGraw-Hill, 1931.

George, Wesley Critz. *The Biology of the Race Problem.* No imprint, 1962.

Giddings, Franklin Henry. *The Principles of Sociology.* New York: Macmillan, 1896.

Gillard, John T. *The Catholic Church and the American Negro.* Baltimore: St. Joseph's Society, 1929.

Gobineau, Arthur de. *The Inequality of Human Races.* London: William Heineman, 1915.

Gossett, Thomas F. *Race: The History of an Idea in America.* Dallas: Southern Methodist University Press, 1963.

Gould, Charles W. *America, A Family Matter.* New York: Charles Scribner's Sons, 1922.

Grady, Henry W. *The New South.* New York: Robert Bonner's Sons, 1890.

———. *The Race Problem.* Chicago: George Shuman, 1889.

Graham, Stephen. *The Soul of John Brown.* New York: Macmillan, 1920.

Grant, Madison. *The Conquest of a Continent, or the Expansion of Races in America.* New York: Charles Scribner's Sons, 1933.

———. *The Passing of the Great Race, or the Racial Basis of European History.* New York: Charles Scribner's Sons, 1921.

Graves, John Temple. *The Fighting South.* New York: G. P. Putnam's Sons, 1943.

Green, Fletcher Melvin (ed.). *Essays in Southern History.* Chapel Hill: University of North Carolina Press, 1949.

Haaskarl, G. C. H. *The Missing Link; or the Negro's Ethnological Status.* Chambersburg, Pa.: Democratic News, 1898.

Hamilton, J. G. de Roulhac. *Reconstruction in North Carolina.* New York: Columbia University Press, 1914.

Hammond, Lydia Hardy. *In Black and White.* New York: Fleming H. Revell, 1914.

Handlin, Oscar. *Race and Nationality in American Life.* Boston: Little, Brown, 1957.

Hart, Albert Bushnell. *The Southern South.* New York: Appleton and Co., 1912.

Harte, Thomas J. *Catholic Organizations Promoting Negro-White Race Relations in the United States.* Washington: Catholic University of America Press, 1947.

Harvey, George. *The Power of Tolerance.* New York: Harper and Brothers, 1911.

Hawk, Emory Q. *Economic History of the South.* New York: Prentice-Hall, 1934.

Haygood, Atticus G. *Our Brother in Black, His Freedom and His Future.* Nashville: Southern Methodist Publishing House, 1881.

Helper, Hinton Rowan. *Nojoque: A Question for a Continent.* New York: George W. Carlton, 1867.

Herbert, Hilary A. (ed.). *Why the Solid South?* Baltimore: R. H. Woodward, 1890.

Herskovitz, Melville J. *The Anthropometry of the American Negro.* New York: Columbia University Press, 1930.

Hicks, John D. *The American Nation.* Boston: Houghton Mifflin, 1955.

Higham, John. *Strangers in the Land, Patterns of American Nativism 1860–1925.* New Brunswick: Rutgers University Press, 1955.

Hill, John Louis. *Negro, National Asset or Liability?* New York: Literary Associates, 1930.

Hirshson, Stanley P. *Farewell to the Bloody Shirt.* Bloomington: Indiana University Press, 1962.

Hofstadter, Richard. *Social Darwinism in American Thought, 1860–1915.* Philadelphia: University of Pennsylvania Press, 1945.

Holley, Joseph Winthrop. *You Can't Build a Chimney from the Top.* New York: William-Frederick Press, 1949.

Holmes, S. J. *The Negro's Struggle for Survival.* Berkeley: University of California Press, 1937.

———. *Studies in Evolution and Eugenics.* London: George Boutledge and Sons, 1923.

———. *The Trend of the Race.* New York: Harcourt, Brace, 1921.

Hooten, Ernest Albert. *Apes, Men, and Morons.* New York: G. P. Putnam's Sons, 1937.

———. *Twilight of Man.* New York: G. P. Putnam's Sons, 1939.

Hosmer, James K. *A Short History of Anglo-Saxon Freedom, The Polity of the English-Speaking Race.* New York: Charles Scribner's Sons, 1890.

Humphrey, Seth K. *Mankind, Racial Values and the Racial Prospect.* New York: Charles Scribner's Sons, 1917.

———. *The Racial Prospect.* New York: Charles Scribner's Sons, 1920.

Huntington, Ellsworth. *The Character of Races.* New York: Charles Scribner's Sons, 1927.

———. *Civilization and Climate.* New Haven: Yale University Press, 1924.

Ingram, T. Robert. *Essays on Segregation.* Boston: St. Thomas Press, 1960.

Ireland, Alleyne. *Democracy and the Human Equation.* New York: Dutton, 1921.

Irwin, John R. *The Crisis, Let's Keep the United States White.* New Orleans: Pelican Press, 1945.

Jarrell, Hampton M. *Wade Hampton and the Negro, the Road Not Taken.* Columbia: University of South Carolina Press, 1950.

Jennings, H. S. *The Biological Basis of Human Nature.* New York: Norton, 1930.

Jervey, Theodore D. *The Slave Trade, Slavery and Color.* Columbia: The State Co., 1925.

Jordan, David Starr. *War and the Breed.* Boston: Beacon Press, 1915.

Josey, Charles Conant. *Race and National Solidarity.* New York: Charles Scribner's Sons, 1923.

Kilpatrick, James Jackson. *The Southern Case for School Segregation.* New York: Crowell-Collier, 1962.

LaFarge, John. *The Catholic Viewpoint on Race Relations.* Garden City: Hanover House, 1960.

Landry, Stuart Omer. *The Cult of Equality.* New Orleans: Pelican Publishing Co., 1945.

Lawton, Alexander R. *The Negro in the South and Elsewhere.* Athens: n. p., 1923.

LeBon, Gustave. *The Psychology of Peoples.* New York: G. E. Stechert and Co.,1924.

Loescher, Frank S. *The Protestant Church and the Negro.* New York: Association Press, 1948.

Logan, Rayford W. *The Attitude of the Southern White Press toward Negro Suffrage, 1932–1940.* Washington: Foundation Publishers, 1940.

————. *The Negro in American Life and Thought: The Nadir, 1877–1901.* New York: Dial Press, 1954.

Lonn, Ella. *Reconstruction in Louisiana after 1868.* New York: G. P. Putnam's Sons, 1918.

Lytle, Andrew Nelson. *Bedford Forrest and His Critter Company.* New York: Minton, Balch and Co., 1931.

McCord, Charles H. *The American Negro as a Dependent, Defective and Delinquent.* Nashville: Benson Printing Co., 1914.

McCulloch, James E. (ed.). *Battling for Social Betterment, Southern Sociological Congress . . . 1914.* Nashville: Southern Sociological Congress, 1914.

————. *Democracy in Earnest, Southern Sociological Congress 1916–1918.* Washington: Southern Sociological Congress, 1918.

————. *The South Mobilizing for Social Service, Addresses Delivered at the Southern Sociological Congress . . . 1913.* Nashville: Southern Sociological Congress, 1913.

McDougall, William. *The Group Mind.* New York: G. P. Putnam's Sons, 1920.

————. *The Indestructible Union.* Boston: Little, Brown, 1925.

————. *Is America Safe for Democracy?* New York: Charles Scribner's Sons, 1921.

[McKinley, Carlyle]. *An Appeal to Pharaoh, The Negro Problem and Its Radical Solution.* New York: Fords, Howard and Hulbert, 1890.

McKitrick, Eric. *Andrew Johnson and Reconstruction.* Chicago: University of Chicago Press, 1960.

Mallison, George. *Color at Home and Abroad.* Boston: Christopher Publishing House, 1929.

Mangum, Charles S., Jr. *The Legal Status of the Negro.* Chapel Hill: University of North Carolina Press, 1940.

Masters, Victor Irvine. *The Call of the South*. Atlanta: Southern Baptist Convention, 1918.

Mayo, Marion J. *The Mental Capacity of the American Negro*. New York: Science Press, 1913.

Mecklin, John Moffatt. *Democracy and Race Friction, A Study in Social Ethics*. New York: Macmillan, 1921.

Meier, August. *Negro Thought in America, 1880–1915*. Ann Arbor: University of Michigan Press, 1963.

Men versus The Man, A Correspondence between Robert Rives LaMonte, Socialist, and H. L. Mencken, Individualist. New York: Henry Holt, 1910.

Merriam, Charles Edward (ed.). *A History of Political Theories*. New York: Macmillan, 1924.

Michael, W. E. *The Age of Error*. New York: Vantage Press, 1957.

Michie, Allan A. and Ryhlick, Frank. *Dixie Demagogues*. New York: Vanguard Press, 1939.

Miller, Robert Moats. *American Protestantism and Social Issues, 1919–1939*. Chapel Hill: University of North Carolina Press, 1958.

Mims, Edwin. *The Advancing South*. New York: Doubleday, Page, 1926.

Minutes of the University Commission on Southern Race Questions. No imprint, 1912–1917.

Montgomery, Harry Earl. *Vital American Problems*. New York: G. P. Putnam's Sons, 1908.

Morris, Charles. *The Aryan Race*. Chicago: S. C. Griggs, 1888.

———. *The Old South and New*. Washington: n. p., 1907.

Murphy, Edgar Gardner. *The Basis of Ascendancy*. New York: Longmans, Green, 1909.

———. *The Problems of the Present South*. New York: Macmillan, 1904.

Murphy, John C. *An Analysis of the Attitudes of American Catholics toward the Immigrant and the Negro, 1825–1925*. Washington: Catholic University of America Press, 1940.

Murray, William H. *The Negro's Place in the Call of Race*. No imprint, 1948.

Myrdal, Gunnar. *An American Dilemma*. New York: Harper and Brothers, 1944.

Neff, Lawrence W. *Race Relations at Close Range*. Emory University: Banner Press, 1931.

Northen, W. J. *Constructive Christianity and the Negro Problem*. No imprint, n. d.

Nott, J. C. and Gliddon, George R. *Types of Mankind*. Philadelphia: Lippincott, Grambo, and Co., 1855.

Odum, Howard W. *Race and Rumors of Race*. Chapel Hill: University of North Carolina Press, 1943.

———. *Social and Mental Traits of the Negro*. New York: Columbia University Press, 1910.

Oldham, J. H. *Christianity and the Race Problem*. New York: George Doran Co., n. d.

Otken, Charles H. *The Ills of the South.* New York: G. P. Putnam's Sons, 1894.

Page, Thomas Nelson. *The Negro: The Southerner's Problem.* New York: Charles Scribner's Sons, 1904.

————. *In Ole Virginia.* New York: Charles Scribner's Sons, 1910.

Papers Read at the Meeting of Grand Dragons, Knights of the Ku Klux Klan, At their First Annual Meeting. . . . Asheville: n. p., 1923.

Patterson, Raymond. *The Negro and His Needs.* New York: Fleming H. Revell, 1911.

[Payne, Buckner H.] *The Negro: What is His Ethnological Status?* Cincinnati: n. p., 1872.

Percy, William Alexander. *Lanterns on the Levee.* New York: Knopf, 1946.

Persons, Stow. *American Minds.* New York: Henry Holt, 1958.

Phillips, Ulrich Bonnell. *American Negro Slavery.* New York: Appleton and Co., 1918.

————. *Life and Labor in the Old South.* Boston: Little, Brown, 1937.

Pickett, William P. *The Negro Problem, Abraham Lincoln's Solution.* New York: G. P. Putnam's Sons, 1909.

Popenoe, Paul, and Johnson, Roswell Hill. *Applied Eugenics.* New York: Macmillan, 1918.

The Possibilities of the Negro in Symposium. Atlanta: Franklin Printing Co., 1904.

Price, John Ambrose. *The Negro Past, Present, and Future.* New York: Neale Publishing Co., 1907.

Priest, Josiah. *Bible Defense of Slavery.* . . Glasgow, Ky.: W. S. Brown, 1851.

The Pro-Slavery Argument; as Maintained by the Most Distinguished Writers of the Southern States. . . . Philadelphia: Lippincott, Grambo, and Co., 1853.

Putnam, Carleton. *Race and Reason: A Yankee View.* Washington: Public Affairs Press, 1961.

Ramsdell, Charles W. *Reconstruction in Texas.* New York: Columbia University Press, 1910.

Randall, James G. *The Civil War and Reconstruction.* Boston: Heath, 1953.

Randle, E. H. *Characteristics of the Southern Negro.* New York: Neale Publishing Co., 1910.

Raper, Arthur F. *The Tragedy of Lynching.* Chapel Hill: University of North Carolina Press, 1933.

Record, Wilson. *The Negro and the Communist Party.* Chapel Hill: University of North Carolina Press, 1951.

Reed, John C. *The Brothers War.* Boston: Little, Brown, 1905.

Reuter, Edward Byron. *The American Race Problem.* New York: Crowell, 1938.

Rhodes, James Ford. *History of the United States from the Compromise of 1850.* . . . 7 vols. New York: Macmillan, 1904–1920.

Ripley, William Z. *The Races of Europe, A Sociological Study.* New York: Appleton and Co., 1923.

Robertson, William J. *The Changing South.* New York: Boni and Liveright, 1927.

Roche, Richard J. *Catholic Colleges and the Negro Student.* Washington: Catholic University of America Press, 1948.

Roosevelt, Theodore. *American Problems.* New York: Charles Scribner's Sons, 1926.

Ross, Edward Alsworth. *Foundations of Sociology.* New York: Macmillan, 1905.

Rowland, Dunbar. *A Mississippi View of Race Relations in the South* Jackson: Harmon Publishing Company, 1902.

Royce, Josiah. *Race Questions, Provincialism and Other American Problems.* New York: Macmillan, 1908.

Sadler, William S. *Long Heads and Round Heads.* Chicago: A. C. McClurg, 1918.

Saveth, Edward Norman. *American Historians and European Immigrants.* New York: Columbia University Press, 1948.

Sayers, James Denson. *Can the White Race Survive?* Washington: Independent Publishing Co., 1929.

Schultz, Alfred P. *Race or Mongrel.* Boston: L. C. Page, 1908.

Sellers, Charles Grier (ed.). *The Southerner as American.* Chapel Hill: University of North Carolina Press, 1960.

Semple, Ellen Churchill. *Influence of Geographic Environment on the Basis of Ratzel's System of Anthropo-Geography.* New York: Henry Holt, 1911.

Shaler, N. S. *The Neighbor, The Natural History of Human Contacts.* Boston: Houghton Mifflin, 1904.

Shannon, A. H. *The Negro in Washington.* New York: Walter Neale, 1930.

Sheehan, Donald, and Syrett, Harold C. (eds.). *Essays in American Historiography, Papers Presented in Honor of Allan Nevins.* New York: Columbia University Press, 1960.

Shuey, Audrey M. *The Testing of Negro Intelligence.* Lynchburg, Va.: J. P. Bell Co., 1958.

Shufeldt, R. W. *America's Greatest Problem: The Negro.* Philadelphia: F. A. Davis Co., 1915.

―――. *The Negro, A Menace to American Civilization.* Boston: Gorman Press, 1907.

Simmons, Enoch Spencer. *A Solution of the Race Problem in the South.* Raleigh: Edwards and Broughton, 1898.

Simmons, William Joseph. *The Klan Unmasked.* Atlanta: Thompson Publishing Co., 1924.

Smith, Robert Edwin. *Christianity and the Race Problem.* New York: Fleming H. Revell, 1922.

Smith, William Benjamin. *The Color Line, A Brief in Behalf of the Unborn.* New York: McClure, Phillips and Co., 1905.

Solomon, Barbara Miller. *Ancestors and Immigrants.* Cambridge: Harvard University Press, 1956.

Sorokin, Pitirim. *Contemporary Sociological Theories.* New York: Harper and Brothers, 1928.

The South in the Building of the Nation. 13 vols. Richmond: Southern Historical Publication Society, 1909.

Stanton, William. *The Leopard's Spots, Scientific Attitudes Toward Race in America, 1815–1859.* Chicago: University of Chicago Press, 1960.

Stephenson, Gilbert Thomas. *Race Distinctions in American Law.* New York: Appleton and Co., 1910.

Stoddard, Lothrop. *Clashing Tides of Colour.* New York: Charles Scribner's Sons, 1935.

————. *The French Revolution in San Domingo.* Boston: Houghton Mifflin, 1914.

————. *Racial Realities in Europe.* New York: Charles Scribner's Sons, 1924.

————. *Re-Forging America, The Story of Our Nationhood.* New York: Charles Scribner's Sons, 1927.

————. *The Revolt Against Civilization: The Menace of the Under Man.* New York: Charles Scribner's Sons, 1923.

————. *The Rising Tide of Color Against White World Supremacy.* New York: Charles Scribner's Sons, 1920.

Stokes, W. E. D. *The Right to be Well Born, or Horse Breeding in its Relation to Eugenics.* New York: n. p., 1917.

Stone, Alfred Holt. *Studies in the American Race Problem.* New York: Doubleday, Page, 1908.

Strong, Josiah. *Expansion.* New York: Baker and Taylor Co., 1900.

————. *The New Era.* New York: Baker and Taylor Co., 1893.

————. *Our Country: Its Possible Future and Its Present Crisis.* New York: American Home Missionary Society, 1885.

Studies in Southern History and Politics Inscribed to William Archibald Dunning. New York: Columbia University Press, 1914.

Suksdorf, Henry F. *Our Race Problems.* New York: Shakespeare Press, 1911.

Sumner, William Graham. *Folkways.* Boston: Ginn and Co., 1911.

———— and Keller, Albert Galloway. *The Science of Society.* New Haven: Yale University Press, 1927.

Taft, William H. *Political Issues and Outlooks, Speeches Delivered between August, 1908 and February, 1909.* New York: Doubleday, Page, 1909.

Talmadge, Herman E. *You and Segregation.* Birmingham: Vulcan Press, 1955.

Tate, Allen. *Jefferson Davis: His Rise and Fall.* New York: Minton, Balch and Co., 1929.

————. *Stonewall Jackson, The Good Soldier.* New York: Minton, Balch and Co., 1928.

Thomas, William Hannibal. *The American Negro, What He Was, What He Is, and What He May Become.* New York: Macmillan, 1901.

Thompson, C. Mildred. *Reconstruction in Georgia.* New York: Columbia University Press, 1915.

Thompson, Holland. *The New South.* New Haven: Yale University Press, 1919.

Tourgee, Albion W. *An Appeal to Caesar.* New York: Fords, Howard and Hulbert, 1884.

Twelve Southerners. *I'll Take My Stand, The South and the Agrarian Tradition.* New York: Harper and Brothers, 1930.

Van Deusen, John G. *The Black Man in White America.* Washington: Associated Publishers, 1938.

Vertrees, John J. *The Negro Problem.* Nashville: Marshall and Bruce, 1905.

Ward, Lester F. *Pure Sociology, A Treatise on the Origin and Spontaneous Development of Society.* New York: Macmillan, 1907.

Warren, Robert Penn. *John Brown, The Making of a Martyr.* New York: Payson and Clarke, 1929.

Washington, Booker T. *The Future of the American Negro.* Boston: Small, Maynard and Co., 1899.

———. *Up From Slavery.* New York: Doubleday, Page, 1901.

Weatherford, W. D. *Negro Life in the South.* New York: Association Press, 1918.

Weismann, August. *Essays Upon Heredity.* Oxford: Clarendon, 1889.

———. *The Evolution Theory.* London: Arnold, 1904.

Weyl, Nathaniel. *The Negro in American Civilization.* Washington: Public Affairs Press, 1962.

——— and Possony, Stefan. *The Geography of Intellect.* Chicago: Henry Regnery, 1963.

Widney, Joseph P. *The New World.* Volume II of *Race Life of the Aryan Peoples.* New York: Funk and Wagnalls, 1907.

Wiggam, Albert Edward. *The Fruit of the Family Tree.* Indianapolis: Bobbs-Merrill, 1924.

———. *The New Decalogue of Science.* Indianapolis: Bobbs-Merrill, 1922.

Wilson, Woodrow. *Division and Reunion, 1829–1909.* New York: Longmans, Green, 1910.

Wish, Harvey. *The American Historian.* New York: Oxford University Press, 1960.

Woodruff, Charles E. *The Effects of Tropical Light on White Men.* New York: Rebman Co., 1905.

———. *Expansion of Races.* New York: Rebman Co., 1909.

———. *Medical Ethnology.* New York: Rebman Co., 1915.

Woodward, C. Vann. *Origins of the New South, 1877–1913.* Baton Rouge: Louisiana State University Press, 1951.

———. *The Strange Career of Jim Crow.* New York: Oxford University Press, 1957.

———. *Tom Watson: Agrarian Rebel.* New York: Macmillan, 1938.

Workman, William D. Jr. *The Case for the South.* New York: Devin-Adair, 1960.

PERIODICALS

The issues of *The Crisis* for the period 1920–1930 were used extensively. Articles from other periodicals which proved most helpful follow:

Abrams, Richard M. "Woodrow Wilson and the Southern Congressmen, 1913–1916," *Journal of Southern History*, XXII (November, 1956), 417–37.

Adams, Charles Francis. "Reflex Light from Africa," *Century Magazine*, LXXII (May, 1906), 101–11.

Alderman, Edwin A. "The Growing South," *Worlds Work*, XVI (June, 1908), 10373–83.

Atkinson, Edward. "The Negro A Beast," *North American Review*, CLXXXI (August, 1905), 202–15.

Baker, Ray Stannard. "The Tragedy of the Mulatto," *American Magazine*, LXV (April, 1908), 582–98.

Bardin, James. "The Psychological Factor in Southern Race Problems," *Popular Science Monthly*, LXXXIII (October, 1913), 368–74.

Beale, Howard K. "On Rewriting Reconstruction History," *American Historical Review*, XLV (July, 1940), 807–27.

Bean, Robert Bennett. "The Negro Brain," *Century Magazine*, LXXII (October, 1906), 778–84.

――――. "Some Racial Peculiarities of the Negro Brain," *American Journal of Anatomy*, V (September, 1906), 353–432.

――――. "The Training of the Negro," *Century Magazine*, LXXII (October, 1906), 947–53.

Bilbo, Theodore G. "An African Home for Our Negroes," *Living Age*, CCCLVIII (June, 1940), 327–35.

Boddy, J. M. "The 'Kinks' in the Negro's Hair," *Scientific American*, CII (April 30, 1910), 359.

Boyle, James E. "Has the Fifteenth Amendment Been Justified?" *Arena*, XXXI (May, 1904), 481–88.

Bratton, Theodore DuBose. "The Christian South and Negro Education," *Sewanee Review*, XVI (July, 1908), 290–97.

Breckinridge, William C. P. "The Race Question," *Arena*, II (June, 1890), 39–56.

Brooks, R. P. "A Local Study of the Race Problem," *Political Science Quarterly*, XXVI (June, 1911), 193–221.

Brough, Charles Hillman. "Work of the Commission of Southern Universities on the Race Question," *The Annals*, XLIX (September, 1913), 47–57.

Brown, Sterling A. "Negro Characters as Seen by White Authors," *Journal of Negro Education*, II (April, 1933), 179–203.

Bruce, Philip Alexander. "Evolution of the Negro Problem," *Sewanee Review*, XIX (October, 1911), 385–99.

――――. "Race Segregation in the United States," *Hibbert Journal*, XIII (July, 1915), 867–86.

Bryce, James. "Thoughts on the Negro Problem," *North American Review*, CLIII (December, 1891), 641–60.

Castle, W. E. "Biological and Social Consequences of Race," *American Journal of Physical Anthropology*, IX (April, 1926), 145–56.

Closson, Carlos C. "The Hierarchy of European Races," *American Journal of Sociology*, III (November, 1897), 314–27.

Cook, O. F. "The Negro and African Colonization," *Forum*, XXVII (March, 1890), 114–19.

Coon, Carleton S. "New Findings on the Origin of Races," *Harper's*, CCXXV (December, 1962), 66–74.

Crowell, Chester T. "A Message to the North," *Independent*, LXX (May 11, 1911), 990–94.

Curry, J. L. M. "The Negro Question," *Popular Science Monthly*, LV (June, 1899), 177–85.

Davenport, C. B. "Are there Genetically Based Mental Differences Between the Races?" *Science*, LXVIII (December 21, 1928), 628.

———. "Influences of Heredity on Human Society," *The Annals*, XXXIV (July, 1909), 16–21.

———. "Race Crossing in Jamaica," *Scientific Monthly*, XXVII (September, 1928), 225–38.

Davidson, Donald. "Still Rebels, Still Yankees," *American Review*, II (November, 1933), 58–72.

Donald, David. "Why They Impeached Andrew Johnson," *American Heritage*, VIII (December, 1956), 20–25.

Dublin, Louis I. "The Health of the Negro," *The Annals*, CXL (November, 1928), 77–85.

East, E. M. "The Future of Man in the Light of his Past: The View of a Geneticist," *Scientific Monthly*, XXXII (April, 1931), 301–308.

Edwards, Lyford P. "Religious Sectarianism and Race Prejudice," *American Journal of Sociology*, XLI (September, 1935), 167–79.

Evans, Hiram Wesley. "The Klan: Defender of Americanism," *Forum*, LXXIV (December, 1925), 801–14.

———. "The Klan's Fight for Americanism," *North American Review*, CCXXIII (March, 1926), 33–63.

———. "Where Do We Go From Here?" *Papers Read at the Meeting of Grand Dragons, Knights of the Ku Klux Klan at Their First Meeting . . . July, 1923*. Asheville, 1923.

Ferguson, George Oscar. "The Mental Status of the American Negro," *Scientific Monthly*, XII (June, 1921), 533–43.

Fleming, Walter L. "The Servant Problem in a Black Belt Village," *Sewanee Review*, XIII (January, 1905), 1–17.

Frank, Glenn. "The Clash of Color," *Century Magazine*, XCIX (November, 1919), 86–98.

Garrett, Henry E. "Facts vs. Opinions on 'Race and Reason,'" *The Citizen*, VII (February, 1963), 7–12.

———. "One Psychologist's View of Equality of the Races," *U.S. News and World Report*, LI (August 14, 1961), 72–74.

Garth, Thomas R. "Race and Psychology," *Scientific Monthly*, XXIII (September, 1926), 240–45.

Giddings, Franklin H. "The American People," *International Quarterly*, VII (June, 1903), 281–99.

Goodenough, Florence L. "Racial Differences in the Intelligence of School Children," *Journal of Experimental Psychology*, IX (October, 1926) 388–97.

"Governor Vardaman on the Negro," *Current Literature*, XXXVI (March, 1904), 270–71.

Graham, James L. "A Quantitative Comparison of Rational Responses of Negro and White College Students," *Journal of Social Psychology*, I (February, 1930), 97–121.

Grant, Madison. "The Passing of the Great Race," *Geographical Review*, II (November, 1916), 354–60.

Grantham, Dewey W. "Southern Congressional Leaders and the New Freedom, 1913–1917," *Journal of Southern History*, XIII (November, 1947), 439–59.

Gregg, William W. "The Mulatto—Crux of the Negro Problem," *Current History*, XIX (March, 1924), 1065–70.

Guild, Walter. "A Plea from the South," *Arena*, XXIV (November, 1900), 483–88.

Hall, G. Stanley. "The Negro in Africa and America," *Pedagogical Seminary*, XII (September, 1905), 350–68.

Hall, H. N. "Are the Various Races of Man Potentially Equal?" *Proceedings of the American Philosophical Society*, LXIII (1924), 208–14.

Hammond, L. H. "A Southern View of the Negro," *Outlook*, LXXIII (March 14, 1903), 619–23.

————. "The White Man's Debt to the Negro," *The Annals*, XLIX (September, 1913), 67–73.

Hampton, Wade. "The Race Problem," *Arena*, II (July, 1890), 132–38.

Hawley, Walter L. "Passing of the Race Problem," *Arena*, XXIV (November, 1900), 467–78.

Hemphill, J. C. "The President, the South, and the Negro," *Harper's Weekly*, LIII (January 9, 1909), 10, 31.

Hoffman, Frederick L. "Race Traits and Tendencies of the American Negro," *Publications of the American Economic Association*, XI (August, 1896), 1–329.

————. "Vital Statistics of the Negro," *Arena*, V (April, 1892), 529–42.

Hooten, E. A. "Methods of Racial Analysis," *Science*, LXIII (January 22, 1926), 75–81.

Hopkins, Albert A. "Which Races Are Best?" *Scientific American*, CXXXII (February, 1925), 77–79.

"Intelligence of Negroes as Compared with Whites," *Current Opinion*, LXXI (November, 1921), 640–41.

"Is the Negro Race Dying Out," *Review of Reviews*, V (May, 1892), 469.

Jelks, William Dorsey. "The Acuteness of the Negro Question," *North American Review*, CLXXXIV (February 15, 1907), 389–95.

Jordan, David Starr. "Biological Effects of Race Movements," *Popular Science Monthly*, LXXXVII (September, 1915), 267–70.

———. "War and Race Decadence," *Independent*, LIX (December 21, 1905), 1475–77.

Jordan, H. E. "The Biological Status and Social Worth of the Mulatto," *Popular Science Monthly*, LXXXII (June, 1913), 573–82.

———. "The Inheritance of Skin Color," *Science*, XXXVI (August 2, 1912), 151–52.

Krogman, Wilton Marion. "Is There a Physical Basis for Race Superiority," *Scientific Monthly*, LI (November, 1940), 428–34.

Krug, Mark M. "On Rewriting of the Story of Reconstruction in the U.S. History Textbooks," *Journal of Negro History*, XLVI (July, 1961), 133–53.

Lacy, L. D. "Relative Intelligence of White and Colored Children," *Elementary School Journal*, XXVI (March, 1926), 542–46.

Lindbergh, Charles A. "Aviation, Geography, and Race," *Reader's Digest*, XXXV (November, 1939), 64–67.

Lytle, Andrew Nelson. "John Taylor and the Political Economy of Agriculture," *American Review*, III (September, 1934), 432–47.

McCulloch, J. E. "Another View of the Washington Riots," *Outlook*, CXXIII (September 3, 1919), 28–29.

McCurley, W. S. "The Impossibility of Racial Amalgamation," *Arena*, XXI (April, 1899), 446–55.

McGovern, J. Montgomery. "Disfranchisement as a Remedy," *Arena*, XXI (April, 1899), 438–46.

McGurk, Frank C. J. "Negro vs. White Intelligence," *Harvard Educational Review*, XXIX (Winter, 1959), 54–62.

———. "Scientist's Report on Race Differences." *U.S. News and World Report*, XLI (September 21, 1956), 92–96.

Mayo-Smith, Richmond. "Theories of Mixture of Races and Nationalities," *Yale Review*, III (August, 1894), 166–86.

Mecklin, John Moffatt, "The Philosophy of the Color Line," *American Journal of Sociology*, XIX (November, 1913), 343–57.

Meyers, William Starr. "Some Present-Day Views of the Southern Race Problem," *Sewanee Review*, XXI (July, 1913), 341–49.

Michaud, Gustave. "What Shall We Be? The Coming Race in America," *Century Magazine*, LXV (March, 1903), 683–90.

Miller, Robert Moats. "The Attitudes of American Protestantism toward the Negro, 1919–1939," *Journal of Negro History*, XLI (July, 1956), 215–40.

———. "The Protestant Churches and Lynching," *Journal of Negro History*, XLII (April, 1957), 118–31.

"Mind in the White and the Negro," *Literary Digest*, XLVIII (January 17, 1914), 101–102.

Mitchell, John. "Immigration and the American Laboring Class," *The Annals*, XXXIV (July, 1909), 125–29.

Morse, Josiah. "A Comparison of White and Colored Children Measured by the Binet Scale of Intelligence," *Popular Science Monthly*, LXXXIV (January, 1914), 75–79.

Murphy, Edgar Gardner. "The Task of the Leader," *Sewanee Review*, XV (January, 1907), 1–30.

"The Negro and His Creator," *Outlook*, LXXVII (July 16, 1904), 635–36.

Neifeld, M. R. "The Race Hypothesis," *American Journal of Sociology*, XXXII (November, 1926), 423–32.

Newby, I. A. "The Southern Agrarians: A View After Thirty Years," *Agricultural History*, XXXVII (July, 1963), 143–55.

————. "States Rights and Southern Congressmen During World War I," *Phylon*, XXIV (Spring, 1963), 34–50.

Odum, Howard. "Negro Children in the Public Schools of Philadelphia," *The Annals*, XLIX (September, 1913), 186–206.

Osborn, Henry Fairfield. "The Evolution of Human Races," *Natural History*, XXVI (January, 1926), 3–13.

"Out of the Heart," *American Magazine*, LXIII (December, 1906), 216–19.

Owsley, Frank L. "The Old South and the New," *American Review*, VI (February, 1936), 475–85.

————. "The Pillars of Agrarianism," *American Review*, IV (March, 1935), 529–47.

————. "Scottsboro, The Third Crusade: The Sequel to Abolition and Reconstruction," *American Review*, I (June, 1933), 257–85.

Page, Thomas Nelson. "The Disfranchisement of the Negro," *Scribner's Magazine*, XXXVI (July, 1904), 15–24.

————. "The Negro: The Southerner's Problem," *McClure's Magazine*, XXII (March, 1904), 548–54.

————. "The Negro: The Southerner's Problem," *McClure's Magazine*, XXII (April, 1904), 619–26.

————. "The Negro: The Southerner's Problem," *McClure's Magazine*, XXIII (May, 1904), 96–102.

————. "The Old-Time Negro," *Scribner's Magazine*, XXXVI (November, 1904), 522–32.

————. "A Southerner on the Race Question," *North American Review*, CLIV (April, 1892), 401–13.

Park, Robert E. "Mentality of Racial Hybrids," *American Journal of Sociology*, XXXVI (January, 1931), 534–51.

Percy, Leroy. "A Southern View of Negro Education," *Outlook*, LXXXVI (August 3, 1907), 730–32.

Phillips, Ulrich Bonnell. "The Plantation as a Civilizing Influence," *Sewanee Review*, XII (July, 1904), 257–67.

Pierce, David H. "Is the Jew a Friend of the Negro?" *The Crisis*, XXX (July, 1925), 184–86.

"President Harding Discourses on the Color Line," *Current Opinion*, LXXI (December, 1921), 704–708.

"President Harding on Negro Education," *School and Society*, XIV (November 5, 1921), 393–94.

Putnam, Carleton. "Evolution and Race: New Evidence," *The Citizen,* VI (July–August, 1962), 7–10.

"Race Discrimination at Washington," *Independent,* LXXVI (November 20, 1913), 330.

Reddick, Lawrence D. "Racial Attitudes in American History Textbooks," *Journal of Negro History,* XIX (July, 1934), 225–65.

Reuter, E. B. "The American Mulatto," *The Annals,* CXL (November, 1928), 36–43.

————. "The Superiority of the Mulatto," *American Journal of Sociology,* XXIII (July, 1917), 83–106.

Ripley, William Z. "Races in the United States," *Atlantic Monthly,* CII (December, 1908), 745–59.

————. "Race Progress and Immigration," *The Annals,* XXIV (July, 1909), 130–38.

Roosevelt, Theodore. "The Progressive and the Colored Man," *Outlook,* CI (August 24, 1912), 909–12.

Rose, John C. "Negro Suffrage: The Constitutional Point of View," *American Political Science Review,* I (November, 1906), 17–43.

Ross, Edward A. "The Causes of Race Superiority," *The Annals,* CXVIII (July, 1901), 67–89.

———— and Ingraham, Sidney. "Deucalion and Company, Ltd.," *Saturday Evening Post,* CXCVIII (February 6, 1926), 174, 209.

Rutledge, Archibald. "It's a Dark Business," *Saturday Evening Post,* CCXII (December 16, 1939), 23, 44–47.

Saveth, Edward Norman. "Race and Nationalism in American Historiography: the Late Nineteenth Century," *Political Science Quarterly,* LIV (September, 1939), 421–41.

Scott, Anne Firor. "A Progressive Wind from the South, 1906–1913," *Journal of Southern History,* XXIX (February, 1963), 53–70.

Shaler, N. S. "The African Element in America," *Arena,* II (November, 1890), 660–73.

————. "The Future of the Negro in the South," *Popular Science Monthly,* LVII (June, 1900), 147–56.

————. "The Nature of the Negro," *Arena,* III (December, 1890), 23–25.

————. "The Negro Since the Civil War," *Popular Science Monthly,* LVII (May, 1900), 29–39.

————. "Our Negro Types," *Current Literature,* XXIX (July, 1900), 44–45.

————. "Science and the African Problem," *Atlantic Monthly,* LXVI (July, 1890), 29–39.

"Shall We All Be Mulattoes," *Literary Digest,* LXXXIV (March 7, 1925), 23–24.

Shannon, A. H. "The Racial Integrity of the American Negro," *Contemporary Review,* CXLIV (November, 1933), 581–92.

Sherwood, Henry N. "Early Negro Deportation Projects," *Mississippi Valley Historical Review,* II (March, 1916), 484–508.

Simkins, Francis Butler. "Ben Tillman's View of the Negro," *Journal of Southern History*, III (May, 1937), 161–74.

———. "New Viewpoints of Southern Reconstruction," *Journal of Southern History*, V (February, 1939), 49–61.

Simmons, Donald C. " 'Scientific' Racism," *New Republic*, CXLVIII (January 5, 1963), 9–10.

Simmons, F. M. "The Political Future of the Southern Negro," *Independent*, LX (June 28, 1906), 1521–26.

Smith, Anna Tolman. "A Study in Race Psychology," *Popular Science Monthly*, L (January–March, 1897), 354–60.

Smith, Charles H. "Have American Negroes Too Much Liberty?" *Forum*, XVI (October, 1893), 176–83.

Stoddard, Lothrop. "The Impasse at the Color Line," *Forum*, LXXVIII (October, 1927), 500–19.

———. "The New Realism of Science," *Saturday Evening Post*, CXCVII (September 6, 1925), 38, 121.

———. "Racial Realities in Europe," *Saturday Evening Post*, CXCVI (March 22, 1924), 14–15, 156–58.

———. "Worthwhile Americans," *Saturday Evening Post*, CXCVII (January 17, 1925), 23, 146–48.

Stone, Alfred Holt. "The Mulatto Factor in the Race Problem," *Atlantic Monthly*, XCI (May, 1903), 658–62.

Styron, Arthur. "A Southern View of Northern Reformers," *North American Review*, CCXXXVIII (August, 1934), 149–57.

Tate, Allen. "A View of the Whole South," *American Review*, II (February, 1934), 411–32.

Taylor, Griffith. "The Evolution and Distribution of Race, Culture, and Language," *Geographical Review*, XI (January, 1921), 54–119.

Terry, Robert J. "The American Negro," *Science*, LXIX (March 29, 1929), 337–41.

Thomas, William I. "The Psychology of Race Prejudice," *American Journal of Sociology*, IX (March, 1904), 593–611.

Tillinghast, Joseph Alexander. "The Negro in Africa and America," *Publications of the American Economic Association*, Third Series, III 1902), 1–231.

Tillman, B. R. "Causes of Southern Opposition to Imperialism," *North American Review*, CLXXI (September, 1900), 439–46.

Underwood, Oscar W. "The Negro Problem in the South," *Forum*, XXX (October, 1900), 215–19.

Van de Graaf, A. S. "Unaided Solution of the Southern Race Problem," *Forum*, XXI (May, 1896), 330–45.

Vander Zanden, James W. "The Ideology of White Supremacy," *Journal of the History of Ideas*, XX (June–September, 1959), 385–402.

Viteles, Morris S. "The Mental Status of the Negro," *The Annals*, CXL (November, 1928), 166–77.

Walker, Francis A. "The Colored Race in the United States," *Forum*, XI (July, 1891), 501–509.

Waterman, T. T. "The Subdivisions of the Human Race and their Distribution," *American Anthropologist,* XXVI (October, 1924), 474–90.

Watson, J. J. "Churches and Religious Organizations," *The Annals,* XLIX (September, 1913), 120–28.

Watson, Richard L. "The Defeat of Judge Parker: A Study in Pressure Groups and Politics," *Mississippi Valley Historical Review,* L (September, 1963), 213–34.

Watson, Thomas E. "The Negro Question in the South," *Arena,* VI (October, 1892), 540–50.

Weatherly, Ulysses G. "Race and Marriage," *American Journal of Sociology,* XV (January, 1910), 433–54.

Weinstein, Jacob J. "The Jew and the Negro, *The Crisis,* XLI (June, 1934), 178–79.

Weisberger, Bernard A. "The Dark and Bloody Ground of Reconstruction Historiography," *Journal of Southern History,* XXV (November, 1959), 427–47.

Wesley, Charles H. "The Concept of Negro Inferiority in American Thought," *Journal of Negro History,* XXV (October, 1940), 540–60.

"What the South Thinks of Northern Race-Riots," *Literary Digest,* LXII (August 16, 1919), 17–18.

Williams, John Sharp. "The Glory of the State, Mississippi," *American Magazine,* LXXXI (February, 1916), 45, 81–82.

Winston, George T. "The Relation of the Whites to the Negroes," *The Annals,* XVIII (July, 1901), 105–18.

Winston, Robert Watson. "Should the Color Line Go?" *Current History,* XVIII (September, 1923), 945–51.

Wright, R. Charlton. "The Southern White Man and the Negro," *Virginia Quarterly Review,* IX (April, 1933), 175–94.

Yerkes, Robert M. "Testing the Human Mind," *Atlantic Monthly,* CXXXI (March, 1923), 358–70.

INDEX